HENRY WEMYSS, M.M.

DESTINY

If God Be For You

Published by Distinction Publishing House
Dover, Denver, Colorado
United States of America
www.distinctionpublishinghouse.com

ISBN: 979-8-9894214-6-6

This book is printed on acid-free paper.

Printed in the United States of America

Dedication

This book is dedicated to my wife, Judy Anna Wemyss, nee Lockhart, who faithfully journeyed with me throughout life's ebbs and flows as a constant source of strength, support, and encouragement.

What then shall we say to these things?
If God be for us, who can be against us?
Romans 8:31 (KJV)

Table of Contents

Foreword

Winding is often used to describe something with many twists and turns. When someone compares their life to a long winding road, we immediately realise it has not been an easy journey for them. That is how this book recounts Henry Wemyss' life through some of his most painful experiences. It also faces the reality that, despite our best efforts, life does not always pan out the way we expect. On the brighter side, it demonstrates how God used adversities, as a springboard, to propel him forward.

As a law enforcer in the Royal Bahamas Police Force for 31 years, Henry served with passion and excellence, upholding his reputation as one of the cleanest officers of his time. While his career did not end the way he envisioned, his contributions as a Chief Instructor at the Police College in Nassau, The Bahamas, live on through the many exemplary officers whom he trained. These fine men and women have excelled, some to the highest ranks in policing and others in various sectors of the Bahamian society. This is a legacy of which he can be proud.

Losing one's freedom can be a devastating blow for anyone and re-entry into society is not an easy transition. However, Henry believed in himself and fought to regain his reputation and dignity. True to his character, he diligently applied himself to whatever opportunities came his way. One such opportunity paved the way for him to establish his own security firm. Through his business, he continues to contribute to the well-being and security of the Bahamian people. This is another legacy of which he can be proud.

With a deep faith in God, Henry nurtures a loving, generous and forgiving heart. Undoubtedly, these qualities afford him a blessed life. If there was a price for success, Henry paid it with disappointments, hardships, and tears. He is an over-comer, and I am proud to call him a friend. I applaud him for allowing his story to be used to change lives. It is a source of encouragement for people, from all walks of life, to persevere through the ups and downs of life. Read on. You will be inspired.

The Paul Farquharson, QPM †

Commissioner of Police (Ret), Royal Bahamas Police Force (2000-2008)
Former Bahamas High Commissioner to Great Britain and Northern Ireland (2008-2013)

Foreword

Destiny: If God Is For You is a remarkable book about Henry Wemyss which details his phenomenal life and captures the harsh realities of the challenges he confronted and surmounted to achieve the success and significance that he enjoys today. Henry's story is inspirational, and it captures the essence of what it means to persevere. He has added tremendous credibility to this body of work by tapping into the testimonies of nation-builders and community leaders from law enforcement and various spheres of public life in The Bahamas.

Henry Wemyss served as an instructor at the Police College during the mid-1970s and into the 1980s. I first met him when I joined the Royal Bahamas Police Force as a recruit Constable on 11th May, 1979, as part of "A Squad 79." Over a training period of 6 months, he and other instructors moulded us into a cohesive team of fit, knowledgeable, competent, and respectful young police officers, who were prepared for the challenges attendant with our profession and our society. Suffice it to say, "A Squad 79" was an impressive squad and it delivered to the Bahamian people the 6th Commissioner of Police in an independent Bahamas.

Hearing the name, Henry Wemyss, invokes compelling and positive images for me. It brings to mind stellar leadership and characteristics such as integrity, professionalism, competence, confidence, poise, and distinction, among many other traits. He was a transformational leader, who also possessed excellent servant-leader attributes. He did not merely say what one should do, he modelled the behaviours, skills set, and attitudes, that he expected. He set an excellent example for dress and deportment and was consistently neatly groomed.

Despite the challenges that confronted him in 1990, the quotation that, "His head was bloodied, but unbowed," seems to be an appropriate description of his perseverance. Those challenges would have toppled the average man, but he demonstrated to all of us that he was no average man and rose like the proverbial Phoenix. In 2000, he embarked on a new and exciting phase in his life, which again illuminated him as a stellar leader and a major contributor to the Bahamian economy. He established WemCo Security & Collections Limited and immediately captured the attention of both the private and public sectors. His employees are well trained, well attired, well equipped, and they exude confidence. Quality was and is the hallmark of WemCo.

Henry Wemyss is an unsung Bahamian hero, and I am most inspired by his legacy of perseverance, determination, courage, and vision. Therefore, it is with a tremendous amount of pride that I extend the invitation to you to turn the pages of this book.

H.E. Ellison Greenslade, C.D., QPM, Dr.h.c, MBA
Former Bahamas High Commissioner to
Great Britain and Northern Ireland
Commissioner of Police (Ret.)
Royal Bahamas Police Force (2010 – 2017)

Acknowledgements

Henry Wemyss has a story that begs to be told and because of the support of many, you are holding this book today. He is a Bahamian, who has earned his place in history as a nation-builder.

As a husband, father, brother, friend, colleague, mentor, employer, businessman and philanthropist, his influence has spanned the social spectrum. His story is intertwined with their stories, and this book is a collection of their memories, experiences, and thoughts about him.

Because of their willingness to participate in this written work, Henry Wemyss' legacy of leadership, altruism, faith, and human resilience was captured.

A debt of gratitude, beyond words, is owed to:

1. Hon. Frederick A. Mitchell, Minister of Foreign Affairs & the Public Service; Member of Parliament;
2. Mr. Paul A. Farquharson (posthumously), Retired Commissioner of Police;
3. Sir Albert Miller (posthumously), Former Deputy Commissioner of Police, Former Chairman of the Board of Directors of Batelco;
4. Paul Thompson, Sr.(posthumously), Retired Assistant Commissioner of Police (Crime);
5. Bishop V. G. Clarke, Pastor Emeritus, Calvary Deliverance Church;
6. Bishop Dr. James Newry, Senior Pastor, Calvary Deliverance Church;
7. Darnley Sealey, Retired Sergeant, Her Majesty's Prison;
8. Ms. Marina Knowles- Retired Educator;

Former Recruits:

9. H.E. Ellison Greenslade, Former Bahamas High Commissioner to Great Britain and Northern Ireland/ Retired Commissioner of Police;
10. Ismella Davis-Delancy, Retired Deputy Commissioner of Police;
11. BK Bonamy Jr, Retired Assistant Commissioner of Police;
12. Mary Mitchell, Retired Superintendent of Police;
13. Clarence Russell, Former Superintendent of Police/Past Director of Immigration;
14. Philip Don Wilson, Retired Superintendent of Police/ Entrepreneur;
15. Randy Lightfoot, Retired Superintendent of Police;
16. Elaine Sands, Retired Superintendent of Police;
17. Edric Poitier, Retired Police Inspector; Head Volleyball Coach, Bowie State University;
18. Kendal Rahming, Retired Police Constable;
19. Clayton King, Former Police Officer; Bank Manager;
20. John Pople, Retired Police Sergeant; Manager, Investigations & Intelligence WemCo Security & Collections Ltd.;
21. Luke Lawrence Bethel, Retired Chief Petty Officer, Royal Bahamas Defence Force;

Royal Bahamas Police Force 1988 Cadets – 'A' Squad:

22. Tyrone Archer, Cadet # 2 - Boat Captain;
23. Will Hart, Cadet #9 – Chief Superintendent of Police;
24. Berkley Neely Cadet #17 – Assistant Superintendent of Police;
25. Gamal Newry, Cadet #18 – President, Preventative Measures Ltd.; Assistant Superintendent of Police (Reserve);
26. Dr. Waldon Russell, Cadet #20 – Chief Operating Officer, URCA;
27. Jeremy Saunders, Cadet #22 – Engineer;

28. Deon Simms, Cadet #23 – Manager/Trainer/Actor/Writer & Rapper;

1989 Cadets:

29. Truman Butler, Cadet #32 - International Attorney-at-law;
30. Glennis Knowles, Cadet # 108 – Senior Administrator, Bahamas Global Academy;
31. David Cox, Cadet #54 – Chief Superintendent of Police & Attorney-at-Law;

Family:

32. Wife: Judy Wemyss, Retired Educator;
33. Children: Ingrid Wemyss, Keisha Wemyss, Acribba Lightbourne, Casey Wemyss, Assistant Superintendent of Police, Freddie Lightbourne (Son-in-law), Assistant Superintendent of Police;
34. Siblings: Roselda Sawyer, Mildred Butler, Raphael Whyms Jr., Theresa Burrows;
35. Nephew: Kenneth Whyms – Architect/Entrepreneur;
36. Business Associates: Brenda Ferguson-Dean, Accountant/ Consultant;
37. Terrance Bain – Accountant/Advisor Consultant;
38. Bishop Arlington Rahming – Former Senior Manager, Batelco; Senior Pastor, Christian Discipleship Ministries International;

Long Term Friends:

39. James Lewis (Jimmy Lou) (posthumously) - Former Police Officer;
40. Anthony Gibson – Businessman;

WemCo Security & Collections Ltd. Employees:

41. Jewel Fulford, General Manager;
42. Irene Smith, Security Manager;
43. Gerelene Meadows, Security Manager – Administration;

Medical Team:

44. Dr. Nicholas Fox, GP – The Medi Center Clinic, Nassau;
45. Dr. Frank Hull, Pulmonologist, Florida;
46. Andy Dorcely, Therapist, Kindred Hospital, Florida;

Caretakers:

47. Islande Desauguste, Florida;
48. Dyrine Ennis, Florida;
49. Marco Smith Jr., Bahamas; and

Last, but not least, special mention to Sebrena Bullard, writer, for her tireless effort and dedication in compiling the story. As a result of her persistent focus, Henry has finally told his story - a desire he has had since 1993.

Thanks to each of you, the "Henry Wemyss Story" has come to life.

Chapter 1

A Life Graced By God

On 19th September 2020, a flock of blackbirds sat perched on the side fence of Henry and Judy Wemyss' home, like permanent fixtures. Earlier as he gazed out his bedroom window, Henry observed them with curiosity, knowing that they were considered a bad omen. He could not imagine proving that true before the end of the day. It was also the first thing Acribba noticed when she arrived at her parents' home that day.

Equally unnerving was the stillness that hung over the yard and the airy scent that made her wonder if it was the smell of death. At the thought, she burst into tears. It was the height of the unprecedented global pandemic, and the COVID-19 death toll was steadily rising. The virus was wrecking families across The Bahamas and had made its way to the Wemyss' household. Five days earlier, Henry had tested positive.

Keisha and Acribba were assisting Judy with monitoring his symptoms, and while he had experienced fevers and chills, there had been no reason to panic until that day. They had hurried over after she had called to say he was having breathing difficulties. While Acribba prayed and paced outside, Keisha went inside to persuade him to go to the hospital. He was stubbornly against it, and unable to change his mind, they reached a compromise by getting an oxygen tank to treat him at home. That plan quickly fell through when they discovered that there was no oxygen in the tank. They would later come to see it as a blessing in disguise because he was then forced to go to the hospital.

As Henry protested, Keisha drove him to Doctor's Hospital, while Judy and Acribba followed in a separate vehicle. Sobbing all the way, Keisha was terrified that she would lose her father. The situation had escalated far too quickly. Earlier, she had cooked him breakfast, and before she left, he had assured her that he was fine. As soon as she got home, she had to rush back to the house. Knowing him, she suspected he had been suffering silently, even as he claimed otherwise. "If you knew you weren't feeling well, you should've said something," she scolded him between sobs. "Are you trying to leave us?"

By the time they reached the hospital, Henry could barely breathe. He was quickly admitted for what they expected to be a few days' stay. At 2:00 a.m., Acribba was still at the hospital, sitting in the lobby texting with her father and trying to console him. He was upset about being hospitalized, and she remembered his words at the onset of his illness, "Kiki, whatever happens to me, let me die at home." At the time, she had quickly assured him, "You're not going to die."

It was difficult to picture life without her father. For as long as she could remember, they had shared an extraordinary bond. She enjoyed being a 'daddy's girl.' As she got older, the two of them could talk about anything. He was not only her father, but also her best friend. In desperate need of intercession, she contacted Prophetess Mattie Nottage, her pastor. "We will pray," the pastor said calmly after hearing about Henry's hospitalization. Before the call ended, she asked to be kept updated. More at ease, Acribba returned home, hoping her father would recover quickly.

The hospital had a 'No Visits' COVID-19 policy, so they maintained contact throughout the day by cell phone. Soon, those conversations had to be cut short because Henry was becoming easily winded. He also appeared to be suffering from brain fog, as Acribba explained, "He was coming in and out, and because of the lack of oxygen, Daddy was losing a lot of his memory." Henry would later reflect, "I was told that my oxygen levels were so low that I was calling and texting people without knowing who I was communicating with. Someone showed me a text message I had sent to them from the hospital, and I had no idea what it meant—it was not English." Henry seemed to be getting worse rather than better, and this led to a series of unexpected turn of events.

"Daddy had called me on the morning of the 22nd, telling me to get him out of that place because he didn't want to die," Acribba recalled. "The call came in at 9:11, so I saw it as a '911' emergency, and if we don't get Daddy out of here, he's going to die! So, he continued pleading, 'Kiki, get me out of here; I don't want to die.' I replied, 'Daddy, listen to me. Don't talk, just listen. You are not going to die. You will not die.'" Despite her own concerns, she wanted to reassure him. Judy was also pushing for him to go, telling her daughters, "We can't let your Daddy stay here, and we got to get him off."

Since their father's hospitalization, Keisha and Acribba had reached out to the two US-based hospitals where he was already registered as a patient. With restrictions on family calls and visits, both facilities were quickly ruled out, as the family wanted daily updates on Henry's condition. As a third option, Keisha remembered the Holy Cross Hospital in Fort Lauderdale. She had recently watched a news report about a former boxer who had been released from the hospital after surviving a COVID-19 near-death experience. She also remembered that one of her local friends was the hospital's international coordinator. Calling her friend, she explained their situation and was immediately referred to a hospital administrator, who was also a physician.

The administrator told them exactly what they wanted to hear. Not only would they be able to call at any time to check on their father, but they could also have unlimited video chats and hospital visits when possible. He also emphasized that the hospital had recently added a state-of-the-art COVID Unit and that saving lives was the facility's top priority. Having wondered where God was since her father's admission, Acribba began to see His hands at work. She believed the name Holy Cross held spiritual significance. Convinced that it was a divine choice, she was willing to entrust her father's care to them. Keisha, on the other hand, was a bit hesitant because, unlike the other two hospitals, no one at Holy Cross knew them. "When God wants to see how much you trust Him, He will allow you to venture into unfamiliar territory," Acribba explained to her.

"We must trust God in everything, so that is what we have to do." Later, she would reaffirm their decision, "Holy Cross is a state-of-the-art hospital. It looks like a five-star hotel and that means everything was first-class. I felt good, and told Keisha, 'We did Daddy well. We did him proud. This is what he would have done if it was one of us. He would have made sure we got the best care.'"

On 23rd September, 2020, plans for Henry's departure were finalized, notwithstanding opposition to his release from the hospital. One of the doctors argued that the local hospital could provide him with the critical care he needed, just as well as any facility abroad, but the family was unwilling to take that chance. They wanted to do for him what he would have done for them - pull out all the stops. "Daddy, you're going to be okay," Keisha assured him as he was being carried out of the hospital and down the ramp to the waiting ambulance. "I'm taking you out of here." He was unconscious, but she hoped he had heard her. Like Acribba, she could not imagine life without her father. She considered him to be the family's protector and someone they could always depend on because he never broke a promise. Even though she was an adult, she realised how much she still needed her father.

Keisha referred to herself as "Medevac" because she often accompanied relatives who were receiving medical treatment abroad. As she was unable to join her parents at the time, she drove her mother to the airport. With a curfew in effect, the streets were deserted, so the drive to the airport was shorter than usual. Standing close, she used her phone to record her father as he was being transported across the airstrip to the air ambulance. As they prepared him for boarding, they switched his oxygen supply, and what happened next sent Keisha into hysteria.

"Daddy's body was fluttering like a chicken," she explained. "They had to hold him down, or he would have fallen off the stretcher." With her mother out of sight, she called Acribba, wailing, "Kiki, our Daddy is going to die!" she shouted, assuming they had run out of oxygen and her father had gone into cardiac arrest. "His body is jumping all over the bed. He's

8

fluttering." While on the call, Keisha blacked out and collapsed. Picking her up, one of the nurses revived her with oxygen. As soon as she regained consciousness, Keisha questioned whether she needed to get more oxygen for her father. Still on the other end, Acribba could hear a female's voice in the background saying, "Calm down. Mr. Wemyss is going to be okay. His body just needs to settle down. We have everything that he needs. We're going to get him over there safely."

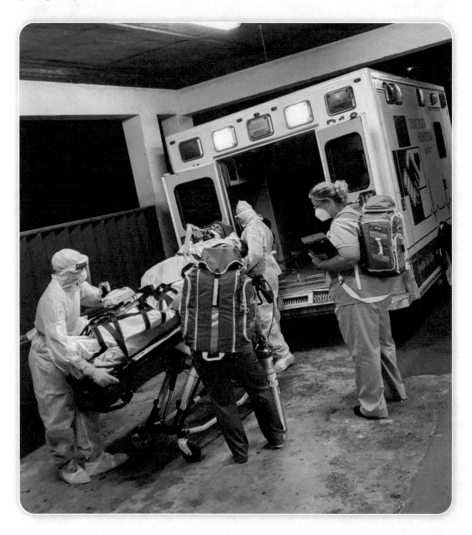

By 12:30 a.m., the air ambulance was ready for take-off, and before closing the door, the attendants gave Keisha the thumbs-up. As soon as the plane took off, Keisha sobbed bitterly. She followed its course as far as the Airport Industrial Park until she lost sight of the plane's light in the sky. When she returned home, Acribba was sitting outside, so she joined her, and together they waited for word from the hospital that their father had been admitted. About two hours later, they received that call and were relieved; believing his chances of recovery had significantly increased.

As soon as the plane landed in Fort Lauderdale, Henry was rushed into another waiting ambulance. Looking on, Judy lost count of how many machines were being connected to him, but estimated it to be about "20 machines." With all the wires protruding from his body, she realised the severity of his condition. Refusing to give in to tears, she clung to her belief that he would make a full recovery. After everything they had already survived together, she saw it as just another challenge the family had to endure. That steadfast faith continued to sustain her.

At Holy Cross Hospital, a team of ICU doctors assessed and treated Henry. By that time, his condition had intensified, and he was battling multiple complications. Both of his lungs were damaged, causing severe bilateral viral pneumonia. His oxygen levels were dangerously low, and the ventilator had to be set to fully support his lungs. Eventually, that was not enough. His lungs were filling up with fluid and becoming very stiff. If they were to get any worse, his death would become imminent.

Dr. Frank Hull, a pulmonary and ICU physician, was part of the team. "The team of ICU doctors at Holy Cross who cared for Henry included Dr. Coopersmith, Dr. Scott, and others. Things looked hopeless for Henry and having seen so many patients like him pass on from COVID-19, this looked inevitable," Dr. Hull explained. "Henry's kidneys had shut down, and he was not making any urine. A giant catheter was placed in his neck into the main vein, called the vena cava. He was started on dialysis to take over from the failed kidneys. Henry could not eat, and a feeding tube was placed directly into his stomach to feed him. The virus continued to try to kill Henry. His pneumonia was worsening, and a tracheostomy tube was placed in his neck. In desperation to keep Henry alive, the doctors placed him in a medical coma, and his muscles were paralysed so vital oxygen could be diverted to his heart and lungs."

In the days that followed, Keisha and Acribba continued checking in with the hospital from The Bahamas, getting updates on their father's condition, and keeping their mother, who was still in Florida, informed. All the while, they shared responsibility for overseeing the operations of WemCo Security & Collections Limited - the family's business. On the surface, everything appeared to be fine, but they were emotionally drained.

Keisha recalled, "I had lost a good 30 pounds for the first month and had no appetite. I was just working and drinking Gatorade, going without sleep for days, but no one could tell. The staff at the office had no idea what was going on or what we were going through. I told Kiki, 'We're going to run this place as though Daddy is here making the call.'"

There were times when they cried, but they did so privately, and their shared grief brought the two of them closer. Besides his children and close family members, few people knew about Henry's illness. Keisha and Acribba stayed tight-lipped while putting up a strong front to carry on with their usual routines. Later, a physician jokingly referred to them as, "The Gestapos."

On 4th October, 2020, Keisha and Acribba joined Judy in Florida. No one had seen or spoken to Henry since he had left The Bahamas, and there was no hope of seeing him soon. He had not come out of the coma and was still receiving medical care within the COVID Unit. They could only see him if they were called in to say their final goodbyes. Religiously, they called the hospital every day, hoping to hear good news about their father's condition, but his status remained grim. Fortunately, there was a physician in the family, Dr. Sharmaine Butler, Henry's niece, who joined in on the calls with the physicians. With her assistance, they were able to understand the medical jargon and the specifics of Henry's fight for his life. Being included on those calls, Dr. Butler knew her uncle's life was hanging in the balance. As a Christian, her faith joined medicine, and she led her immediate family to fast and pray.

"We had never fasted and prayed so much in our lives," Terry, Henry's sister, shared. "During that time, no one could have heard from anyone because you couldn't visit. Although they were there, they couldn't visit him. I didn't need to know what was happening. I just prayed to God and asked Him to bring Henry back to us and raise him up because he is a faithful servant. I prayed and cried because that was so touching." Keisha also shared, "Daddy's COVID episode drew me closer to the Lord; I learnt how to pray, I learnt how to fast, and I paid more attention to the Bible, church, and the likes."

"I was mortified when he was stricken with COVID and was extremely worried because he had a grim time," Dr. Nicholas Fox, Henry's local personal physician shared. "I diagnosed and treated him, but by then, it was a bit too far gone. I was updated daily by his daughters, sometimes from the hospital, and addressed any questions they had. It was a really tough struggle – a scary one because we thought he would die."

On 7th October 2020, at about 10:00 a.m., Acribba and Keisha called the hospital as they normally would, but were unprepared for what they heard. "I don't know who has been giving you all the news, but this man is going to die. He's not doing good at all, and he hasn't been doing well since he arrived," the nurse blurted out. "He's not going to make it through the night. How soon can you all get here? We don't want you all to miss out on the opportunity to see him one last time." There was no quick route to get to the hospital because they lived roughly a two-hour drive away. Besides, nobody was in a hurry to say goodbye. Emotions were running high.

As soon as they arrived, one of the physicians asked what action the hospital should take if Henry 'coded.' The reality of that question hit them hard, sending Acribba into a tearful panic attack. "My father is not dying, and you'll have to take every means to revive him because that's why he's here," Keisha stated emphatically. "You all will not call and tell me or my family that my father has passed." She was ready to do whatever it took to keep her father alive, even if it meant selling everything they owned.

Somewhat reluctantly, they made their way to Henry's room. "We need to go inside, so Daddy knows we are here, and he is not alone," Keisha told Acribba. "Since the 22nd of September, he has not heard any of our voices." Opting not to go in, Acribba gave her phone to Keisha, which had a recorded prayer from Prophetess Nottage and asked Keisha to play it over their father. She had been holding on to the prayer since he had been airlifted to Florida, but she had no idea how he would get to hear it. Although bad news had brought them there, she saw the opportunity as a Godsend.

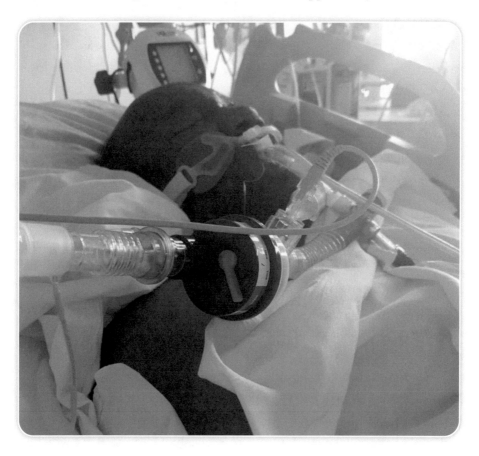

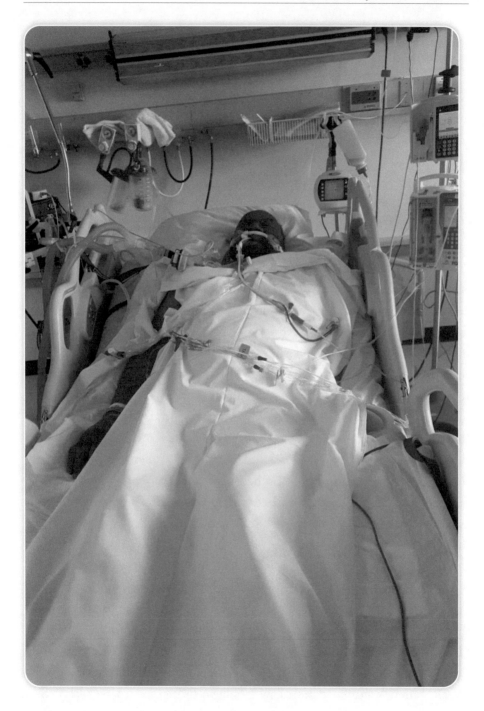

From where she stood outside, Acribba could see her father through a glass opening. "When I saw my dad in that bed, one side of his body was a totally different man. It looked like he had already departed this earth. And the other side looked as if he was still here fighting for his life. It was him on one side, and on the other side, I didn't know who that was so swollen," Acribba recalled. The extent to which COVID had physically afflicted their father was troubling. "It was heart breaking to see him lying there in that bed, swollen beyond recognition and hooked up to about 27 machines, knocked out and not able to look at me standing there," Keisha shared. "My Daddy was so helpless."

Teary-eyed, Keisha tried to sound cheerful as she greeted him, "Daddy, we're here you know. This is your big girl. I love you." There was no reaction, but she knew he could possibly hear what was going on around him. Placing the phone under his pillow, she played the prayer, which spoke healing to all his body parts affected by the virus and called him to rise from his sleep. Keisha also anointed his head and feet with the olive oil that the prophetess had sent. As the prayer played, she noticed his stomach quivering. Becoming excited, she asked, "Daddy, can you hear me?" His stomach quivered again. She motioned to Acribba to speak over the intercom. Acribba also called out, "Daddy, can you hear me?" Every time he heard their voices, his stomach moved. When they questioned the nurses, they were told that he had not shown any previous reactions. Seeing it as a turning point, they became optimistic. Before leaving, Keisha assured him, "Daddy, you're going to be okay. You're going to pull through this, and you're going home."

Although the nurse's earlier news had upset them, they were relieved that it did not turn out to be their last goodbyes – their father was still fighting to stay alive. After several weeks of being isolated from them, they were happy that he got to hear their voices. Rallying up, Acribba said, "Daddy is going to be okay you know." But Keisha reminded her, "Our Daddy doesn't look good in there." Affirming her faith, Acribba said, "Yeah, but he's going to be okay. I believe he's going to be okay." She felt hopeful, knowing that he heard the prayer. Shortly after their visit, they all returned to The Bahamas to await word that Henry had regained consciousness.

Whether it was hearing their voices, listening to the prayer, the combined prayers of others or divine timing, Henry opened his eyes three days after his daughters visited. Something he had not done in almost a month. Waking up in an unfamiliar place, he was disoriented. "When I came to know myself, there were tubes stuck all over my body, but I didn't know where I was. I was being fed through one of the tubes," Henry reflected. "The last thing I recalled was that Keisha took me to the emergency room at Doctor's Hospital, but I didn't want to go there, and I never came back. When I caught myself again, I was in another place, and I didn't know why I was there or how I got there. I had been on my back for so long that I had developed a bedsore that covered my entire back. I later saw a picture of it, and the hole was so big, a fist could fit inside of it. It was always bleeding, and I don't know how I survived. It was that bad." He knew he had COVID-19, but was shocked to learn about the other debilitating challenges he was facing.

In reflection, Dr. Hull said, "Henry was a strong man and fought for his life with every ounce of strength he could muster. The virus thought it had the upper hand and was trying to add Henry to the list of millions it had already killed. Henry's family prayed that Henry's soul would not leave him. The Lord must have heard. At that point, Henry required 100% oxygen, and the ventilator was set to fully support his lungs. If his lungs got worse, Henry would die. The virus must have thought it had done enough damage to kill Henry and moved on. Henry then tested negative for the Coronavirus. Unfortunately for Henry, his body and lungs looked like the aftermath of a war zone. His arms and legs had lost the ability to move on their own. He was now lying in bed paralysed."

Regaining consciousness was the first of many miracles for Henry. His family had taken a huge leap of faith by consenting to the medically induced coma. After being told he had awakened, they were eager to see him, but had to make do with talking over the phone until he was cleared for visits. With the tube in his throat, Henry could not speak, but he would sob whenever he heard their voices. In early November, Judy and Acribba returned to Florida. By then, Henry had been awake for two weeks and was anxious to see his family.

When they entered, Acribba brought joy into the room with balloons and a blue teddy bear. At the sight of his wife and daughter, Henry wept with relief. Overwhelmed with gratitude, Acribba fought back her own tears. "Now listen here, big guy, don't cry because you are alive," she said. "We give God thanks, and we give God praise. Don't cry." Unable to respond, he continued to cry inconsolably. "Knowing my Daddy, he had so many things he wanted to say, so many questions he wanted to ask, and he couldn't ask anything," Acribba recalled. "His body was paralysed; he could only blink his eyes to say yes he understands or nod his head, but he couldn't do anything else."

It was difficult to envision him regaining the strength and vitality he had before COVID-19 had struck him down. He had wasted away, having lost so much weight that he had become a shadow of his former self. His complexion had darkened, and he looked considerably older. Seeing him like that was hard, but Acribba managed to mask her true feelings. "We couldn't show our emotions when we saw him, because we had to be strong in front of him," she explained. "I cried a lot when he was in the hospital. I cried a lot when he was in a coma. But when he came out of the coma, it was like God dried up the tears because he realised that I had to go and deal with him. So, it was without emotions. God gave me the strength."

The doctors were concerned that Henry, like most patients recovering from a coma, might have experienced memory loss. Although he could not speak, it was clear from the way he reacted when he saw his family that he was fully aware of who they were and what his relationship with them was. Miraculously, he did not suffer any cognitive dysfunction. "Henry woke up from his medical coma and became lucid," Dr. Hull confirmed.

Henry looked forward to seeing his family every day. Acribba always showed up, wearing bright and cheerful colours. During her visits, she pampered and groomed him and occasionally entertained him with dances. She did anything she could to put a smile on his face. "Boy, I know one thing, you want to know that you look good in this bed," she joked. "I know that's in your head."

Despite his restrictions, Dr. Hull observed, "When allowed to see his family, he would somehow put on a brave face and smile at them. Henry wanted to be strong for his family, not wanting them to worry about him. His family tried to smile back as best as they could. Sometimes tears came instead. Henry's family continued to pray. They had not given up hope, knowing that Henry was a strong man both in mind and body and though recovery chances were slim, it was still possible."

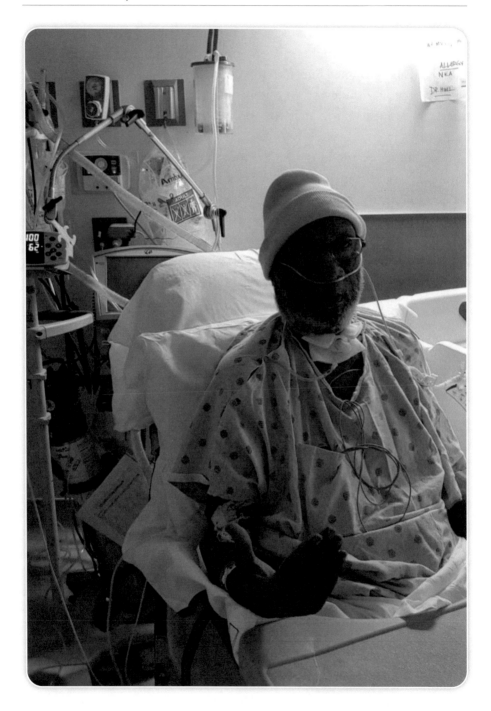

When she saw Henry's bedsore, Judy was horrified. "I visited him one day while they were doing his dressing, and when I saw the hole, I asked, 'What's happened here? What's this big hole in his back?' So, they explained that it was a bed sore where he was lying down," she recalled. "And I pointed out that I could almost see his organs and may be looking at his kidneys. They said, as long as it didn't affect his spine or anything like that, they would be able to treat it. And they would pack it." After his release, she took on the responsibility of treating and dressing the wound until new skin was formed.

Henry had been in Holy Cross for six weeks, but his recovery was going much slower than expected. He was still ventilator-dependent, and his chances of survival hinged on his ability to breathe on his own. To be able to do that, he required specialized care. "Henry was transferred from Holy Cross to the ICU at Kindred Hospital in Fort Lauderdale. This hospital specializes in the recovery of patients stuck on a breathing machine. I became Henry's personal physician there," Dr. Hull explained. "Again, most people in Henry's condition would not survive. I had written 35 death certificates for COVID-19 at Kindred."

"I reviewed Henry's history and examined him. His lungs were severely injured, he was on full ventilator support, and his kidneys had shut down. He remained paralysed and could not move. I also noted that at that point, Henry had a full-thickness skin wound on his buttocks the size of a small pizza. In the fight for his life, Henry had lost over 50 pounds of weight. At Kindred, a team of physicians and allied staff were set up to try to save Henry. We consulted an infectious disease doctor, renal doctors, a wound care physician, and a nephrologist. Great attention was paid to every detail of Henry's care. Labs and X-rays were done almost daily.

"I met all his family, including his loving daughters Keisha and Kiki, and Mrs. Wemyss, his wife. They looked frightened and tired. They had seen many other patients at Holy Cross in Henry's condition not survive the Corona Virus. They knew that most patients transferred with COVID-19 on a ventilator to Kindred Hospital did not survive, despite best efforts,"

He continued. "We now all prayed for a miracle that Henry would not become one of these dreadful statistics. We knew that Henry was very frail and could die at any time. If Henry was to recover, it would be a very slow process with many battles to fight. 'You can get better' is the message we used every day to encourage Henry. Even though his consciousness was clouded from sleep deprivation, I saw the spark of life in Henry's eyes and knew there was a chance."

Being totally dependent, Henry was in such poor form that rehabilitative treatment was crucial to getting him back on his feet. "When I did the evaluation, he was a patient that pretty much needed total care," Andy Dorcely, a therapist who worked with him, recalled. "There was nothing he could do for himself. He couldn't talk, but could mouth some words. He was barely able to move his hands, and all he really could do was move his eyes. When I asked how he felt about doing therapy and whether he wanted to work on getting stronger so he could go home, his face just kinda lit up like he was saying, 'Yes.' I could see he was trying to tell me he wanted to get stronger."

That was a green light for Andy, as he explained, "Just having the will to get better is one of the most important things when you're working with therapy." It was tough getting started because Henry was in such a vulnerable state. "Everything was a struggle," Andy said. "Trying to get him to the point where he could finally just sit up on the side of the bed took a while, and then getting him into a chair so that he could start sitting. It took a few days for him to simply tolerate all these things."

"Daddy got so small that he was just skin and bones. There were days when I didn't want to see him because I felt he wouldn't make it," Acribba admitted. "But I would go and pray with him, and he would raise his hand to receive the prayer. I had plastered photos of the robust person he once was all over the wall around his bedside. And there was one photo of him wearing a suit and praying, with his hand up in the air. I placed that there because I wanted him to remember where his help came from. I told him that every time he looked at that photo, that's what the goal was. And that photo ministered to everyone in the hospital because they spoke to me about it."

Henry was defenceless, so his family worried about how he was being treated, especially as he could not communicate. As family members were not permitted to stay with him, they hired two caretakers—Dyrine Ennis and Islande Desauguste—to provide him with personal attention and companionship. "So, he had a sitter from 7:00 a.m. to 7:00 p.m. and one from 7:00 p.m. to 7:00 a.m. just to have company and someone to call us and tell us what was going on with him," Keisha explained. "That helped with his recovery because he had company. Many people were dying from COVID because of loneliness."

"When I first saw him, I was like, oh my God, this guy is not going to make it, and I'm so sad for his family because they love him so much and there's nothing they can do," Dyrine recalled. "He had the trach. He wasn't speaking. He was just lying down there, and sometimes he wanted to say something so bad, but he couldn't say anything. I used to feel sorry for him."

Islande was astonished as she looked back and forth between the photos plastered on the wall and the man lying on the bed. "He really did not look like the man in the photos at all. Even when he was discharged and left to go home," she said.

The caretakers became extended members of Henry's family. Despite their doubts that he would make it or even walk again, they encouraged him and made him as comfortable as possible. After being on the ventilator for so long, Henry was frequently disoriented and hallucinating, and as soon as he was able, he attempted to pull the tube out of his throat or get out of bed by rolling. Some days, he had to be strapped down because he managed to pull the tube out of his throat. Other days, he demanded that he be taken home or to his office as he had to go to work. They had their fair share of challenges, but both caretakers enjoyed working with the Wemyss family. It was an experience neither of them would soon forget.

"It changed me because I got to meet such sweet people because some of the clients who I work with can be mean. But I became attached to Henry's family. They treated me like family, so they became family. I was happy I stayed because I didn't think I could do it," Dyrine shared. "When the agency asked me how it was, I told them I didn't know how much longer I could do it because it was beyond me. I was frustrated most of the time, but still looked forward to going because I didn't want to leave this man because, in my head, I didn't think anyone else would put up with his behaviour. I don't know if the pain medicine caused him to hallucinate so much. But as time went on and he transformed into himself, I could not leave. Then you get to see the real Henry. He was just a humble, sweet man, and I don't think he remembered everything that happened."

Others may have questioned whether Henry would recover, but Judy remained optimistic that he would fully recover. "While we were over there, Keisha and Acribba cried every day, and I would ask them, why are you crying? Your father is not dead. He is very much alive. He has more life than you or me," she recalled. "Instead of crying, you all pray." Keisha stated, "Whilst Acribba and I were tearing and breaking down, she had that mustard seed faith. My mother was in Walmart shopping for Daddy. She said, 'Your Daddy is going to need these when he comes out.' I told her, 'We don't dispute, he's coming out, but look at him now.' Her response was, 'I'm not worried about that, my husband is coming home.'" Acribba's four-year-old daughter, Skylar, also shared her grandmother's sentiments, and rebuked them, "Stop this! Stop this crying y'all. Nothing is going to happen to my Papa. My Papa is going to live and not die."

After great efforts, Henry got strong enough to transition to acute rehabilitation, where he had to endure three-hour sessions. He underwent more aggressive therapy and rehabilitation for the next three months, gradually becoming stronger. "We started to pick up the intensity of what we were doing, but it was still based on what he was able to tolerate. Some days he was happy to do it, and some days he needed extra pushing and motivation because he was tired," Andy recalled. "But he kept getting better, and then he had family who would come and visit with him and stay by his bedside, and that really made a difference in his progress." Andy remained optimistic because he continually saw Henry's determination to get better. "At some point, he was working with speech therapy. The only way he couldn't talk was because he wasn't able to breathe on his own, so he had a tube in his throat. So as his lung got stronger, I had to start working on taking the trach out."

24

"Things were still against Henry, but we believed he could live, and we all prayed for a miracle. Maybe someone did hear, as at that point, the miracle of his recovery started," Dr. Hull explained. "This was not a rapid miracle, as we read in the Bible, where paralysis is suddenly cured, and people get up and walk. Henry's miracle occurred over many weeks. At first, it was a flicker of strength. He was able to start to flex his arms and legs and later move his hands. Initially, movements were very weak, and he could not lift his arms or hands off the bed. His strength improved slowly, and soon Henry was pointing to the tracheostomy tube in his neck. Henry gestured he wanted it out. I explained to Henry that his lungs were far too weak for this.

"Next, a slow trickle of watery urine started. It was like finding an oasis of water in the desert. Soon, this flow turned into a strong stream of urine. Henry's kidneys had discovered the fountain of youth and were recovering. Next, the miracle moved to the lungs, the very organ that COVID-19 initially infected and had caused the most damage. The lungs were cleaning up the war zone damage left by the virus and were rebuilding. We cut down the oxygen levels and support from the ventilator, and Henry's lungs were allowed to do more work. Slowly, we were able to wean him off the breathing machine, and Henry was breathing on his own! His lungs were still very scarred and damaged, and he required a lot of oxygen that was now supplied by a nose cannula."

Having the breathing tube removed was a major milestone on his journey to recovery. Judy was there and recalled, "They took out his trach and feeding tube in front of me and gave them to me. They took everything out of him and gave them to me, and I kept everything they pulled out of him as a souvenir."

Henry needed speech therapy to regain the ability to swallow, take food, and drink by mouth. "The speech therapist assessed his swallow, and Henry had improved such that he was allowed to eat real food again. Henry was a man who loved food, and boy, did this make him happy. I believe Henry's mood improved tenfold with that first mouthful of ice cream," Dr. Hull stated. "The miracle continued. It was plain to see Henry was now gaining strength and weight. His strength had gotten to a point where he could sit up and walk with assistance. No longer being bedbound."

"Daddy spoke his first words on my birthday, the 30th of December 2020," Keisha said. "On the week of my birthday, we kept asking the doctor, 'When is he going to talk?' 'We want to hear him.' On my birthday, I dressed up and went there. I asked, 'Hey, Pappy what's up?' I asked, 'Do you know what today is?' He said, 'Yes, happy birthday, my daughter.' I exclaimed, 'What! You remembered?' He said, 'Yes, of course.' I replied, 'Thank you, Daddy,' and that made my whole day because I had already told everyone that I was going to have the worst birthday ever, but that made my whole day."

Relieved to regain his voice, Henry became an inspiration to everyone around him, sharing his faith from his hospital bed. Islande observed, "He was always talking to everybody there and all the nurses who were taking care of him. When they came to his room, they did not want to leave because of the way he spoke to them. He had that vibe. He talked about God, and they felt that he cared enough. And that was the first time they experienced a patient like that." She noticed that he listened in on a prayer line every morning and even shared the link with her. "While gazing through the window, he would say, 'Oh God, I give you thanks', and he would always tell me that God is good." Also being a person of faith, she said, "He was the first person I worked with who really believed like that."

Dyrine was primarily responsible for keeping Henry clean. "When he first talked, he told me that he felt bad for me because no one should have to do all that I was doing," she said. "I told him not to worry because that was my job. And he said he didn't care because nobody should have to do that." Reflecting on Henry's journey, she said, "I think it took a toll on him mentally. I don't think he ever gave up and never said he knew he was dying, but it was just a lot for him. All he wanted to do was to go home. God is just good because I never thought that he would have made it. I never got the opportunity to see someone in that state on my job before, but I will do it all over again."

Recognizing that recovery cases like Wemyss are scarce, Dr. Hull called him the "miracle patient" saying, "Praying and believing make miracles possible." He also attributed Henry's recovery to his family, who never gave up and allowed the miracle to happen. He was discharged from Kindred Hospital on 28th January, 2021. Even though he was still quite ill, he was strong enough to continue to recuperate at home.

"They had a farewell celebration for him," Islande said. "Because he was so nice and always said, 'thank you'. He gave every single nurse who took care of him something to say thank you to the hospital. Many of the people I work with didn't care and never said thank you. He even called me after he left to thank me for pushing him to exercise and encouraging him when he didn't want to go." Andy also observed, "Henry is a humble guy and is definitely about family and cares about family a lot. He appreciates people. A lot of people came in and out, and he was thankful for everyone, but there were some people he felt impacted him differently, and he showed his appreciation.

"That last week he kept on working hard; he understood that he was not done, but he understood at that point he could go home and continue therapy and just be in his own environment," Andy said. "He had a plan. He would talk about all the things he was going to do to be more active and put his weight back on so he could fit into his suits. He was determined, and he really stuck with it. A lot of people say that, and when they get home, it's not the case. But he went home, and he and his daughters put some work in, and they would send pictures of him in the pool doing exercises. His road to recovery was amazing, and I was happy to be a part of it. It was good to see how his family stuck with him and just wanted him back home. Not everybody who goes through all that would stay strong. I just love getting updates and pictures of him continuing to work on getting better and stronger. You don't get to be as weak as he got and lose all your strength and muscle and get it back within a month. His recovery was remarkable. He shared his story about how he persevered, and he tied it back to his faith."

Marco Smith Jr., a family friend who became like one of Henry's sons, also assisted the family. Two weeks before Henry was discharged, he flew to Florida to ensure that Henry was able to get around. "Because the house where they were staying was on the second floor, they were concerned about how he would get up and down the stairs," he explained. "So, I told them that instead of hiring someone, I could volunteer to lift him up and down the stairs in his wheelchair." He also set out to get Henry back on his feet. "When he came out in January, I told him, 'Don't worry, we will have you walking in no time. You will be strong again; you won't need any wheelchair, and you won't need any oxygen mask. You won't need any of that.'"

Marco also worked out with Henry to assist him with getting stronger, so he would be able to walk up and down the stairs. "We usually had conversations while working out, so it took his mind off how long we were exercising or trying to give up," Marco explained. "I tried to encourage him every day, adding some humour when he was feeling down and didn't want to get up. I would say, 'Man, Daddy let's go for a long walk. You can't be in the house all day, like furniture. Only furniture stays in the house all day.' So, I think that's what motivated him to get up every day because I was there to push him."

Henry returned to The Bahamas on 5th February, 2021. Although still dependent on oxygen 24 hours a day, he was in much better condition than when he had left. He was happy to be home and continued his slow journey to recovery. Over the next several months, he was completely weaned off the oxygen supply, and with an increased appetite, he started regaining weight. "He has recovered tremendously," Marco said. "When he first came out of the hospital, he was frail and really did not have any strength at all. It was quite easy lifting him up the stairs."

Freddie Lightbourne, Henry's son-in-law, Acribba's husband, also reflected on Henry's battle with COVID-19, "That was terrifying for everybody because it went so far so fast. One day he is in Doctors Hospital, and we expect him to be there for a couple of days and then come home. Then the next day, he is in the air ambulance, and then he's in a coma. And I remember one day they called me to say the hospital had called them to come in. When the hospital calls you to come in, that's it. That was a rough day."

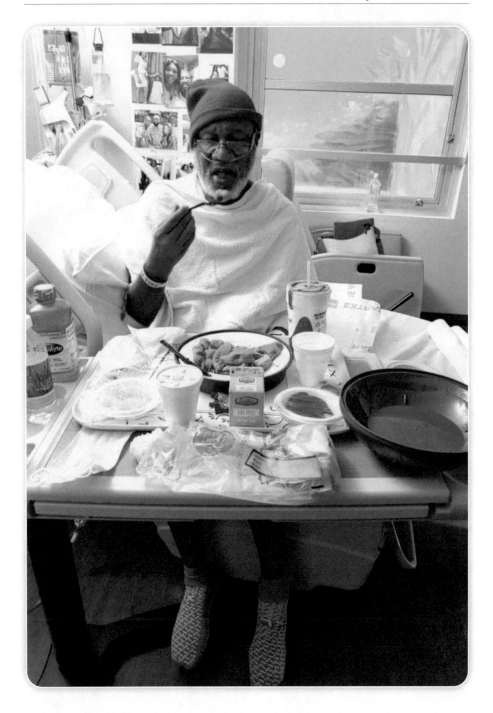

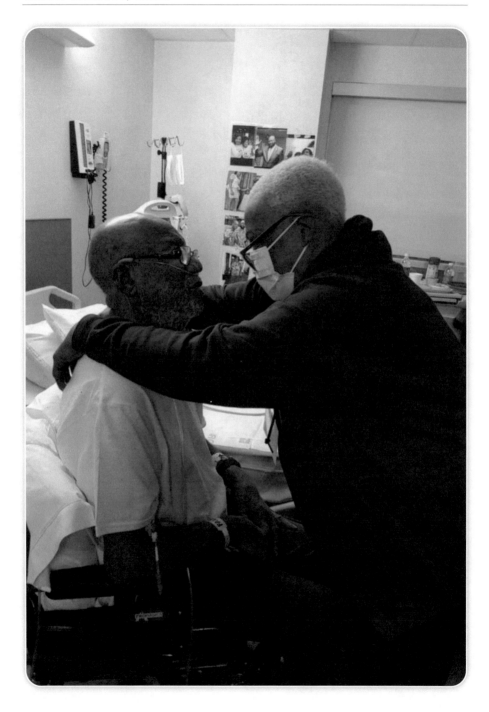

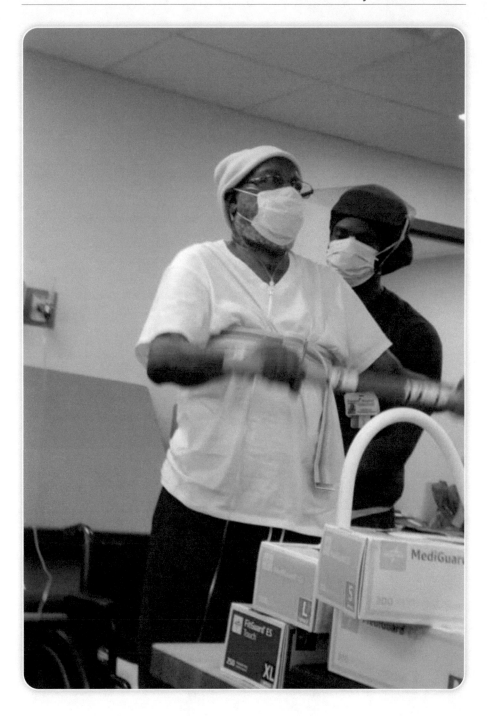

31

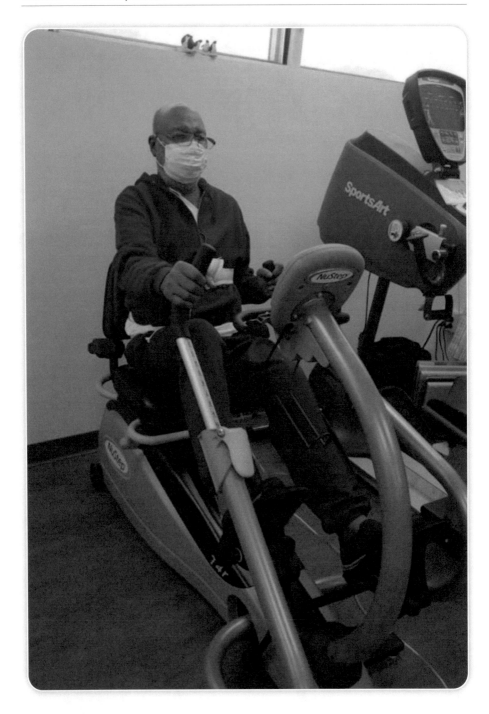

Freddie continued, "His illness affected the family deeply. Everybody was afraid that he was going to die, and you couldn't really prepare for it. If anybody prepared for death, it was him, but as a family, no one was prepared to lose him. I kept wondering how I would deal with him dying, like with Kiki and Skylar and the rest of the kids, how they would handle it. I would have to deal with Acribba losing her daddy, especially in such a way, you know. And it was terrifying. When they called me that day, saying the hospital had called them, I thought that was it, but thankfully it wasn't."

Summing up her father's miraculous recovery, Acribba said, "My Dad's physical appearance is better than when he went into the hospital. The way he looks now, he looks healthier than he was before. It is something to think about. He looks very youthful. He's always looked younger than he is or good for his age. But to come out of a situation that was supposed to take you to your grave, or the enemy intended to put you in your grave, but God intended to raise you up better again."

"He didn't die but lived to tell the tale, and that right there is a sign of his utter determination to succeed at everything he does," Dr. Fox said of Henry's recovery. "With determination, vim, and vigour, I knew that he would pull through. It is mind over matter, and I've proven that personally. He wanted to live, and he did."

Sadly, as the family celebrated Henry's miraculous recovery, there was a dark cloud hanging over their heads, While Henry was fighting for his own life, his oldest son, Conrad, had lost his battle with COVID. When he returned to The Bahamas, Henry had been asking for Conrad and thought it strange that he had not seen or heard from him. Out of concern for him, his family had told him that Conrad was off the Island.

When he did find out, it was shortly before the first anniversary of Conrad's death. A close family member let it slip during a telephone conversation. The news sent Henry's blood pressure skyrocketing and his oxygen level dangerously low. "I felt that something strange was going on with Conrad, but never expected to hear of his passing. That hurt me a lot," he shared.

Like anyone who survived a near-death experience, Henry reflected on his life's journey and how God had kept him during two of life's most tragic events—losing his freedom and almost losing his life. "When I look back on my life, there are good times, bad times and times that I wish had never happened," he noted. "Whenever I get to heaven, I want permission to ask God, what I did to deserve this? What I went through, did I deserve it? What he had me become, did I deserve that? Was it because of me or for others that he kept me? Despite all I have been through, I have already surpassed the lifespan of any other male in the Wemyss' clan."

Henry continued, "There were times when I felt lonely, but I later realised that even when I was lonely, I was never truly alone, because God promised never to leave us. 'When you pass through the waters, I will be with you; and when you pass through the rivers, they will not sweep over you. When you walk through the fire, you will not be burned; the flames will not set you ablaze,' Isaiah 43:2 (NIV). God had his hands on me from day one. His mercy and extravagant grace brought me from where I was to where I am today."

He recalled, "In 2011, I began writing my story, but had to stop for various reasons. I began again in 2019, but it came to a standstill in 2020, because of my COVID-19 experience. Originally, I had intended to publish the book later, but my recovery made me realise that I had been through too much and had too much to say to remain silent. I believe that God wanted me to share my story with the world, and if it could help even one person, it would be worth it. Looking back, I now understand that God was still writing my story during the time the book was on hold. My life is like a crossword puzzle that has come together in a way that I never imagined, and perhaps after reading my story, you will see why I feel this way."

CHAPTER 2

A Proud Family Heritage

On 14th April, 1947, Henry Anselm Wemyss was born, the seventh child and fourth son of Raphael Emmanuel Wemyss Sr. and Nathalie Pinder-Wemyss. April 14th would also commemorate two other significant events that happened later in his life. As was customary at the time, Nathalie gave birth to Henry at home with the assistance of a midwife. Their home was a three-room stone house with a thatched roof in Behring Point, Central Andros. Built on a hilltop, there was a panoramic view of the sun-kissed ocean that was located a stone's throw away. The house, which rested on seven acres of land, was passed down to Raphael Sr. from his father, Henry Wemyss, Sr.

During childbirth, all windows and doors were closed. "On the island, houses were closed two times when a funeral procession was passing the house to keep the spirits out," Henry recalled. Also, when a woman was having a baby and she and the midwife were in there, they didn't want any air to come in on the mother and baby, so they would patch up the houses and doors with pieces of old clothing."

Children were banished to the outside, and to preserve childhood innocence, parents never admitted where babies came from. Instead, they told a white lie, "The baby was dropped through the roof by a plane." Until they realized otherwise, children grew up believing this because they trusted their elders' words completely. This was the era into which Henry was born—one of innocence and great respect.

Despite having his grandfather's name, Henry is said to resemble both his grandmother, Malvease Brennen-Wemyss of Fresh Creek, Central Andros, and his mother. Whenever this was brought up, he was told that a man would live a blessed life if he looked like a woman in his family. In his case, looking like two women could only bring double blessings for him.

Henry would never get to meet any of his grandparents, as they had all died by the time he was born.

Three siblings followed Henry, but the Wemyss clan would have been 15-strong if all his siblings had survived childhood. The surviving 10 were Ambrose, Maria, Samuel (Big Sam or LO), Roselda (Rosie or Maggie), Joseph (JD), Mildred (Millie or Nancy), Henry (The Goose), Raphael Jr. (Rafe), Michael (Toodie), and Theresa (Terry). By the time Henry arrived, Ambrose, Maria, and Samuel were adults, having already branched out on their own, and except for Maria who had moved to Fresh Creak, they had relocated to Nassau.

From an early age, Henry cherished his close-knit family, and his parents were primarily responsible for the unbreakable bond between the Wemyss siblings that existed then and remains the same. Raphael Sr. and Natalie were their greatest example of how to live together lovingly, without bickering or disrespect. Rosie remembers, "My mother taught us that if your finger hurts, that means your brother's finger hurts. Or if his feet hurt, you should feel it. That's how much you should love them. That's the way our parents brought us up, and we've maintained that as adults—we love one another." Reflecting on her father's relationship with his siblings, Ingrid said, "They are close. They were tight when they were children, and they are tighter now if that's possible."

Elder sisters would help parent their younger siblings, and at one year and six months, after being weened, Henry was handed over to Rosie. She was 11 years his senior, and the oldest sister living at home. Besides caring for Henry, she looked after Millie, who was two years older than Henry. "At nights, I would sit in the rocking chair that once belonged to our grandfather, Old Henry Wemyss, and holding Henry in one hand and Millie in the other, I would rock them to sleep, usually until midnight," Rosie reminisced. "Wherever I went, I had to take them with me, even when I slept over at my mother's sister, Aunt Daisy's, house." It was a big responsibility for someone her age, but she did not mind, "I loved caring for him. I used to bathe and powder him before dressing him in the shorts and pants my mother had made for him." Through caring for Henry, Rosie developed a special bond with him, and he would grow up to acknowledge her as his 'other mother.'

Raphael Sr. and Nathalie were both born and raised in Behring Point, but became acquainted at St. Mary's Catholic School, the island's only educational institution at the time. Raphael Sr. was a junior teacher, and Nathalie was one of his students. She was two years younger than him. He became smitten with the girl, whom he observed as having both inner and outer beauty. "My mom was of medium stature, light-skinned, and beautiful," Millie said. "As a young man growing up in Andros, my father's parents thought he was too good for any girl, but my mother won him over," Millie added. Of course, other girls were vying for Raphael Sr's attention, but he particularly liked that Nathalie was not as 'forward' or 'fast' as some other girls her age.

Living in such a small community, Raphael Sr. knew Nathalie's family history. Her father, Shadrach Pinder, had abandoned them after leaving to work on 'the contract' in the United States of America, and her mother had since died. Her older sister, Georgiana, was left to raise Nathalie and her siblings. They were farmers, and life was tough for them. Raphael Sr., who was better off financially, often helped them. When Natalie was old enough, he asked Georgiana for permission to pursue her. In 1930, when she was 18 years old, they were married and were only separated by Raphael Sr.'s death 53 years later. Their relationship was the epitome of partnership and teamwork, illustrating the kind of marriage Henry would grow up to desire in his own life.

Raphael Sr. was a great catch and a man who stood out from the rest. Being the youngest child and only son living at home, he became the sole heir to his father's estate. "My dad had about seven sisters and two brothers, but his brothers went to the USA and never came back," Millie explained. "The sisters liked and respected him so much that they didn't want to call him by his first name, so they called him My Bulla. I also call Henry, My Bulla."

"He was an imposing figure, tall, dark, and handsome," Millie said of her father. "And he took great pride in his appearance and mannerisms." As a gentleman in his own right, his suits were either tailor-made from gabardine, which he imported from Oxford, England, or ordered from the Sears Roebuck catalogues. He completed his look with a Paramore straw hat and a gold chain link watch.

Henry's father had a significant influence on him, and through simple observations, he learnt many important life lessons. "Daddy was well-respected in the community," He stated. "He was a teacher by profession, but he was also a catechist, postmaster, justice of the peace, and just like his father before him, a local constable. He was responsible for just about everything going on in the island, from recording all deaths and births to overseeing mail boat shipments in and out of the island."

Raphael Sr. was also a businessman, being the sole proprietor of 'Dem Boys Bar,' a local hangout and the settlement's only bar at the time. As Rosie recalled, "Mostly, he hired someone to run it instead of doing it himself." Henry thought it was remarkable that, despite being a liquor merchant, his father never drank alcoholic beverages or smoked anything. "As children, we were not allowed to go near the bar, which was only a few feet away from our home," he reflected.

Henry also described his father as being "very quiet, no-nonsense, and having a serious demeanour." An avid reader, Raphael Sr. read the daily papers, Catholic publications, and any other books that captured his interest. He was well-spoken, and according to Henry, "his diction and penmanship were of another time." Similarly, Henry's penmanship has been described as "excellent, writing clearly and concisely," a skill only he and Rafe are said to have inherited. "Daddy had this air about him and stood out among the other fathers in the settlement," Henry boasted. "He never wore his shirts out of his pants. Whether he was wearing a t-shirt, pullover, or cotton shirt, they were always neatly tucked into his pants." Following in his father's footsteps, Henry would tuck his shirt into his pants until he reached advanced adulthood and was told that it was no longer fashionable.

"Mummy and Daddy insisted that we practice good hygiene and show pride in our appearance," Henry recalled. "Every morning, we would have to get washed up and fully dressed before having breakfast." After learning the value of maintaining a neat and clean appearance from his parents, Henry adopted those characteristics as his personal trademark. Most of the life lessons he learned were not solely based on what his parents told him to do, but also from watching their actions. "They did some things, and they said some things," he pointed out.

Reflecting on the traditional role of his parents in the home, Henry said, "Daddy preferred not to be involved in any housework and focused mostly on his business and community work. When he was at home and Mummy was busy around the house, he would sit on the porch, looking out into the settlement." Raphael Sr. had soft hands, indicating that he never farmed, fished, or worked hard. While being Androsian is often associated with crab catching, Raphael Sr. was cut from an altogether different cloth and never caught or even knew how to catch crabs. "I never learnt to catch crabs because when other children in the settlement went crabbing, my father never allowed us to go," Henry explained.

Nathalie, on the other hand, did not mind laborious tasks. Coming from a family of farmers, she knew how to farm, fish, and catch crabs. Preferring her not to work so hard, Raphael Sr. hired a man Henry and his siblings referred to as 'Old Uncle Reggie,' to handle the strenuous workload for her. He ploughed the farm, planted the peas and corn, and hauled all the trash away. Although Raphael Sr. also hired others to catch and clean fish for her, Nathalie enjoyed doing her own fishing. Her favourite spot was in the shallow waters of the Creek that ran through the front of their land, where multiple schools of bonefish could be found swimming.

Henry recounted, "As a young boy, I often went fishing with Mummy. She would raise her dress and tie it around her waist as we waded out into the sea. I always held the bucket with the bait in it as I stood next to her in water that almost covered my shoulders. Whenever I looked down into the water, I saw little sharks swimming close by and became frightened. I watched silently as Mummy threw the line out and skilfully pulled in her catch. By the time we left, the bucket was usually filled with enough fish for our meal or to share with another family or two." Back then, they never imagined that one day their island would boast of being the bone-fishing capital of The Bahamas, attracting tourists from all over the world.

Nathalie was also a dedicated homemaker who enjoyed caring for her husband and children. Recounting found memories, Millie said, "My mom was the best homemaker and catered to her family at all levels. Her husband was truly the king of the home, and she ensured that he received all he deserved. She looked after us, cooked, cleaned, managed the family farm, sewed the clothing, and shared with those in need." Being an exceptional seamstress, Nathalie made undergarments and denim pants for her husband and most of her children's clothing. She also made clothes for people in the community, including wedding dresses.

Whatever meals her husband wanted, Nathalie prepared, but her children had no choice as Rosie explained, "At that time, there were no favourite meals; whatever your mother fixed for you, you would have to eat, and Henry never made a fuss." On school days, she always had hot meals waiting for them. As Millie attested, "After school, my mother always had dinner prepared: peas n' rice, steamed fish or peas n' dough or any soup, baked crab, crab n' dough, potatoes, and cassava." Rafe recalled, "Mom baked bread better than anyone on the island. When Mom baked bread in the oven, it's like the bread you would get in the bakery now."

Sunday mornings were Henry's favourite because that was when his mother prepared stew fish and Johnny cake, and baked a variety of breads - potato bread, cassava bread, cornbread, and flour cake. However, they had to attend church before they could enjoy breakfast, and until then, they had to contend with a cup of tea. As children, they only drank bush tea with sugar. Carnation cream was a privilege exclusively for adults. According to their parents, it was not good for children because it made them 'brazen' and 'hardheaded.' Like anything else adults told them, they accepted that as a fact. When most families ate peas n' rice for Sunday dinner, Raphael Sr. wanted peas n' grits, and that was what they had. Nathalie prepared two types of meats—chicken for the children and ham for her husband. Since he had grown up with parents who farmed chickens, he never ate it.

Even though Raphael Sr. was able to provide for his family more than most fathers in the community, they lived a modest life. He believed in earning one's way and never splurged on his children. Instead, he preferred to extend his reach to benefit as many people as possible. According to Henry, "Growing up with the Benedict Priests, he was very conservative." Material-wise, nothing caused Henry and his siblings to stand out amongst other children in the community. "We lived with the essentials and never realised that life could have been better for us. Like everyone else, we had an outside toilet and took our baths in the back of the yard using a tin tub. We always walked around barefooted, except when going to school or church. Later, when we found out he could have given us more, we called him "cheap and mean," but quickly realised that he always provided for our real needs. I admired Daddy most for the way he carried himself and how dependable he was when it came to caring and providing for us. There was never a day when we went to bed hungry or lacked anything we needed."

During the day, a stick kept the wooden windows in their home open. At nights when they were closed, the house was in total darkness, except for a kerosene lamp that was lit in their parents' room. There was one bed in the other bedroom that the children shared. As everyone could not fit, some slept sprawled across the wooden floor. They had to be in bed by 7:00 p.m. and awake by 6:00 a.m. every day, at which time they had family devotions.

Eventually, Sam made life a little more comfortable for them. After relocating to Nassau, he established himself as a building contractor and returned home to Andros to construct a bigger house for his parents. The new house had two bedrooms, a kitchen, a dining room, and a living room. They were all excited about their new home, which also had a shingled roof, sliding glass windows, an oil stove, and a gas refrigerator. Before the oil stove, Nathalie had cooked on an outside stove built from buttonwood and steel.

Raphael Sr. ran an extremely strict household. "We weren't afraid of our parents, but had the utmost respect for them," Rosie explained. "We knew that when their friends visited to talk, we could not stay in the house but had to go outside. We knew how strict our father was. Mummy was easier on us, but Daddy was very strict." Strangely, their father was never the one to dish out punishment. "My Daddy never beat us. He spoke to us, and we knew what that meant. Daddy was in charge," Millie said.

However, their mother would send them to "go to the tamarind tree and bring back the biggest switch you can find." Not wanting to be sent back a second time, they did as they were told. When they got back, she would plait it up before whipping them until they cried. She would give them a drink of water to 'calm their passion' whenever they cried until they gasped for breath.

Afraid of getting punished, Henry tried his best to avoid it. Reflecting, Rosie said that Henry was "a well-behaved child." Rafe claimed, "Henry never got beaten because I got beaten for everyone." As Henry recalled it, "Rafe got a lot of punishment, but Rafe was kind of mischievous. As a child, I practiced self-discipline because I was afraid of being punished, so I tried to always do what was right. I was always fearful of problems."

At the time, adults in the community had the right to discipline children other than their own. The saying "it takes a village to raise a child" was in full effect. Adults were sticklers for good manners, and if word got home that any child passed an older person without a greeting, that child would be punished for being ill-mannered. Children were trained to say, "Yes sir," "Yes ma'am," "No sir," and "No ma'am." Rosie also recalled, "My parents used to tell us to respect the elderly and give respect to whom respect is due. They instilled values of being honest, being nice to others, and having self-respect because if you respect yourself, people will respect you." Grateful for his upbringing, Henry said, "My parents taught us good manners, self-respect, and that respect for others would take us around the world. When they said that, I always took it literally. Those lessons formed my core values and still influence everything that I do today."

On the Wemyss property, native fruits such as sugar cane, sugar apple, sapodilla, soursop, banana, sweet potato, coconut, and corn grew in abundance. Henry and his siblings were free to eat the fruits that fell to the ground but could not pick anything directly from the trees without parental consent. Adults also used a scare tactic to prevent children from raiding the trees. Every child in the community understood that bottles filled with water and sand hanging from trees indicated that evil spirits lived within the trees. They would scurry away whenever they saw the bottles, not daring enough to pick anything from those trees.

However, children could freely pick the plums, dillies, and tamarinds that grew wild on unoccupied properties. Henry took full advantage of this freedom. "I especially liked picking tamarinds and placing them in a pot on the fire. I would mix a little sugar in it and keep stirring it to make tamarind sauce," Henry said. "That was a speciality of mine and probably the only thing I ever learnt how to cook."

Henry grew up in an environment that also nurtured his sense of kindness. He recalled, "Behring Point was a close-knit community of givers. Even though there was not much to give, everyone willingly shared what little he or she had. Most families were self-sufficient, surviving on fishing and farming. Whenever someone went fishing or slaughtered a pig, they were eager to share their provisions with others. No one complained about not having anything because they either went without or borrowed from a neighbour, who willingly shared."

While Raphael Sr. was kind, it could be said that Nathalie had a double dose of generosity. She often went out of her way to be kind to others, always offering food. "I remember Mummy as a loving, kind, and gentle person. She was compassionate, also caring for the other children in the community," Henry said. Rosie, like all his siblings, agreed that Henry was a combination of both parents. "Henry is kind like my mother, who was more generous than my father. Mummy loved everyone and loved giving away things. He is smart like my father, who was well educated." She described Henry as, "a nice and kind person. He would give you his heart if he could take it out."

Henry also attributes some of his most endearing character traits to his mother. "She taught me how to be kind, how to be gentle, how to share everything with your sisters and your brothers, and how to care for elderly people and others. She taught me that nothing is too good to give away. Don't give them what you don't want, give them the best; give them what you want. If you can't do that, don't give them anything at all. These are things that I did not learn in school but learnt through watching her," he reminisced.

There were about 20 houses scattered throughout the settlement, and everyone was family, not necessarily by blood relations. Henry recalled, "The families living in the settlement were the Coakleys, Mackeys, Braynens, Thompsons, Whites, Neymours, Whyllys and the Wallaces. And men usually referred to one another as "Bruh"—an abbreviated term for brother. Imitating them, I also used it amongst my peers," he stated. "There was a visible sense of camaraderie, friendship, and togetherness in the settlement. They practised 'love thy neighbour as thyself.' As crimes were unheard of, the only reason people locked their doors before leaving home was to prevent them from flying open in the event of wind, rain, or during hurricane seasons. Back then, no one in their right mind would think of stealing anything from a church, so there was no need to secure it."

Every week when the mail boat arrived from Nassau, the community at large would flock to Raphael Sr.'s office, which was located at the dock. They were eager to find out whether they had received mail or boxes of groceries from family members in Nassau. The older Wemyss children, who had relocated to Nassau, sent boxes of groceries and other essential supplies for the family back in Andros. "My father used to order his groceries from E. L. Sawyer, which was located on Bay Street in Nassau. At that time, the maple leaf butter was in a yellow and gold can. And the groceries came by mail," Rosie recalled. Whether she really needed to or just wanted to assist families who did not have much money, Rosie remembered her mother bartering for fish. "Sometimes when people went out to fish, Mummy exchanged grits, flour, rice, or whatever they wanted for the fish."

During Henry's childhood, hardly much ever happened in Behring Point. "Forty seemed old back then, and grown-ups mostly sat around bragging about their children, who had moved to the capital, waiting for letters from them," Henry said. "There were no special days in the year. Christmas was just another ordinary day without gifts, decorations, or Christmas trees. I only knew it was Christmas because, as a family, we spent most of the day at church singing Christmas carols. Birthdays went by unnoticed - no parties or dancing - and the first birthday gift I ever received would be at 18 years old from my girlfriend, who eventually became my wife." The only time he could recall any type of celebration was when the Catholic Bishop came down for mass, once every two years. That was a major event, and everyone dressed up in their Sunday best for the occasion.

Life was simple, and there was little, if any, outside influence. Nobody in the community had a television, so Henry had no idea that such a thing existed. He knew about radios, as he recalled, "My father had a turn-handle radio that he used exclusively, and we were not allowed to touch it. He only turned it on to listen to the daily news. As soon as the news was finished, he switched it off. I don't believe he ever needed to charge the battery." There was never music of any kind playing in their house. "The first secular song I ever heard was while visiting Aunt Estelle, my father's sister, who lived close by," Henry recounted. "Her daughters had a radio and were listening to Elvis Presley's 'Love Me Tender.' They had also bought a booklet with all the lyrics and used to sing along with the radio. Other than that, I only knew church hymns."

Raphael Sr. was not so keen on playtime, and whenever he allowed them to go outside, they had to remain in their own backyard. He never wanted them to go anywhere else. Henry recalled "If we wanted to go down the road, we would go to Mummy, and she would say, 'Go to your Pa,' and your Pa would send you back to your mother, and she would send you back to him, and he would ask, 'You came back?' And you would know what that means: don't come back; it meant no." Their mother was more lenient, so they enjoyed most of their playtimes when their father was out, attending to his numerous duties.

Unlike other children, Henry and his siblings could not run around the settlement, getting dirty, or wander over to the neighbours' yards, as they liked. Sometimes, they were allowed to visit relatives who lived nearby. They often ran errands for their mother and delivered items to the neighbours, but she would spit on the ground and warn them to get back before it dried. Being surrounded by water and having a beach just a few hundred yards from home would be a privilege for any child, but Raphael Sr. was hard set against them playing there. Unlike other boys in the settlement, Henry did not learn to swim while growing up in Behring Point.

Occasionally, children were allowed to come over and play with them. Like most boys his age, Henry enjoyed shooting marbles, playing bat-and-ball, hopscotch, and jumping rope. Back then, they made their ropes with tree twines. Tourists who frequented the area often left behind tennis balls, but otherwise, rolled-up bobby socks were the next best thing. As there were no modern devices, they had to use their imaginations. They created bird traps by constructing a replica house roof out of tree branches and placing a stick with a string underneath it. They used corn seeds to lure the birds inside, and as soon as a bird entered, they yanked the string to trap it. Pulling the bird out, they roasted it over an open fire.

Henry also had his share of fun times that left him bruised and scarred. JD had a knack for creating things. Not only was he skilled at building mud castles, but he also carved three-foot wooden boats out of Kamalame trees. "We would sit in the boats and push them forward as we raced around the yard. Being the best was always important to me," Henry reminisced. "And one day, as I was pushing hard to stay ahead of everyone else, I fell backwards over some sharp rocks and ended up with a large gash on the back of my head that my mother had to treat. There were no doctors or nurses around then, so parents and other adults treated you with natural remedies, like bush medicine, and those things worked."

Empty cardboard boxes became pull carts. "I used to put Rafe in a cardboard box and drag him through the house from the back door to the front door, and that's how I burned my right foot," Henry explained. "In those days, you would light a fire in a pan or some other container and place it in the front of the house to create smoke to prevent mosquitoes from getting inside. One time, as I was dragging Rafe, I stepped back into the pan and screamed so much I thought I was going to die. My mother had to rush to the bay to get some salt water to draw out the heat. Later, it turned out and became swollen but eventually healed." Henry will always remember that incident, which left a mark on the top of his foot that remains to this day.

As a young child, Henry exhibited leadership traits. He was known for collecting shells, washing them, and selling them to other children for rock currency. Although he enjoyed a good competitive game of shooting marbles, he recalled, "I preferred to be the scorekeeper or referee because I didn't like getting dirt on my hands or clothes. I called the shots whenever arguments about specific shots became heated and threatened to end the game if the boys did not play peacefully." The other boys always respected his rulings and followed his orders. Rafe stated, "Henry was always the peacemaker." From an early age, his siblings noticed something different about Henry; their parents also recognized this. He was dubbed, 'the golden child' and was adored. Rosie attested to this, saying, "He was ever the pride and joy of our family. Well-loved." According to Millie, "Henry was an ambitious child, very inquisitive, and always wanted to know what his older brothers and sisters were talking about."

It was no secret that Henry had little enthusiasm for his household chores, but all the Wemyss' children were expected to do their fair share of work around the home. Everyone had tasks to do, whether they were scrubbing the wooden floors, washing dishes, or fetching water from the well. Before going to school, Henry and Millie were responsible for drawing water for bathing and filling the drums for cleaning, washing, and cooking. As the well was located some distance away, they had to walk back and forth through the bushes many times, something Henry never looked forward to doing. After school, they also assisted with the farm work, such as roasting potatoes and corn with their mother or picking and shelling peas with Rosie, who recounted, "Henry was kind of lazy to do that and Mummy never insisted. Sometimes, when she asked him to do anything, he did it without a kick."

They were devout Catholics and attended St. Mary's Catholic Church, which was at the center of their lives. They spent a lot of time attending mass and praying at home. One of Raphael Sr.'s favourite sayings was, "A family that prays together stays together." At 6:00 a.m. daily, they had morning devotions as a family, and Rosie recalled, "When we were younger, at nights before going to bed, my father made everyone kneel around the bed, join hands, and pray. We had to pray as a family before going to sleep." Terry recalled overhearing her father reciting his personal nightly prayer, "He would say the Lord's prayer, then Hail Mary, and then a prayer coming from 2 Timothy v 7: 'I have fought a good fight, I have finished my course, I have kept the faith', and then he would continue saying, 'Oh my God, have mercy on me. Forgive me for my sins and let me die in your friendship and favour.'"

As a catechist, Raphael Sr. was the point of contact for the Diocese and was responsible for distributing the items coming in from the Catholic mission - milk, cheese, and other necessities. He was very active, taking care of the church and the school and getting his family involved. Like his older brothers before him, at seven years old, it was Henry's responsibility to ring the church bell at 6 o'clock every evening. Although the church was not on the main road, it was within walking distance of their home. Houses were scattered around, but none were near the church. To get there, Henry had to pass a graveyard. Even though he had never seen a ghost, older people in the community claimed they had, and gripped by fear, he kept looking around. There were also ghost stories he had heard from his father, who recounted walking on the road at night and a man passed by, but when he turned to see who it was, the man had strangely disappeared. Hearing such stories from his elders, he developed a fear of the unknown, which he would carry with him throughout his life.

"Once, Millie and I went to the back of our house to pick yams and trailed the yam string hoping to find yams at the end of it. After walking for a while, we thought we were lost because we had no idea how to get back home," Henry recalled. "There were snakes crawling all over the trees, and Millie said that a ghost had lost us. She then suggested that we turn our clothes inside out to ward off bad luck. She then climbed one of the trees and started yelling, 'Hello,' and I also yelled with her, but our voices just echoed back, and nobody answered or came looking for us. When she came down, we decided to walk in another direction, and within a few steps, we were back in our own backyard."

Henry was too short to reach the church bell, so he had to climb up on a wooden bench. From there, he proceeded to ring the bell ninety-nine times—10 times in chimes of nines and nine times in singular chimes. By the time he was done, it was dark, so he always ran back as fast as he could to the main road. He also served as an altar boy, and by the time he was 10, he could recite the entire Catholic Mass in Latin and had memorized all the priests' routines. Millie recalled, "Henry also enjoyed assisting at church and looked forward to participating." Although he never thought about what he wanted to be when he grew up, his father decided that he should be a priest. In Raphael Sr.'s eyes, serving the church and the people was a respectable duty. With this mindset, he sent Rosie and Millie to Nassau to join St. Martin's Convent as postulant nuns. They only stayed for about a year because Nathalie missed them and wanted them back home.

Buying into his father's dream that he would become a priest, Henry held his own play-play mass at home. Taking two buckets, he laid a piece of wood across them and covered them with one of his mother's tablecloths - this was his altar. He took a second tablecloth and draped it over his shoulders - that was his priestly robe. To make himself seem more like a priest, he tied his robe with tree twines. His congregation was made up of Millie, Rafe, and any other children who happened to be around at the time. As a child, his understanding of God was limited to his observations of the priests and their seeming dedication to serving the church.

In addition to church work, Raphael Sr. was also passionate about education. He taught all his children, who attended St. Mary's Catholic School - the same school where he had met their mother. He was serious about academics and no matter what else was going on, he expected them to spend quality time studying or reading. He would often tell them, "Pick up your books or your Bible and do some reading." Henry grew up knowing that his father expected nothing less than excellence, and he never tolerated mediocrity. He was determined not to disappoint his father and always strived to make him proud. Reflecting on Henry's early education, Rosie said, "He was a very good student, although he never studied much. He glanced through his books. But whenever he took exams, he came tops. He was very smart."

Just about everyone in the vicinity referred to Raphael Sr. as "teacher." "My father taught for the Catholic school for 40 years or more," Millie recalled. "In 1957, The Bahamas Government opened an all-aged public school between Cargill Creek and Behring Point. The government hired Mr. Frederick Curry, a teacher from Nassau, and provided him with housing. The parents moved all the children between those settlements, who used to attend my father's school, and sent them to the new school. My father was hurt by the parents' actions because they did not inform him."

At the time, Raphael Sr. could not see the necessity for a second school. He was heartbroken because being a teacher was his pride and joy. "Prior to Mr. Curry's arrival, there were no government schools on the island, so the Catholic Church made sure that an education system was in place," Millie explained. "My father became upset because he felt that he had been teaching all the while, and there was no need for another teacher. He felt as if he had lost his power."

Raphael Sr. decided to continue teaching Millie, Henry, and Rafe until they were ready for high school, at which time he planned to send them to Nassau. However, Nathalie persuaded him otherwise, telling him it would be better if they attended 'The Curry School.' Mr. Curry also met with him to encourage him to enrol the children in the new school, pointing out that he would then have more time to devote to his church and other community-related duties. Eventually, Raphael Sr. agreed, and soon, Mr. Curry became a close acquaintance of the family, whom he referred to as "the aristocrats of Behring Point."

Henry found it to be an exciting, brand-new experience after only having his father teach him. He was grouped with the older boys and continued to do exceptionally well in all subjects. A year later, Henry received a scholarship to attend a Catholic school in Nassau, and his father also made plans for Millie to go with him. Sending Henry to a Catholic school in Nassau was all part of Raphael Sr.'s plan for his eventual entry into the priesthood. With no say in the matter, Henry had no choice but to accept his father's plans as his own. Besides, he was not opposed to the idea since he had observed how highly respected priests were in the community.

Henry had always wanted to visit Nassau, so when he learnt that he would not only be going, but staying as well, he was overjoyed. The one damper was that it meant living away from his parents. Raphael Sr. also struggled with his choice because as Rosie stated, "He felt that his minor children should not be anywhere without him." As they prepared to leave, there was a bittersweet excitement in the air. "I didn't know if I would ever return to Behring Point and that made me sad. I had a wonderful upbringing there because of all the love and kindness that was around me - the spirit of community," Henry reminisced.

Growing up, Henry became aware that being a Wemyss carried certain expectations, particularly from his father. He would come to appreciate that his parents did everything they could to raise him and his siblings to be responsible and respectable adults. He would never forget the morals and values that had shaped his character. What he remembers most clearly from his childhood is a simple life, in a peaceful place where everyone was treated as family. It would become the 'good old days,' as he never imagined life could be any other way.

Millie also looked back fondly on their childhood, "Growing up in Andros, in those days, was very exciting. We watched the beautiful waters as we walked to and from school. They were our best days, and when you're small you never think that those days are coming to an end."

Raphael Senior & Nathalie Wemyss

CHAPTER 3

Embracing A New Way Of Life

In the summer of 1959, Henry and Millie travelled to Nassau with their father aboard the M/V Madam Elizabeth, a mailboat that sailed between Andros and Nassau. After spending their entire lives in Behring Point, they were looking forward to new experiences in Nassau.

"When I came to Nassau, the first thing I saw that stood out was the big white man - the statue of Columbus - at Government House," Henry recalled. At the time, he did not realise that it was a statue. "The boat came in at the Woodes Rogers Wharf, where the straw market is right now, and we rode from there and drove up George Street." By the time that ride was over, Henry had already realised that compared to Nassau, Behring Point was a sleeping town. "It was too big to comprehend with all the cars, and I noticed that people were driving from the left of the car instead of the middle as I had earlier envisioned."

There had been no cars in Behring Point, so anytime Henry drew cars, the steering wheel would be in the centre because he could not imagine driving it from any other position. Henry's prior exposure to modern amenities happened when he spent a summer with his sister, Maria, in Fresh Creek. "She lived in a place called The Lost City. I was about 10 years old at the time, and that was the first time I saw a refrigerator, felt air conditioning, or saw electrical lights. I was so amazed," Henry recalled. "We went to a food store called the commissary. When I walked through the glass doors, the inside was so cold that I was frightened but excited because I had never felt anything like that before. It would also be my first-time seeing cars."

In Nassau, they moved in with Sam, who lived with his wife on Rupert Dean Lane in the Bain Town area. They had a three-bedroom, modern clapboard house, which he had built. Their brother Joe, who was five years older than Henry, had relocated some time earlier and was also living there. It was a comfortable place and one of the best in the area, at the time. After not seeing his brothers for a long time, Henry had to get to know them all over again. When his father returned to Andros, Sam immediately assumed the fatherly role, taking care of Millie and Henry. Like their father, he ran a liquor store but only part-time because he was also working as a building contractor. Spending time around Sam, Henry gained respect for him and looked up to him as a role model. He thought Sam was brilliant, sharp, and quick on his feet. Anytime he needed advice, he went to Sam, who because of his brilliance, the family nicknamed 'LO' after the first Bahamian Prime Minister, whom he also resembled slightly.

It took some time for Henry to adjust to his new surroundings. Streetlights were still a mystery to him, especially as they only lit up at night. Growing up with kerosene lamps, it was fascinating to turn on the house lights at the flip of a switch. Curious, he had stayed up many nights trying to figure out the workings of electricity. Back home, he was accustomed to walking on dirt roads, but in Nassau, the roads were nicely paved. After moving to Nassau, Henry experienced many firsts, but he was especially delighted to discover ice cream and candies.

Although Nassau was crowded and moved at a faster pace than he was accustomed to, he never worried about his safety. Crime was relatively low, and people seemed comfortable moving about, even at night. Everyone appeared friendly, but Henry noticed they kept to themselves more than the people in Behring Point. He also saw children in the area doing things he had never done before, like riding bicycles and skating. He realised he had a lot of catching up to do.

Soon, Henry would meet James Lewis, nicknamed Jimmy Lou, who lived nearby. He was a skinny boy and the tallest one around at the time. Initially, he would just stand around watching Henry and the other boys shoot marbles without saying a word. Henry assumed that he could not speak until he finally did. Over time, they grew closer and formed a lifelong friendship. In reflecting, Jimmy said, "Back in those days we didn't go out;

we stayed at home, shooting marbles and flying kites. We stayed out of trouble and never ventured too far from home. Now and then, we went to the movie theatre but when it got dark, we stayed in. As the years went by, we became closer and closer." Henry also reflected on his time with Jimmy Lou, a brother, and a friend, who unfortunately predeceased him, "We became best friends, and as we got older spent a lot of time together, travelling and attending church, sitting side by side in the same pew. My family became his family, and my children called him "Uncle Lou" and his family also became my family."

When Raphael Sr. brought Henry and Millie to Nassau, he expected that they would both attend Aquinas College. But as Millie explained, "In 1959, my father took Henry and me to Aquinas College to attend high school. Henry was too young for enrollment, so the principal, Sister Maria Patricia, recommended that he be enrolled at St. Thomas Moore, which was across the street." So, Mildred went to Aquinas College and Henry was sent to St. Thomas Moore, which he described as a "predominantly white environment." Before then, the only white persons he had ever seen were the Catholic Priests or the Bishop, who visited the island every two or three years. Being a friendly person, Henry embraced everyone and addressed them as "Bruh". After a while, he himself became branded with the nickname, "Bruh".

Henry was especially good at mathematics and had a knack for calculating figures. Noticing this, Sam hired him as a timekeeper for his work crew. Before dropping him off at school in the mornings, Sam took him down to the job sites to take attendance. Then, at the end of the week, Henry tallied up the hours and calculated each worker's wages. "I liked working with figures and saw a future there," Henry stated.

Henry and Millie missed the nurturing care they had received back in Andros. Finding it hard to adjust without it, Millie sent word back home for their parents to send Rosie to Nassau. In 1960, Rosie left Behring Point, where she had just started working as a third-grade class monitor, to join her siblings and care for them. She was not ready to leave her hometown but knew that her family needed her. In Nassau, Rosie ensured that her younger siblings received their meals on time. Having learnt basic sewing from her mother, she enrolled in a sewing school on Hospital Lane to improve her skills. Eventually, she opened a shop of her own on Market Street and Cordeaux Avenue. In addition to sewing clothes for her customers, Rosie enjoyed sewing shirts for Henry, as well, "After school, he would wear his white tennis and the nice shirts that I made for him. He was a handsome little guy in Khaki pants," she recalled.

About a year later, Henry was old enough to sit the entrance exams for Aquinas College, which he passed with honours. He also had the option to attend St. Augustine's College, but after hearing rumours about certain priests, his father did not take to the idea, at the same time changing his mind about Henry joining the priesthood. Instead, Henry joined Millie at Aquinas, where the Dominican Nuns from Georgia and Boston taught them. Millie reflected on his time in school and said, "Henry was one of the most popular students. He was not only smart but also well-mannered, outspoken, and well-liked. In fact, the nuns were so fond of him that they trusted him to carry their books and bags. He would also assist them by carrying heavy objects, always willing to help." Henry also became active in school activities, participating in some of the school plays, like the HMS Pinafore.

Henry enjoyed his high school experience, perhaps a little too much. While he stood out for academic excellence, he was also known for goofing around. To the annoyance of his teachers, he was always 'cracking jokes' during class and making his classmates laugh. "I just wanted to make everyone happy," Henry explained. But his teachers saw it differently. Although they liked him, they continually cautioned him about disturbing the class. Still, Henry did things to make everyone laugh. "I never saw anything as challenging in school. The teacher would say it once, and then I would just pick it up. And when asked, I could explain it," Henry said. "When the other students were cramming for exams, I never had to study." Henry valued his academic success, especially as it pleased his father.

Eventually, Sam encouraged Raphael Sr. and Nathalie to move to Nassau. It was a hard decision for both parents, who preferred living in Behring Point, not caring much for city life. Also, with Raphael Sr. being relied on so heavily on the island, nobody was anxious to see him go. However, Sam insisted that they relocate because they were getting older. In preparation, Sam, with his father's assistance, began constructing a bigger home—a two-storey structure on the corner of Oxford Avenue and Market Street, with living quarters upstairs and downstairs comprising a food store on one side and a bar and restaurant on the other. Heeding Sam's concerns, Raphael Sr. and Nathalie moved to Nassau, bringing Rafe, Toddie, and Terry, the only children still living at home in Behring Point.

In 1961, the family moved to their newly constructed home. While the family lived upstairs, Raphael Sr. ran his business downstairs, opening a food store and a restaurant and bar called 'Summer Moon.' Relocating to the area commonly referred to as 'The Grove,' Henry had to readjust once more. Soon, he realised that many people from other family islands were also living there, bringing with them a sense of community. People greeted each other in passing and got along. Homeowners kept their homes well maintained by painting them regularly, keeping their yards weed-free, and ensuring that no trash lined the area. Upholding the same strict house rules they had in Andros, his parents did not allow them to roam around the area or keep company, especially with individuals they considered to be a bad influence. Henry still could not venture beyond the yard, at least not with his parents' knowledge. Having never learnt to drive, Raphael Sr. hired Ed Moss, owner of Taxi 105, to take him around. Moss was an organist at Our Lady's Church and a regular customer at the restaurant. In addition to taking him wherever he needed to go, he often hired Moss to take Henry and Millie to school.

Raphael Sr.'s business attracted lots of foot traffic, and as a result, Henry met other children within his age range. However, unlike Henry, these children did not seem to have many parental restrictions. Like the other boys, Henry wanted to go exploring and one Saturday, Ralph and Anthony, two brothers who lived across the street, convinced him to sneak off with them to Bay Street. "Without a father in their home and a mother who was always at work, they were raising themselves," Henry explained. "They had a shoe-shine box, which they used to hustle money from tourists coming off the cruise ships."

While they were on Bay Street, whenever they saw a police officer, they would duck behind a bush, a building or anything to avoid getting caught. "Shining shoes on Bay Street was forbidden, but they took the risk of earning money to support themselves," Henry stated. "Not needing to shine any shoes, I just stood around and watched. Just as we feared, a police officer chased us away from Bay Street. Afraid of being arrested, I ran back home. That was the first and last time I went with them. In those days, the police were so revered and respected within the community that just the sight of their uniform was a deterrent that instilled fear."

Raphael Sr. was a strong believer in integrity and honesty. Henry learned just how strongly his father felt about these values through an incident that left a long-lasting impression on him. "My father had sent me downstairs to get lunch money for Millie and me from a drawer in the shop," Henry recounted. "While I was doing that, I decided to take a few extra threepence to buy Noxzema to treat my pimples. My father walked in and said, 'I caught you stealing. Put it back.' As a punishment, he stopped giving me lunch money for about six months." At the time, Henry felt his father had overreacted, but he understood the importance of following instructions and the consequences of being dishonest.

Basketball was growing in popularity, and at age 14, Henry had more than a passing interest in the sport. Standing on the sidelines, he often watched other boys playing, wishing he could play as well as they did. His chance came when he met Cynthia Moxey, a girl who would grow up to become the first female Deputy Prime Minister and the 12th Governor General of The Bahamas. She lived in the Coconut Grove area, and her family frequented his father's grocery store. "She was two years older, but being athletic, she could play just about every sport, including basketball," Henry recalled. Cynthia, Henry, Rafe, Sammy Gardiner, and another boy they remember only as Earl would meet by the Oakes Field hanger, where Cynthia taught them how to play basketball. They would sneak away without their parents' knowledge. "To get there, we would ride a bicycle that either my father or Sammy had bought. It was a two-seater with a back stand," Rafe recalled. "Henry would pedal, Earl would be on the hand bar in front, and I would be sitting or standing on the axle."

After playing for a while, Henry uncovered a natural talent and fell in love with basketball, practising as often as he could. He and Rafe also began 'shooting hoops' with other boys on the basketball courts at St. Barnabas Church. Wanting to be like Goose Tatum from the Harlem Globe Trotters, Henry practised long hours. He practised with the basketball so much that he was soon able to do spinning tricks with it. "Eventually, I could dribble the ball and turn it around on my back and throw it under my leg and all that," he said. Soon, everyone began calling him "Goose" or "Goosey" and the nicknames stuck with him.

When not playing basketball, Rafe recalled, "We would join other boys in a ditch, which the then Bahamas Electricity Corporation had cut out, near the school in Big Pond, to keep the turbine engines cool. Some parts were oily and dark, but we went to the clear part, which was about 10 feet deep." It was there in the ditch that Henry finally learnt how to swim. He was happy to finally be able to swim and thought back to a frightful incident that occurred a few years earlier, while he was in Andros.

He had gone out in a fishing boat with JD and some cousins. The blue water was so deep that he could not see the bottom, but his cousins dived from the boat. "I saw them jumping overboard, so I decided to do it as well, only to realise that it was not as simple as it looked," Henry recalled. "They all went head down, and I tried that and ended up on my stomach in the water, and I almost drowned. Simeon, the youngest one, caught me and swam back to the boat with me, using one arm. I could not swim then."

After swimming in the ditch, they would go into the pond and play on the thread mills, the empty spools from the underground cables that were discarded in the pond or at the back of the building. Rafe also recalled, "We played King of the Treadmill. You would get on the treadmill and try to push everybody else off. There was talk of quicksand there, but we never encountered any, so we figured that was just the talk." Again, their parents had no idea where they were or what they were doing.

As a teenager, Henry got to experience a bit of the nightlife as well. At the time, The Cat and Fiddle nightclub on Nassau Street was one of the hottest places for going out, often featuring internationally acclaimed artists. When he was about 15 years old, JD took him there to see a James Brown and Jackie Wilson concert. Although Henry was a minor, and JD could not afford it, that did not stop them. The club was surrounded by a three-storey wall and access was only possible from the front, but children in the surrounding area had found a way to enjoy the concerts for free.

They discovered that by climbing a lamp pole in the back street, they could scale the wall to reach the roof. Once there, they could sit on the beams under the rafters. It was the perfect spot, from which they had a clear view of the stage and the performers. Looking back, Henry said, "I don't know how I got up there because I was never so good at climbing."

As the police were aware of this, they randomly patrolled the area, chasing children off the roof whenever they caught them. But whenever the children heard approaching footsteps, they would run off on their own. "This may have happened to us once or twice," Henry said. "We went there about three times, but only when they brought the stars over like James Brown and Jerry Butler—maybe once a year."

In just a few years since leaving Behring Point, Henry's life had changed considerably. There was never a lack of places to go or things to do in Nassau, and he was proud of his basketball skills. But despite all the attractions of the city, Henry was still an island boy at heart, as he explained, "Everything was exciting, but I sometimes missed the quiet life on the island because Nassau was just too noisy for me." He would also come to realise just how sheltered his life had been in Behring Point.

CHAPTER 4

Encountering Societal Ills

Henry was fortunate to have spent most of his adolescent years free from violence or aggression, either within or outside his home. As Millie attested, "There was no shouting or fighting in our home." Their parents had never argued or even raised their voices at each other, and aside from friendly wrestling matches, there was never any sibling rivalry. "The closest I ever came to a fight was the day Rafe stole my marbles while we were shooting marbles," Henry recalled. "He then ran off, hiding behind a garbage bin. I picked up a stone and waited until he held his head up and threw it at him, cutting him across his eyes. When I saw that he was hurt, it frightened me because I never really wanted to hurt him. Even though I repeatedly told him how sorry I was, my parents still punished me because they wanted to discourage that kind of behaviour."

Few arguments and acts of violence had occurred among residents of Behring Point, and heinous crimes were highly unlikely. When he was eight years old, Henry witnessed a drunken brawl between his brother-in-law and another man. The men had fought all the way to the beach from the front of his father's bar. They were throwing bottles and blows at each other, stumbling as they went. Henry found their actions disturbing, as he recalled, "It frightened me because I never expected people to behave that way." He had also heard about another incident where a man had been stabbed. Even though the man did not die, the community saw it as a violent tragedy. However, Henry would soon learn just how hostile Nassau could be.

In the 1960s, teenagers flocked to The Cinema Theatre, which was located on the corner of East and Lewis Streets. It was a good walking distance from where Henry lived, but he enjoyed going there to watch movies. He recalled watching one of his first Western movies, "Every time the guns were pointed, and the shots were fired, I hid under the seat because I believed I was in danger." However, getting into the theatre was occasionally problematic. A group of brothers from Mason's Addition, who were known bullies, often hung out near the theatre. They would rough up and rob young boys on their way there. Bystanders never got involved because the brothers would say, "Give me back my money!" as though the money belonged to them. Knowing this, if Henry spotted them from a distance, he would quickly turn around and return home. "I didn't like confrontations, so I always tried to avoid any form of trouble," he explained.

Around 12:30 p.m. on a Saturday, Henry was on his way to the matinee when he was ambushed by the brothers. Before taking his money, one of them slapped him hard. "Because I was not one to fight, I could not defend myself, so I just walked away," Henry recalled. That incident shook him up because it was the first time he had experienced something like that. To avoid future run-ins with the brothers, Henry began going to the Capitol Theatre, which was located on Market Street, across from the Southern Recreation grounds. Later, he would learn that the brothers were no longer a threat because a police officer had been posted at The Cinema Theatre.

Henry always had a good sense of humour. However, his humour once led to a misunderstanding that got the police involved. One evening, just before dark, Rosie sent him to buy Apex grease from a pharmacy on Palm Tree Avenue. "I was riding down Market Street on my brother's bike when I noticed a small crowd gathered around a woman lying unconscious in the road, near the intersection of Market Street and Coconut Grove Avenue," he recalled. "As I passed, I overheard someone saying that a rental car had knocked her down and left the scene. When I saw a guy, who usually hung around my father's bar, I asked him, 'Did you knock that woman down?' I was just being funny, but he took it seriously and said, 'You better be quiet and get from around here!' Thinking nothing of it, I laughed and rode off."

As Henry headed back home, someone flagged him down to tell him that the police were looking for him. "I became so frightened and asked them why. And they told me the police had heard that I knew who had knocked the woman down," he said. "When I heard that, I rushed home to tell my parents that the police were looking for me. My father asked me why, and I assured him that I had not done anything wrong, so he said, 'We'll just have to wait and see.' Because I didn't know if the police would come looking for me, I was on pins and needles."

Later that evening, two motorcycles pulled into their yard, and two officers in black uniforms knocked on their door. When his father answered, they informed him that they were there to question Henry about a hit-and-run accident. Although Henry insisted that he knew nothing about the accident and was not even there when it happened, they persisted in getting a statement. So, he told them about his earlier conversation with the guy. Surprisingly, it turned out that the guy with whom he had joked had been a passenger in the car that had knocked the lady down. After that experience, Henry had no desire to have anything else to do with police officers, especially as he was unfamiliar with the ins and outs of policing. But it seemed that his connection with them was fated.

When Henry moved to Nassau, he got to meet family members who had never visited Behring Point. Alphonzo, who was a year older than Henry, was one of the cousins he had met. Alphonzo worked on The Bahamas Star, a cruise ship that sailed between Miami and Nassau twice a week. "I admired Alphonzo because he was a sharp dresser, and he had much more guts than me," Henry reminisced. "Whenever he came in from Miami, he either brought me a tin of Murray's hair cream to keep my crimps styled or the latest fashion in pants, shirts, or shoes. I enjoyed being around him and always looked forward to his visits."

On a Saturday afternoon in 1963, Alphonzo stopped by for a visit and accompanied Henry to Miller's High Life, a nearby restaurant, where Rosie had sent him to buy her a hamburger. When they got there, music was playing, and a few people were on the dance floor. After placing the order, Henry waited at the counter while Aphonzo went over to ask a girl he had noticed for a dance. When he did this, a young man, who had been standing nearby drinking from a beer bottle, approached him. Although Henry could not hear their conversation, he could see the guy becoming agitated. The situation quickly escalated, and the guy shoved Alphonzo off before smashing the beer bottle against his forehead. He then stabbed him in the chest with a broken piece. In disbelief, Henry noticed Alphonzo's blood dripping to the floor. Everyone started screaming, including Henry. Someone called an ambulance, and Henry and others assisted Alphonzo outside. As they waited for the ambulance, everyone just stood around, frightened, watching the blood gushing and not knowing what else to do. Sadly, Alphonzo died before the ambulance or the police arrived.

Shaken, Henry returned home to deliver the tragic news to his family. Coping with his cousin's death was the most traumatic event of Henry's adolescence, especially as he felt his cousin, who was only 18 years old at the time, had done nothing to deserve it. "There was no provocation or self-defence, and the girl did not appear to be connected to the other guy," he recalled.

Going through that trauma was terrifying enough for Henry but being probed by the police again added to his anxiety. He had to give a witness statement at the Criminal Investigations Department, which was then located on Bank Lane. Despite not being guilty of any wrong, sitting in front of the officers was a scary experience for him. He told them what he had observed and described the culprit, who was already known to the police. Eventually, the guy was arrested and sentenced to prison for manslaughter. Later, Henry would hear that he was back on the streets after only serving seven years.

That encounter with the police had such a devastating effect on Henry that he became even more fearful of them. "I was so terrified that if I saw a police cyclist or a patrol car while walking, I ran to the nearest yard and hid until it passed. It got so bad that whenever a patrol car pulled up in the schoolyard, I immediately asked to be excused and dashed into the restroom to hide. I knew that I hadn't done anything wrong, but I had the crazy notion that they were looking for me. I couldn't figure out why I felt that way because they had not done or said anything to intimidate me." Before then, he had never noticed the police cars before, even though they regularly patrolled the campus. Reflecting, he would attribute his unexplained fear to a lack of exposure. It was a fear that lasted until he wore the uniform and understood the nature of police work.

Eventually, the teacher questioned Henry about his reasons for constantly asking to be excused. He could not give a logical answer, and because the teacher was already frustrated with him for always joking around during class, he was sent to see Sister Jane Patricia McGowan, the school's principal at the time. When Henry got there, he had to stand in the office until the class had ended so the teacher could explain why he was sent there.

After the teacher explained the situation, Henry was suspended for a week and asked to return with his father. He dared not tell his father what had happened, so he never returned to school. Since graduation was a few months away, he was able to avoid getting caught by his father. Some 59 years later, he contacted the school to complete the subjects that he had never finished. Although finding the records proved a futile task, he wanted to demonstrate to anyone who may have fallen off the grid that it was never too late to pursue old goals.

With high school out of the way, Henry needed to find a job, and that summer, he began working as a busboy at the Emerald Beach Hotel. Based on his performance, he was quickly promoted to a room service waiter. He enjoyed working in the hotel and interacting with the tourists, especially since he looked clean and neat in his waiter's jacket. Although his time there was brief, it served as a springboard for him to cultivate a heart for service.

CHAPTER 5

On Becoming A Man

In June 1964, Millie graduated from Aquinas College and, soon after, went job hunting. Taking Henry along, she went to Bay Street, where most of the lucrative businesses were at the time. They took their resumes to several places, including Batelco. Their last stop was the office of Sir Robert McAlpine Construction. At the time, it was the largest construction company in The Bahamas, with one of its major projects being the Adderley Building on Bay Street, which housed the Treasury Department.

On entering, Millie met a lady, whom she later knew as Mrs. Sybil, and promptly informed her that they were looking for work. As fate would have it, the company needed someone with clerical skills to replace Mrs. Sybil, who was leaving. When she noticed Henry, she inquired about his experience, and Millie boasted, "He is smarter than I am, and he is an accountant." Saying that the company could use both of their services, Mrs. Sybil took their resumes and telephone contact, promising to forward them to the department responsible for hiring.

Within a week, the company called to inform them they were both hired. They were so excited to hear such good news that they forgot to ask about the salary. Henry would later learn that the company would pay him about five pounds weekly. On their first day on the job, they showed up smartly dressed, and Henry began working as an accounting trainee in the accounts section under Mr. Basil L. Sands, one of The Bahamas' first Black chartered accountants. "I felt fortunate to be working there and thought I had found my true calling because I always liked working with numbers," he reflected. "And having studied bookkeeping and accounting at Aquinas, I was able to perform at the level they expected."

As part of his job, Henry was privy to the salaries of the accountants who were training him. When he realised that he was getting paid much less compared to what they were making, he grew discouraged. At the end of that year, he asked for a raise but was disappointed to receive only a few shillings more. Believing that he could do better, he resigned immediately. "I was still too green to realise that salary was determined by experience and qualifications, both of which I lacked at the time," he noted. "Despite not having any other job prospects, I walked away."

After hearing about Henry's resignation, Raphael Sr. immediately decided on his future, "Son, I want you to be a police officer," sealing Henry's fate. "Despite not having any plans," he explained. "Becoming a police officer was not one of them." At nearly 18 years old, Henry was not man enough to speak out or 'back talk' his parents. "In those days, parental authority was never questioned," he explained, adding that, "Despite society's flaws, the church and parents were the cornerstones of the community, each having considerable power."

It was no secret that Raphael Sr. admired and always spoke highly of police officers. He was friendly with numerous police officers who frequented his restaurant and bar. Among them was Lance Corporal Bernard K. Bonamy, who lived a block away. Henry had noticed him and considered him to be very mature and immaculate in his appearance. In passing, Henry had overheard him telling his father, "He will make a good police officer." Hearing that, Henry recalled, "I felt flattered because I admired that officer, who rose through the ranks to become the 3rd Commissioner of Police, after independence."

Henry dared not express his thoughts to his father that policing was not a notable career; or that he and his peers looked down on someone who graduated from high school and joined the Force. "That was considered going backwards—maybe customs or some other jobs, but not the Police Force," Henry explained. "As kids, whenever there was a break-in around the community, and the crime could not be solved, we would suspect the police. Although there was a reverence for law and order, we had limited knowledge about the nature of police work."

Raphael Sr. wasted no time finding out the necessary requirements for Henry to become a police officer. In early 1965, he hired his usual driver, taxi 105, and took Henry to the Police Barracks on East Street to sit the entrance examination. At the admittance area, they met Lance Corporal 419 Nelson Stubbs, a customer who frequented his restaurant, and Raphael Sr. proudly explained why they were there. As they walked across the compound, Henry noticed a group of recruits marching up through the Barracks while a man with a cane yelled orders at them. This piqued his interest, and he was impressed by how clean and stiff their uniforms were. "Looking at them, I began to visualise myself as one of them and, being competitive, I felt that I could look better," Henry recalled.

While his father waited outside, Henry took the exam. "Two other young men also took the exam, but I finished first," he recalled. "Because there were only three of us, we were able to wait for the results." In no time, the Lance Corporal, whom they met on their way in, came out and told his father, "You have a smart boy, he passed the exam." Turning to Henry, he said, "I don't care what Daddy says, you have to smile because you passed the exam." Everyone knew that Raphael Sr. rarely smiled, so he assumed that he had told Henry to look serious.

After learning the next steps, his father arranged for him to complete the medical examination the following day at the Princess Margaret Hospital. Shortly afterwards, Henry and his father were back in taxi 105, heading to the Barracks for the screening interview. When Henry entered the room, he saw the English officers and other police personnel and became nervous. Before he could get comfortable, they hammered him with questions:

"Why do you want to be a police officer?"

"That's what my father wants."

"What do you have to offer the Force?"

"I know I don't have any experience, but I have youth, and I am willing to learn. I also would like to do something for my country."

"If a member of your family committed an offence, can you arrest them?"

"Yes, sir," That was a tough one for him, knowing he could never arrest his parents or siblings.

"What rank are you looking to attain?"

"I want to make the Police Force a career."

From their facial expression, it was difficult to tell whether they were impressed by his responses. But when he answered the final question, he noticed them giving each other eye contact and nodding. Then, they all stood up and shook his hand, confirming that he had passed.

"As I walked away from the headquarters, I already felt like a police officer," Henry said. His father was also pleased, "Son, you've made me proud. You have done well. Now you must go on and continue to do well." Even though Henry was happy to hear his father's encouraging words, he felt pressured to live up to his expectations. At that time, his father's decision for him to join the Police Force seemed insignificant. Not knowing, at the time, it was the start of something big for him. Later in life, he would be grateful to his father for encouraging him to pursue what turned out to be a life-changing career. Reflecting, he said, "I would encourage young people to join the Royal Bahamas Police Force. It is the best career choice for anyone seeking a more disciplined life."

On 16th August 1965, Henry was once again a passenger of Taxi 105 on his way to the Police Barracks to begin a new chapter in his life. As he left the house, Rosie and his other siblings cried. "It was hard on us because we didn't want him to go," Rosie said. "We all cried. But he was excited to go because Daddy wanted him to go; he had his mind made up by then." Henry agreed, "By that point, I was eager to go because it was what my father wanted, and I had already decided to comply."

He arrived at the then Police Training School well-groomed and carrying a suitcase with his personal belongings. He walked through the gates into a world he would have never known as a civilian. He felt ready to begin the six-month training programme but had no idea what was in store for him. The training facilities were located at the back of the compound and consisted of a two-story building with a female dormitory on the top floor and a classroom on the lower floor. Adjacent to that was another building that housed the kitchen, dining, and canteen facilities for recruits and constables, and another section reserved only for sub-officers – corporals and sergeants. Then there was Arthur's House, a building that was once a prison, a part of which was the living quarters for recruits and other single officers. The other dormitory was in Neville's house, which is the current police headquarters, and that was where Henry was assigned to live. There were 10 iron bunk beds in a room.

Before he could settle in, an officer, assumed to be an instructor, walked through the doors, shouting orders at them. By the time the officer got to him, Henry was already shaking with fear.

"What's your name?"

"Henry Wemyss, sir?"

"What are you doing here? I didn't send for you, I sent for your pa. You go in there, and you stay in there!"

Henry was so frightened and confused when he heard it was his father they had sent for that he did not know what else to expect. No one had ever spoken to him like that. Later, he found out that the officer was a senior recruit who was sent in there to intimidate them.

Still having a close-knit mentality, Henry immediately befriended his squad mates. Some of his first friends were 129 Coakley, now deceased, and 549 Smith, from the senior squad; 482 Fernander, now deceased, and 572 Walkine, now deceased, from the junior squad. He also met two recruits, who lived in the Grove – Constables 64 Brown and 364 McKenzie. Both worked in the Fire Branch, which was also situated in Neville House. Henry thought that McKenzie had the best-shined shoes and belt around at that time and was fortunate enough to have him teach him how to 'slick' his shoes and his belt. They remained lifelong friends.

Henry quickly discovered that becoming a police officer required stamina. At 5:00 a.m. the next day, and each subsequent day, excluding weekends and holidays, they woke up to a rigorous exercise routine. A group of recruits stayed behind to clean the yard while another group ran to Long Wharf Beach, now named Junkanoo Beach, across from the May Fair Hotel, on the corner of West Bay and Augusta Streets. After taking a swim, they ran back. It was too much for Henry, "I thought I was going to pass out or die the first morning of training. Not only was the distance longer than I had ever run before, but the sea was so chilly, my teeth rattled."

Returning to the Barracks, they had to make up their beds and clean the room for daily inspections. Inspections were thorough and everywhere was checked for dust, including under the beds and the cupboards. If anyone's area was not cleaned to standard, their roommates would also get punished. This forced them to work as a team to ensure that the entire room could pass inspections. After inspections, they showered and cleaned their uniforms. Then they had breakfast, which usually consisted of grits with sausage, tuna, or corn beef. After several weeks on that menu, Henry noticed that some of the recruits were appearing more rounded and robust.

Breakfast was quick since they had to be on the muster parade at 7:45 a.m. On parade, they were inspected to ensure that they were properly groomed, and their uniforms were clean and correctly worn. During parades, the instructors had a book, and anyone who did not have a Clean Turnout (CTO) received a demerit. At 10:30 a.m., they had a break and by 11:00 a.m. they had to be back on parade to learn drills and precision. After a five-minute break, they were in class until 2:00 p.m. After classes, they had lunch and then returned to their rooms to take a nap.

By 4:00 p.m., they had to be in their physical education gear. Some recruits played volleyball, while others did fatigue, which entailed cleaning the yard and picking up everything, even cigarette butts. If any cigarette butts were missed, the entire team would be punished. The old guns exhibited at the front of the property had to be polished with Brasso every day until they sparkled. At 5:00 p.m., their day ended with supper. Since Henry had never had such a strict routine, it took some time getting used to it, but it eventually got easier.

Everyone looked forward to receiving passes that allowed them to leave the compound between 6:00 p.m. to 10:00 p.m. on weekdays, 10:00 a.m. to midnight on Saturdays, and 10:00 a.m. to 10:00 p.m. on Sundays, except during holidays. "Sometimes everyone would be dressed to go out and when it was time to sign the passbook, there would be a note saying, 'pass stopped', and the instructor would not have given any prior warning," Henry recalled. "And you would have to tell your family that you could not go." They learnt the importance of teamwork because if one member of the squad misbehaved, the entire squad was punished, and passes were revoked. They especially looked forward to going to the Banana Boat Club in Oakes Field, the most popular nightclub at the time. Some recruits often sneaked out just to go there.

One evening, Constable 414 Rigby, an officer living in the Barracks at the time, invited Henry to go with him to the Banana Boat to meet some girls. Even though he did not have a pass, Henry decided to go. To cover his tracks, he propped up his bed to look as if he was in it. As planned, he waited for Rigby at the back of the building. Rigby reversed his Chrysler Studebaker and told Henry to climb into the back trunk to avoid getting caught as they passed through the gates.

That night, he and Rigby were having the time of their lives, not knowing that Instructor Joseph, who was from Barbados and one of Henry's instructors, was there watching. Catching Henry off guard, he warned him, "Don't let me reach the Barracks before you." Leaving his unfinished drink, Henry asked Rigby to get him out of there. As Rigby high-tailed from Oakes Field to East Street, Henry feared they would not make it back in one piece. "The senior recruits would share secrets with the junior recruits, whom they trusted, Henry explained. "One secret was how to 'break barrack,' or get out without a pass. Instead of going through the gate, recruits could get in and out through a hole in the fence." That night when they returned, Rigby did not drive Henry back through the gate for fear of having the car searched but took Henry to the hole.

As a result of that incident, Henry's pass was stopped for two weeks, and Instructor Joseph embarrassed him on parade by telling the other recruits how he was caught 'breaking barrack'. That would be the first and last time Henry did that. Instructor Joseph was famous for going to the club, where he hid in a dark corner, facing the door, to catch recruits who sneaked out at night.

Settling down, Henry became focused on what he came there to do, and realised he was making a good impression when his superiors began using his name as a standard, "Why can't you keep your area clean like Wemyss?" or "Why can't your uniform look like Wemyss?" This eventually created an early rift between Henry, some squad mates, and other recruits, who held it against him. It also did not help that, unlike most recruits, his family brought him home-cooked meals every day and kept him supplied with stiffly pressed shirts and uniforms. They were each given only two uniform shirts.

When payday rolled around, Henry noticed that some recruits' parents showed up to collect their salaries to help with household bills, whereas his father encouraged him to save his money to eventually invest in a piece of property. His older brothers had nice cars, and when the recruits saw him driving around in them, they began to look at him differently. It soon became known that his father owned a food store and a liquor store. And with all the special attention he was getting from home, his squad mates recognized that his family background was better than most of theirs, leading to rumours that he thought he was better than them. Even though he never acted that way, he noticed that some recruits' attitudes toward him shifted, and they began avoiding him. There was a particular recruit from the junior squad who would decline his invitations to go out together, claiming he was not interested, but would later show up at the same place. This bothered Henry, as he wanted to be liked.

Despite becoming uncomfortable, Henry never considered quitting. In fact, he had already decided to pursue policing as a career after only a few weeks into training, and nothing would deter him from that goal. Instead of dwelling on the situation, he became competitive, attempting to outperform all the other recruits. After classes, he studied for long hours and pushed himself harder during physical exercises. He maintained a consistent, disciplined attitude and took extraordinary pride in his appearance. These habits reflected how he saw himself, making it easy for him to uphold them. At the end of the training, he felt confident that he would win the baton of honour, which most of the recruits also believed. Before graduation, Henry approached one of his instructors asking, "Sir did I win the baton of honour?" The instructor replied, "The only baton you would win is a riot baton." Everyone laughed. Even though he could do the work, that was overshadowed by his playful nature of always trying to make others laugh by telling jokes. "However, I must have made a good impression," Henry stated. "Because years later, one of my instructors, Garnet Beneby, who was a Sergeant at that time but retired as a Superintendent and became a Baptist Pastor, wrote an excellent character reference for me."

Retired Assistant Commissioner, Paul Thompson, now deceased, observed Henry as a young recruit and said, "Well I knew him casually when he joined the Police Force. Being on the recruits' square and being a good specimen, he always looked in good shape, I was a detective at CID, and I used to visit the Police College. He was a person who you could have picked out from the group." Former Commissioner of Police, Paul Farquharson, now deceased, also recounted, "As I remember Henry, who was in the senior squad before me, he was the cleanest recruit in his group." About the instructors, he recalled, "While they were extremely tough with us, they were human and tried to instil discipline so that at the end of the training, you would be a well-rounded police officer."

Henry was disappointed when a 28-year-old recruit won the baton. "Being at the maximum requirement age for entrance into the Police Force, he was a mature recruit with working experience as a skilled electrician. That worked in his favour for, unlike the average recruit, he was able to earn extra marks by doing odd jobs around the compound and at the instructors' residence," Henry explained. He considered this as a flaw in the system because even if one recruit excelled in all the examinations, another recruit, who scored significantly lower, could soar higher by getting extra points for physical activities, drills, exercises, and assisting with other non-related duties. Despite not winning the baton, he still believed he had a bright future and told his instructor, "You did not give me the baton of honour sir, but I would be one of the first to be promoted from my squad." He recalled, "When I said that I meant every word, even though I had no idea what challenges were waiting for me within the Force."

In February 1966, Henry graduated from the Police Training School and entered the Royal Bahamas Police Force as Constable 558 Henry Wemyss. His entire family was there to support him, and his mother and sisters cried tears of joy. His father glowed that day, and seeing his face, Henry felt that he must have been the proudest parent there. When he returned home, his family gathered to celebrate what they considered a proud achievement.

Henry also felt that it had been a rewarding experience for him, but his greatest accomplishment was that the six months of military training had changed him from a boy to a man. Having received the discipline and knowledge, he was ready to make his mark on the Royal Bahamas Police Force and The Bahamas at large.

CHAPTER 6

Harnessing A Spirit of Excellence

Constable 558 Henry Wemyss was ready to serve his country, proudly wearing his government-issued uniform. His original plan was to serve for 25 years, advance to the rank of sergeant, and retire at age 43. He eventually developed such a passion for policing that he desired to reach his full potential within the Force. As new recruits, he and his squad mates were rostered on a month-long rotation in each of the major divisions—Central, Southern, Eastern, Traffic, CID, Freeport. He also worked in the Passport Office.

He enjoyed his time at Central Police Station, Bay Street, near the tourist attractions. Working at Southern Police Station, he noticed a higher level of criminal activities, and the Eastern Police Station, East Bay Street, the substation of Central Police Station was a dreaded station. Officers from the Eastern Police Station patrolled by bicycle or on foot, leaving the station and going into the Kemp Road area because there were no patrol cars. Henry, like most young officers, was terrified of going into that area, especially after hearing about the two officers who had returned to the station on foot and bloodied. They were beaten and had their bicycles stolen while patrolling Kemp Road.

Henry preferred working in locations where he was more visible, such as traffic police stations. At these stations, officers would stand on a platform covered by an umbrella to direct traffic on Bay Street and at all major intersections, attracting tourists who would stop to admire the police officers while flashing their cameras. At times, officers had to direct traffic without an umbrella, braving the scorching sun.

After his experience with the Criminal Investigation Department, Henry decided that he would rather wear a police uniform than civilian clothing. "I never wanted to work in plain clothes. I wanted to be in uniform to represent what being a police officer means and to wear it with pride," he explained. From there, he was assigned to the passport office, where he utilized his excellent penmanship skills to assist with writing passports.

Although they wanted him seconded there, he preferred active policing. His final rotation was in Freeport, Grand Bahama. These accumulated experiences opened his eyes to a greater appreciation for a career as a police officer.

While moving throughout the various police stations, Henry met some of the brightest and most brilliant officers, many of them, in his opinion, could have easily excelled in more prestigious professions. Instead, they chose to serve The Bahamas, which inspired him to want to follow in their footsteps. After completing his rotations, his previous perception that joining the Force was not the ideal career quickly changed. "It was amazing how I went from being afraid of them to becoming one of them," he stated.

Henry could tell that the police officers took their duties seriously and strictly upheld law and order. Even though the Force at the time included local Bahamian officers, English Officers held positions of authority. There was an English Commissioner, English Senior Officers, and Officers who were recruited from Barbados and Trinidad, who he felt were stern and harsh enough to arrest their mothers if they walked on the wrong side of the law.

Five months after graduating, Henry and his squad mates returned to the classroom for a one-month refresher course. Throughout the course, they discussed what they learned while working at the various stations, as well as how the commanding officers at the stations had assessed their performance. Based on the field report, the instructor determined which areas of the Force were best suited for each recruit.

In 1966, Henry was posted to the Central Police Station, where he was highly visible to tourists and other high-ranking government officials. At first, he could not tell a politician or government official from a regular businessman, so he saluted any Caucasian male wearing a business suit with a tie and toting a briefcase. He paid respect to many astonished businessmen until he got to know actual politicians.

From the moment he joined the Force, Henry established a code of conduct for himself. Standing out in his stature, dress, and deportment, quickly earned him a reputation for being one of the cleanest and sharpest police officers in uniform. His belt was gleaming, his shoes were 'well slicked', his uniform fitted him like a glove, and his hair was neatly brushed down with crimps all around. He exuded an undeniable sense of self-confidence and pride. "Maintaining that image was not a challenge for me but a reflection of how I saw myself," he explained.

Such admirable attributes led to Henry being chosen as an ambassador to travel throughout the United States of America and Canada with The Bahamas Ministry of Tourism from 1967 to 1978. The Ministry required an officer who not only wore the uniform well, but also had extensive knowledge about The Bahamas. Henry took great pride in representing The Bahamas and thoroughly enjoyed each trip. Wherever he went, public announcements were made to announce that a Bahamian officer would be directing traffic at specific intersections, and traffic lights at those intersections were turned off to accommodate him. Additionally, he attended various boat shows in Florida to interact with the public and promote The Bahamas.

Henry visited Canada about five times and once appeared as a guest on the same talk show as Jose Feliciano, best known for writing, 'Feliz Navidad.' His experience, representing The Bahamas, humbled him, as he shared, "There was a moment while directing traffic in Halifax, Nova Scotia, when it occurred to me how far I had come from Behring Point, Andros to serving my country, as a dignitary, in another country. It was a proud and humbling moment for me." Out of this experience grew a passion and a patriotic eloquence that made him a more excellent officer.

A police officer once stopped Henry as he walked to the train station at midnight in Canada. "I was unaware that I was passing through an area where people of colour never went at that hour," he recalled. "I was dressed casually and caught the attention of a Caucasian police officer, whom I would later know as 1000 Petty. He stopped me and asked for my identification. When I pulled out my warrant card, the officer's attitude changed, and he told me that he recognized me from a television show. He then asked me where I was headed and called into the police control room, requesting permission to leave his location so that he could escort me where I needed to go. When that happened, I realised that it was a great privilege around the world to be a police officer."

Henry represented The Bahamas and the Force so well that the Ministry was unwilling to take a chance on any other officer. When he was invited to go to Sydney, Australia, he could not make it because he was enrolled in classes. Word got back to him that if he was not available, they would settle for placing his uniform on a mannequin instead.

CORPORAL HENRY WHYMS* a member of the Royal Bahamas Police Force, was the first foreign policeman to visit the Fort Lauderdale Police Department in 25 years. The Bahamian policeman was there recently on the invitation of the Fort Lauderdale Chief of Police Leo Callahan. Whyms was also there to represent the Bahamas Ministry of Tourism at the city's International Boat Show held last month at Bahia Mar Hotel and Yachting Centre. Cpl. Whyms took time out to direct traffic on Seabreeze Blvd. In second photo from top Regional Manager of the Bahamas Tourist Office in Miami, Adel Fahmy, welcomes Corporal Whyms to Florida.

Henry's passion for policing was evident and he wanted to be the best. He enrolled in evening classes to study accounting and business administration, but he was no longer passionate about his earlier goal of becoming an accountant. While his skills were put to good use in the payroll office, he was driven by the nature of police work. "At first, I told myself that if I made it to Sergeant and spent 25 years, I could get out at 43 years old as a young man on pension," he shared. "But after I got there, I fell in love with policing, and it became my life and that's all I wanted to do. I prided myself on my work and felt as if I was born to be a police officer." In 1967, Henry was deployed to Turks & Caicos, which at that time, was still being governed by The Bahamas. Even though they had their own police force, it was not fully established, so two Bahamian officers were assigned to assist at two-month intervals. Not being able to go as a constable, Henry was temporarily promoted to a lance corporal, a rank which became redundant in 1969. The Corporal, who he was accompanying, was promoted to sergeant. They went there by The British Frigate, a warship that patrolled the Bahamian waters, sometimes transporting police officers between The Bahamas and Turks and Caicos. After being there for only a month, Henry was asked to investigate a local murder. As a young officer, he found it encouraging that he was asked to do the investigations, instead of the Sergeant, who was his superior. He enjoyed his time there and found the experience unforgettable. Upon his return to Nassau, he resumed working at Central Police Station.

The late Paul Thompson, retired Assistant Commission of Police, was a senior officer at the time, who saw something extraordinary in Henry. "When he worked in the division at Central Police Station, I was then in the senior rank, and I would pass by and take one of the officers from there to patrol with me. Whenever he was there, I would specifically ask for him," Thompson recalled. "I always took him on patrol because I found him to be very alert, and our conversations were always very interesting. He would ask questions and offer his opinions on crime situations. He was always interested in police work and questioned those of us who were senior to him. I got to know him better then. He did his work, and he did it properly." Thompson also saw Henry as an officer, who brought value to the Force, "He was never working in criminal investigation, where I was for 25 years, so we were not connected jobwise, but I always tried to observe police officers, who I felt were a credit to the Force and he was one of those persons."

In 1968, Henry was transferred to the Records Section at Police Headquarters and then to the Payroll Section in the Accounts Department. There he worked along with Constables 550 Smith, 129 Coakley, 409 Laroda, and Sergeant 324 Farquharson. They all got along well, and he enjoyed working with each of them.

One of the Assistant Commissioners at Headquarters, the late Stanley Moir, who was then in charge of the Criminal Investigations Department, would often call young officers, like Henry, as they passed his office, getting their input on some of the cases he was working on or had worked on. He would question them about how they would investigate certain matters and the evidence they would look for. Giving them questions, he would ask them to bring the answers back to him. Moir referred to Henry as "Joe Wemyss", but he would never find out why. Reflecting fondly on that time, he said, "I looked forward to Moir's questions and taking answers back to him. I was always eager to find out whether I was right and if I was wrong, what I needed to do." These off-the-record challenges allowed Henry to sharpen his critical thinking skills. "It meant a great deal to me that Moir took the time to invest in me and I always considered him to be an exceptional senior officer."

In addition to his regular duties, Henry was asked to work as the batsman for the then Assistant Commissioner, who oversaw Administration—the late Sir Albert Miller. He was surprised at this posting because, as far as he knew, only English officers had batsmen. The other officers either did their own cleaning or their cleaning was done by recruits from the Police College.

From a distance, Henry had always admired Miller, who he thought had a stately look and a military walk. Among all the other senior officers, Miller always stood out to him, "He was strict, no-nonsense and knew everybody on the Force. He was a Bahamian officer, who conducted himself with the mannerisms and attitude comparable to the English officers. He played tennis and never hung out in the local bars, like other senior officers. He was an exemplary leader, whom I envisioned would become the commissioner of police someday, as he seemed destined for that position."

While his duties were menial, Henry felt privileged to be working as a batsman for Miller, who he felt was a highly respected, outstanding officer, "As a batsman, it was my responsibility to pick up his laundry, run errands, shine his epaulettes, and any other cleaning tasks that he needed," Henry explained. "I also took his children to and from school. It was a position of envy, and I was paid a small stipend, about five shillings per week." Miller later recounted, "I was looking for a batsman and they said they know just the person, and the next thing I knew they brought him, and he probably thought he was being fired because he was sweating and carrying on and he readily agreed. And, from then on, he kept my uniform clean, took my clothes to the laundry, and took my children to school. He tried very hard to be my son and did not quite make that, but he was part of the family."

Looking up to Miller, Henry wanted to emulate him, "During the years I worked with him, I learnt a lot of positive things by watching him, but we never spoke much. I watched him closely, observing how he spoke with others and the way he conducted himself. He never made me feel as if we were ever equal and always sat in the back seat whenever I chauffeured him." Miller would often point out police officers and ask Henry to identify them, and this encouraged Henry to learn most of the officers' names. Despite working closely with him, Henry never benefited when it came to getting promoted. "Once, I overheard his wife questioning him about why I didn't make the promotion list," Henry recalled. "He told her, 'If he had deserved it, he would have received a promotion.' His response bothered me because I knew how hard I was working."

From all accounts, Miller was pleased with Henry's performance, as he recalled, "Mr. Wemyss was a very smart and very clean officer, very military with a real sense of discipline. He was reliable and got things done when he was asked to do things and that was what I liked about him. He knew when things needed to go to the cleaners, and he had the initiative about doing things without having to be told all the time."

Miller went on to become a deputy commissioner of police, but in 1971, he decided to resign from the Force to take up a position at the Casino in Grand Bahama. At his farewell party, he offered Henry a position to join him in Freeport. "He quoted a handsome amount and said if I had accepted it, I would forget there ever was a pension," Henry shared. "As good as the offer was, I was not ready to leave the Force, having just been promoted to corporal a year earlier. I felt that my future was bright, and I enjoyed what I was doing. Besides, it was never about the money, as I was comfortable just being able to take care of my family and pay my bills. I had no desire for a luxurious lifestyle."

Because he respected Miller highly, it became a tough decision for Henry to make being a police officer a lifelong career. Miller agreed that it was a wise decision for him, "When I left the Force, I wanted him to come to work for me in Freeport because he was a winner and I wanted to stay with a winner. It did not happen because he had a police career. It was better for him to pursue his police career and I thought he had a bright future as a police officer." Henry never regretted his decision to remain on the Force, "Even though I was never an overly ambitious person, I felt passionate about my career and looked forward to serving The Bahamas with pride until my retirement."

In 1971, Commissioner John Marsh called Henry in and informed him that he was chosen to be the chauffeur for the then Prime Minister, the late Sir Lynden O. Pindling. As detailed, he went to the Prime Minister's Office, which was in the Adderley Building on Bay Street. When he entered the

Office, Henry saluted, and the Prime Minister invited him to have a seat. He then proceeded to brief Henry about the nature of his chauffeur duties.

"You are here to chauffeur me, and to look after me and to take care of the vehicle and the surroundings."

"Yes, Sir."

"But my wife will be calling on you from time to time to do small errands. She may ask you to take her to the hairdresser or go to the mail boat to collect some crab boxes from the Family Island. You don't really need to do those favours because that is not what you are sent here for. But if you do, it would be most appreciated."

"Sir, I have no problem doing that."

"Remember in life, it's the small things that really count."

Henry always admired the Prime Minister for his brilliance and eloquence and considered him to be the best leader throughout the Caribbean, at the time. As a young man, whenever he listened to him speak at political rallies, he got goosebumps. He was someone that he held in high esteem. "That day, I walked away with the understanding that no matter how much I protected the Prime Minister and ran errands for him, he would be happier if I catered to his wife by taking her to the hairdresser and the food store." The Prime Minister's words that the small things in life really counted would always resonate with Henry.

Henry considered it an honour to drive The Bahamas' first Prime Minister. When he shared the news with his colleagues, they also considered it a prestigious position. Whenever he was seen driving the Prime Minister's car, which was a 1970 navy blue Ford Marquis, his friends, colleagues, and even civilians would salute him. It was a wonderful experience driving the Prime Minister and getting to meet his family. On weekends, Henry took his two sons for ice cream and taught them to shoot pool by his father's restaurant. He would form a lasting bond with the oldest son, Obie. He and the Prime Minister's wife migrated from Andros, but they had never met before. She was surprised to learn that, as an Androsian, Henry did not know how to clean fish.

As the Member of Parliament representing the South Andros Constituency, the Prime Minister travelled to Andros on most weekends and returned on Monday mornings. When he returned, Henry would go to the airport, escorted by police motorcycle outriders, and drive non-stop through traffic. As Henry drove the Prime Minister from the airport on 25th January, 1971, it was a typical Monday morning, but it would be a day he would never forget.

The drive from the airport was trouble-free, but there was heavy traffic when they reached Prince Charles Drive. As they got closer to the Prime Minister's residence, located on Soldier Road at the time, Henry had to slow down and queue in traffic, but the motorcycle outriders continued ahead. While driving, he noticed a middle-aged man running across the road from the southern side. Quickly applying brakes, he allowed the man to cross onto the grass pavement before accelerating forward. Unexpectedly, the man suddenly reappeared in front of the car, and even though Henry applied the brakes as soon as he noticed him, the car hit him. He watched in disbelief as the man fell to the ground.

The Prime Minister, along with his bodyguard, walked the short distance to his home, which was just around the bend from the accident site. Henry, who was left on his own to manage the unpleasant situation, reported the accident to the police and requested an ambulance. He had to divert traffic until the ambulance arrived, since the body lying on the road was obstructing the flow of traffic. The man was taken to the hospital, but died some five months later.

A coroner's request was held to determine the cause of the man's death. Henry attended the inquest by himself, and as a young corporal, he was required to answer the hard questions posed to him. The victim was represented by eight or more prominent lawyers. At that time, Henry would learn that the victim was Donald W. Davis, a prominent educator. Henry would often wonder whether the accident became a major setback for him and the reason he remained a corporal for the next seven years.

Fortunately, a woman, who was the occupant of the residence in front of which the accident occurred, came forward as a witness. At the time, she had been standing by the gate and testified that the accident was not the driver's fault. The inquest resulted in a $250,000.00 lawsuit. Henry, though, bore no responsibility for the settlement. Even though it was an accident, it traumatized Henry. "As a result of that accident, I was given a week off to regroup. That experience bothered me so much that I had nightmares about it and went into depression," Henry recounted. "It got so bad that I even consulted a medical doctor, who assured me that in time I would get over it." That incident, however, stayed with Henry, and he often wondered if, despite not being at fault, he should reach out to the family and apologize. When he expressed his thoughts, he was advised against it because it would "open a can of worms."

As much as Henry enjoyed the privilege of driving the Prime Minister when he returned to work, he immediately requested a transfer. He was reassigned to the Accounts Department and shortly afterwards was transferred to the Southern Police Division. There, he became the Corporal In Charge of the Grove Police Station, as there was no Sergeant present. This was his first experience as a senior person in charge of an area. While he worked office hours, there were other corporals in charge of their shifts. It was a valuable learning experience that paved the way for his subsequent transfers to lead family island divisions.

CHAPTER 7

Serving The Family Islands

In 1972, Henry had his second attachment, but his first to a Family Island. They could not have chosen a better location for him when they sent him on a three-month stint to his hometown as a Corporal and the Officer-In-Charge of the Central Andros District. It was a large area, and his scope of responsibility was from Behring Point to Mastic Point. There were so many settlements that travelling between them took hours. With one constable and one vehicle, he worked out of Fresh Creek. At the time, he was taking over from another corporal, who would eventually become an assistant superintendent.

It was his first trip back to the island since leaving as a boy, some 13 years earlier. "I didn't know what to expect and was shocked to see that the place was much more developed with more streetlights, modern homes, a vacation resort, and many more people driving around in vehicles— something I never saw as a child." With all the changes, he remembered so little about the island and had to be driven around until he re-familiarized himself. Fresh Creek was some 35 miles from where he grew up. "I was also pleasantly surprised to be able to drive from Fresh Creek to Behring Point, something that was impossible to do when I lived there because of the creek that separated one portion from the next," he stated. "But a bridge had been built over the Creek, connecting Fresh Creek. Bowen Sound, Man-O-War Sound, Cargill Creek, and Behring Point."

By that time, all his immediate family had moved to Nassau, so he was curious to see what had become of his birthplace. He went to see the property and found the walls of the building where his father ran his liquor business still standing, and the painted sign, 'Dem Boys Bar' was clearly visible. At the rear of the property, the walls of their two houses were also still standing. "I was saddened to see what had become of my home and felt homesick, wishing my parents were still there." Everything appeared much smaller, even the huge trees that he remembered as a boy. Within a few minutes, he canvassed the entire settlement and recalled how, as a child, it had taken him much longer. Surprisingly, St. Mary's Catholic Church stood intact.

Going around the settlement, he introduced himself, and everyone expressed their delight at seeing their teacher's son return home as the Police Officer In Charge. His cousins, who still lived on the Island, were also happy to see him. In keeping with the generous spirit that remained on the island, the residents offered him fish, crab, and farm products. Not being able to cook, he packaged the items and shipped them back to his family in Nassau. It felt good to be back in a close-knit community where everybody was family or treated as such.

At that time, one of the resorts there did not use locks on the doors during the day. With no crimes to fight, Henry spent most of his time driving around and getting to know the residents. As he moved around the settlement, some of the elderly people were able to tell him stories about his childhood, even recalling the Sunday on which he was born. Hearing them express their pride in him made him feel proud. "I didn't realise how much I really missed the quietness of the Family Island life until that trip," he says of his return to Behring Point. When his time was up, he was not ready to leave, but he had to return to Nassau, where he resumed his duties at the Southern Police Station.

On 23rd December, 1973, Henry was detailed for an immediate transfer from Nassau to head the North Eleuthera district, again as a corporal. The district comprised Upper and Lower Bogue, Harbour Island, Spanish Wells, The Current and Current Island. Although excited about this assignment, he felt that, as it was too close to Christmas, the timing was inconsiderate. Besides, his family dynamics had changed, and he was looking forward to spending the holidays in Nassau with his then-fiancée and toddler daughter.

Needing advice on how to handle the situation, Henry consulted with his parents. However, they felt that if his job required him to go, he had no choice but to do so. Not satisfied with their response, he then asked his brother, Sam (LO), for his opinion. Sam suggested he speak with someone in authority about postponing the transfer until early the following year. Sam's advice sounded reasonable, so Henry went to the then Commissioner, Salathiel Thompson, now deceased, and explained the situation. The Commissioner agreed that it made more sense for the person already stationed there to stay until after the holidays and directed Henry to go to the then Assistant Commissioner of Police, District Headquarters, Dudley Hanna, now deceased, to inform him that he had sent him there to request that the transfer be delayed until after the holidays.

Knowing that the Force was a rank-conscious institution, Henry felt the Commissioner should have informed the Assistant Commissioner directly. However, he obeyed the orders and did as instructed. He also knew that most officers feared that Assistant Commissioner. He recalled, "No sooner had the words left my mouth, the Assistant Commissioner chased me out of the office, using choice words, telling me that I was expected to be in Eleuthera the next day."

"I walked out of his office feeling as if I had been whipped," Henry said. "Over the years I had accepted and even grown accustomed to the militant ways of the Force, which were often uncompromising. Despite that harsh reality, that day I felt that my personal rights had been violated." Despondent, he mentally weighed his options, "I was relatively young, only about 25 years old. Just three years prior to this, I had been promoted to corporal," he recounted. "After being trained and promoted, I was finally enjoying life as a police officer. I considered it a privilege to be working throughout all the stations and divisions of the Force. Despite this, my spirit was dampened, and I struggled with the decision to either continue as a police officer or to resign and accept Mr. Miller's earlier offer."

Returning to Sam, Henry shared what had happened and that he would resign from the Force. "This is only one Christmas," Sam told him. "You will get to that island, and you may not enjoy this Christmas, but you will like it so much that you will forget that there was a Christmas you missed in 1973. Go ahead, don't worry about it; you will like it." Accepting this advice, he swallowed his pride and complied with the request. Not wanting to disrupt his plans, he decided to take his fiancée and daughter with him.

The next afternoon, Henry and his family boarded the flight to Rock Sound Eleuthera, as it was the only available flight to the island that day. For unknown reasons, he was not booked on a flight directly into North Eleuthera, where he would be staying, or even Governor's Harbour, which would have been closer than Rock Sound. After a gruelling four-hour drive, they arrived in Bouge shortly after 10:00 p.m.

However, the housing provided for him was undergoing renovations, so he was being temporarily relocated to another place. When they arrived at the designated location, Henry noticed that the walls were stained due to a plumbing problem and informed the Constable driving them that the building was dilapidated and obviously unsanitary, so they could not stay there. Consequently, he opted to spend the night at the Current Club. With Christmas the next day, he was relieved to have his family with him.

However, his relief was short-lived, as he received a phone call early the following day from Sergeant Edmond Hall, the Officer In Charge at Governor's Harbour. He relayed a message from Assistant Commissioner Hanna, instructing Henry to leave the hotel because the Force was not responsible for hotel expenses. He was also instructed to take the ferry to Harbour Island, where arrangements were made for him to share an apartment with the Corporal there – 274 George Poitier. When Henry explained to the Sergeant that his expecting wife and daughter were with him, he was told that the Assistant Commissioner had said that, as a single man, the Force was not required to make provisions for anyone other than him. After receiving those instructions, Henry had no choice but to send his family back to Nassau. "It was one of my worst Christmases," Henry recalled. "Although I was extremely disappointed, I put my personal feelings aside and headed to Harbour Island, as expected, until my living accommodations were ready."

Alone in Eleuthera, Henry became worried. "After hearing so many witchcraft stories, I was terrified of living alone in Eleuthera. There was one story that made me feel very uneasy about the transfer," he explained. "I had heard that a fellow officer was transferred to Eleuthera, and a woman became interested in him. She poisoned his food when he did not return that interest, causing him to bleed from every part of his body." Whether that story was true or not, Henry did not want to risk living in Eleuthera by himself since he was not good at household chores. "Growing up, when my mother taught us how to clean the house, make beds, cook, and iron clothes, I was never interested. I felt there was no need for me to know those things." Henry was at a crossroads: he had to quit his job or get married. In Nassau, he lived with his fiancé in his father's apartment, but his parents disapproved of his lifestyle. Before his transfer, his father had given him an ultimatum: get married or move out and go to live in the Police Barracks. Back in Nassau, his fiancé was also doing some thinking, and soon they reached a decision.

On the 19th January, 1974, Henry returned to Nassau and in a ceremony officiated by the late Rev. O. A. Pratt, he married his long-term girlfriend, Judy. She had caught his eye in 1966, when she joined the Police Force. "I had found her outstanding in her appearance—lively, kind, and very attractive," he said. "I was happy to be in her company and thought of her as the crème of the crop." Not wanting her to remain in the Force, he had convinced her to change professions. She initially pursued nursing but eventually became a teacher. Immediately, after getting married, she applied for a transfer to accompany Henry to Eleuthera.

As a married man, Henry was an officer who always travelled with his family, as Judy assured him, "Honey, if they put you to live in a rat hole, I would live with you." He would later remark, "We've had our ups and downs like most marriages do, but I think I have the best wife in the world. And she deserves everything I could give her and more."

Henry and his family settled in Eleuthera, where Judy taught at the government school. Life was so comfortable for them that he never wanted to leave. "Besides the occasional drunken brawls and disorderly behaviour, there were no criminal activities. We once received information that one of the locals was cultivating a marijuana field, but after investigating, we found nothing," Henry recalled. "It was a perfect place to raise children. It was quiet, the air was clean, and we enjoyed eating fresh farm products and seafood." They also had a great network of social friends among the immigration officers and other government employees, including the school principal. He could also spend quality time with his family, enjoying long drives around the island. He may have gotten off to a rocky start in Eleuthera, but it turned out to be a rewarding experience for him.

In terms of his career, Henry saw it as an opportunity for advancement since it was commonly understood that officers who made sacrifices to go to the Family Islands were always rewarded with promotions. The Family Islands provided the officer in charge with immense opportunities for growth and self-development. The duties were expansive, including writing all reports, compiling statistics, making arrests, charging individuals, bringing them before the Family Island Commissioner, and prosecuting cases. "In the long run, I considered the transfer to the Family Island as proof that my superiors thought I could manage a district," Henry explained. "My duties as a Corporal In Charge of a Family Island were comparable to the work of a senior officer in Nassau and made me well-rounded and more qualified than my peers in Nassau. With this realisation, I decided to maximise my time in Eleuthera. And I believed that like all the other officers, who went there previously, I would be promoted before returning to Nassau or being sent elsewhere." He intended to remain in Eleuthera until he was promoted to sergeant. Once again, Henry's plans were disrupted, and he was unexpectedly transferred back to Nassau to become an Instructor at the Police College.

Upon arriving in Nassau, he went to the District Headquarters to see the same Assistant Commissioner, who had sent him to Eleuthera. He wanted to know why he had been transferred back to Nassau. "When he saw me, Assistant Commissioner Hanna became furious and chased me out of his office. He'd just returned from vacation and was of the impression that I'd used that time to request a transfer," Henry explained.

"I later found out that the Superintendent, knowing that the Assistant Commissioner would block his request to have me transferred, waited until he had gone on vacation and applied to the Commissioner for my transfer." It was the kind of police politics that Henry preferred to avoid. However, as instructed, he took up his new position, while still maintaining the rank as a Corporal.

In 1984, Henry applied for a transfer from the Police College because he could not work comfortably under the then Commandant. Despite being brilliant and extremely knowledgeable, he did not, in Henry's opinion, have the appropriate management style nor the professional deportment for the position. It was common to see the Commandant arrive on the compound with tins of corned beef or tuna protruding from his pockets while in uniform.

The Commandant who was said to be "the best legal mind on the Force" used advanced language that Henry felt was not to the recruits' level, placing them at a disadvantage. "He was also known for interrupting parades by snatching rifles from recruits and demonstrating how he felt it should be done," Henry said. Considering the Commandant as a detraction to his efforts, he was no longer motivated to work in the environment. However, the Commandant was not pleased with his decision.

Subsequently, the Assistant Commissioner of Police, Family Islands District, informed Henry that he would be stationed in Cat Island. "I was rather disappointed when I heard the news because I felt that, having only three years earlier returned from completing the General Police Course in England, I could better serve the Force in a more developed setting, like Abaco, Grand Bahama, Eleuthera, or Exuma," he explained. "At that time, the Cat Island district was not fully established, and I had never heard anything about that jurisdiction." Since his last Family Island posting, Henry had received two promotions. He was elevated to Sergeant in 1978 and then to Inspector in 1983.

Despite his initial disappointment, Henry was excited about the refreshing change of pace that the island life offered. When he informed

Judy about the transfer, she said, "If you're going, I'm going," and immediately applied to the Ministry of Education for a transfer to Cat Island. "I loved the out-island life. It was quiet and peaceful, so you didn't have to worry about the kids or anything. Just going to work and then coming home and cooking," Judy recalled. "When you got home, you met all kinds of farm goods at your door from different people. On the family islands, they love police officers, teachers, and nurses. They just love government officers." When Henry's mother heard he would be living near the ocean, she decided to accompany him. His father, on the other hand, wanted to remain in Nassau since he had no interest in travelling at the time.

Henry was expected in Cat Island on 1st January, 1985, but the Inspector he was relieving asked him to come a few days earlier. On his first night, the Inspector took him to the various police stations, officially handing them over to him. "During the tour, I noticed the entire island appeared to be in darkness, and the only streetlights around were very dim. Because there were no lights, he handed one of the stations over to me by searchlight but explained that there was nothing to hand over other than a prison cell and that nothing was written in the diary. So, we drove for several miles to the other station, and he handed over everything to me that night," Henry recalled.

"The next morning, at about 6:30, I drove with him to a private airport, where he turned over his firearms and keys to me. I had expected that he would spend at least a day showing me around and introducing me to some key people. But when I had suggested it, he said there was really no need for that."

Although Henry knew very little about Cat Island, he was confident. "As it was my third island assignment, and being an island boy, I knew how to relate to the people," he reflected. He was assisted by two constables and a reverend, who served as a local constable but only worked the weekdays from nine to five. Another constable was stationed in the north in Arthur's Town. Henry was highly respected by the constables, who worked with him and always made sure that one of them accompanied him wherever he went. After a week on the Island, Henry conducted an assessment and realised that the Island was too large for him, two police constables and one broken-down jeep to secure the airstrips fully. As dedicated as they were, their responsibilities far exceeded their capabilities to monitor an island that was some 48 miles long with four airstrips located at Arthur's Town, New Bight, Hawks Nest, and Cutlass Bay.

"So, I wrote to the Superintendent of Family Islands and requested additional officers and another vehicle," Henry recalled. "In my letter, I also detailed how the officers would be deployed to man the airstrips to deter illegal landings. One of my strategies was to detail the officers daily without letting them know where they would be ahead of time. As no one would have prior information on where the officers would be working, it would become difficult for anyone to conspire to schedule landings." At that time, The Bahamas was still reeling from the 1983 Commission of Inquiry, which tarnished its international reputation, branding it as a 'nation for sale'.

In response to Henry's request, the Superintendent promised to allocate more manpower in February, when a squad of recruits would pass out. As instructed by the Superintendent, Henry also found living accommodations for the incoming officers. However, months later, he was still without the much-needed assistance. "I became overwhelmed working with limited resources and could not perform my duties at the level I wanted to," Henry shared. "It became even more challenging when the only police vehicle stopped working and the rental vehicle that I received, in the interim, also broke down. I was disappointed that I wasn't given the necessary resources, but I continued to work with what I had."

Many nights, Henry jumped out of bed, grabbed his revolver, and went onto the porch, thinking he had heard a plane overhead. Strangely, he could only hear the sound from inside, and it stopped as soon as he stepped outside. Puzzled, he was determined to find the plane and went for the officers. They spent entire nights driving from one end of the

Island to the other, looking for any planes that had landed. "Even as we tried, I knew it was an impossible task," Henry explained. "Because with only one vehicle, a plane could possibly be in the east or north when we were in the south." Still, he persisted in his efforts and refused to give up. Fortunately, he later realised that it was not a plane he had been hearing but the wind blowing the sound from the generator against the window screen in his bedroom Nevertheless, Henry and the officers continued to conduct all-night patrols.

Eventually, officers were sent from Nassau at four to six-week intervals but were restricted to the private airstrip at Cutlass Bay. Even though Henry was the Officer In Charge, he could not place them elsewhere. "With limited manpower and resources, I did my best to guard the airstrips. I became so obsessed with preventing illegal landings from occurring during my watch that I had many sleepless nights," Henry recalled.

They frequented the main airstrips as much as humanly possible, to deter unauthorised planes from coming in. Because there were no lights on the airstrips, if there were any emergencies and people needed to fly in or out at night, the locals would notify the officer in charge and line up vehicles on the side of the airstrip, turning on their headlights so planes would be able to take off or land.

"Cat Island, like most other Family Islands, was a close-knit community, where everyone seemed to be family. They were friendly, loving, and caring and greeted each other in passing, which I appreciated." Henry noted. "Cat Islanders seemed to have more pride in their hometown than people from other Family Islands. They boasted about their island as if it were a paradise, far more than those of us from more developed islands. Nobody spoke on the other. If you were not a Cat Islander, you were considered a foreigner. It was difficult to know whom to ask for information since you didn't know connections and couldn't judge relationships by surnames. Although they had respect for authority, no one trusted you enough to disclose anything to you."

Henry visited the northern section on occasions, either with his officers or on Saturdays with his family. There was a particular male there, who always showed up or singled him out to talk, "At that time, I was happy to be able to interact with someone out there because I didn't know anybody else in that area. Later, I became suspicious that he wanted to be seen socialising with me in public so that it could be perceived that he and the Inspector were buddies." After being on the Island for two months, this man gave him a tip that someone had hidden drugs in the bushes in the north.

Following up on the tip, Henry sent the officers to pick up the man so that he could show them where the drugs were. The officers returned and informed him that the man had led them to an abandoned spot covered in cobwebs that had clearly not been visited in quite some time. They believed he had purposely taken them on a wild goose chase, and Henry suspected he had wanted them in that area for a reason. They also reported that the man had a .38 firearm revolver, like the one he was using. When he questioned why they did not arrest him for it, they said he had told them that, "The Chief knows about it," and assumed he was referring to him. Not wanting to be associated with unlawful possession of armed weapons, Henry arrested the man, and because it was a Saturday, he allowed him to sign bail on his own recognizance. When his case came up, he was fined and given time to pay the fine, but his gun was confiscated. "He was so upset over the incident and stated that he would get me back for what I did," Henry recalled.

Again, Henry received a tip that drugs were hidden in some bushes. Following that lead, he and the officers searched the bushes for miles that night, looking for the drugs. "Looking back today, I realised that we had taken a huge risk back then," he stated. "Because we only had a revolver and a shotgun. We began our search around 9:00 p.m. and did not come out until the next morning, having found nothing. But I didn't want it to be said that someone gave me a lead and I ignored it."

During his tenure, two incidents involving planes required his attention. On one occasion, he and the officers were conducting their regular night patrol when they observed a large fire in the bushes some distance away. When they got to the area, they met the locals gathered on the road and discovered that the fire had resulted from a plane that had crashed. The plane was destroyed, and the body inside was burned beyond recognition. The matter was reported to Nassau for further investigations.

Henry encountered the second incident while driving along the settlement one day around midday. He noticed a DC-3 landing at one of the airstrips and took his firearm and the officers to investigate. They discovered two Caucasian men on board, without any passenger seats. He detained the men at the airport and, after searching the plane, they found enough residue on the ground that was suspected to be marijuana. Henry arrested the men and took them to the station, where they were charged, denied bail, and brought before the Family Island Commissioner the next day. They pleaded guilty and received a hefty fine, which they paid in cash. They were then deported and escorted to the airport, where they were picked up by another aircraft and left the country. The confiscated plane was sent to Nassau.

Assistant Commissioner of Police, B.K. Bonamy Jr. was a constable working on the Island at the time. He recalled, "They had something on Cat Island in the '80s called Cutlass Bay Operation, and we did four to six weeks rotations, but Inspector Wemyss oversaw the island. And he made sure we were at the airstrips." While there, he recalled how serious Henry was about protecting the island, "I remember in 1985, a plane landed on Cat Island, and a Rasta fella walked off, but Inspector Wemyss put him back on the plane. He said, "Ain't no Rasta coming on my island. No, no sir, back on the plane. No Rastas in Cat Island." For six weeks, I never saw a Rasta in Cat Island."

Another officer, Kendal Rahming, who also worked with Henry, stated, "The settlements were far apart. He would call us on the radio and say he was coming, and we would do undercover work. We stayed at the airport at night to disrupt any illegal flights trying to get onto the Island. We protected the airport." Henry had trained both Bonamy and Rahming, as recruits. "I knew what he stood for from in training. I knew he wanted us to come in on time, be clean, and do as we were told," Bonamy stated. "He was stern, and everyone on Cat Island respected him."

There was nothing unusual about the Island. It was relatively quiet, with few incidents requiring Henry's attention. He and his family had adjusted well to the closely-knit environment and enjoyed the serene life. They attended Our Lady's of Zion Catholic Church in Port Howe. Henry was very active, often giving members rides to and from the church, starting a choir, and ensuring the church was cleaned. He enjoyed the fellowship. "It was a small church, and they didn't have any music, so I got them a recorder with some of the hymns that are usually sung in the Catholic churches for their use," he recalled. As they lived in Smith Bay, he and his family rode a long distance to attend church services.

Henry remained in Cat Island for less than a year, before applying for a transfer back to Nassau, due to a personal family emergency. After returning to Nassau, he worked as a court prosecutor in the Prosecutor's Office for about two years. Besides working with limited resources, Henry had enjoyed his brief stay on Cat Island. During his time on the Island, nothing significant had occurred that stayed with him or prepared him for what would transpire four years later. However, some 33 years later, he learnt that, after he left the island, officers from the Drug Enforcement Unit came down and conducted a strip search of the officers who had worked alongside him, uprooting their personal belongings. Cat Island would be Henry's final Family Island attachment. He would always remember it as the most challenging island he had ever been stationed on, not because of the workload but because he wanted to be on top of everything that was going on there.

CHAPTER 8

An International Win, Against The Odds

Since the 1950s, many Bahamian officers were privileged to study alongside their international counterparts for a six-month overseas Police Officer's General Course at the Hendon Police Collège in London, England. For years, Henry had been hoping for such an opportunity because the course prepared officers for career advancement. He knew he had already been recommended three times but was not selected because either he was not yet at the required rank or there was no suitable replacement to compensate for his absence.

In 1982, the then-Commissioner of Police, Gerald Bartlett, now deceased, summoned Henry and two other Sergeants - 604 Francis from Nassau and 404 Major from Freeport - and informed them that they had been selected to go to the training in England. Henry was excited, but with the course scheduled to begin on 5th July, they only had about three days to prepare for the trip. "Normally, we would have been told months in advance because, at the beginning of each year, there is a list of the courses and the names of officers who would be attending. It's never a last-minute thing unless officers who were supposed to go for whatever reasons cannot. But I'm not sure why that happened in our situation," Henry noted. When he was asked whether he could make it, Henry said he could.

They were entitled to a per diem allowance, but it was not available to them until they reached England as it was being transferred through the Crown Agents Bank. Henry did not want to travel without any money. "Even though my mind was made up to go, I was in a dilemma because my salary never allowed for anything extra. I had a wife and three children at home, plus a huge mortgage. I could have borrowed from my family, but I didn't want to do that. Fortunately, I had good credit with the bank where I had my mortgage, so I was able to add another $1,000 to my balance. Everything worked out in my favour because the monthly payment remained the same." When Henry found out that the other officers travelling with him also did not have personal funds, he lent them some money until they could reimburse him.

Henry had taken care of his financial problems but was also concerned about his family's well-being while he was gone. "It meant that I would be away from my family for six months, so it was a tough decision for me," he recalled. "While I felt as if I was abandoning my young family, I realised that a second chance for me was quite slim." Judy was also concerned that he would be too far away if something happened to him, her, or any of the children. "Even though I understood her anxiety, I felt that if I turned down the offer, I would be committing career suicide," he explained. "I hoped that going to England would improve my chances of promotion, which would benefit us."

One of his colleagues, the then Superintendent Paul Farquharson, now deceased, had already taken the course. When he found out Henry was going, he handed over his training materials and notes to him. Farquharson realised that Bahamian officers would perform better if the officers who attended ahead of them shared their knowledge with those who would go next. Henry appreciated his consideration and was grateful for his kind gesture. "It was said that the officers from Hong Kong won the baton twice a year because, before attending the course, they had a refresher course. So, by the time they arrived, they were already familiar with the material," Henry explained. On his return, he followed suit and passed his notes on to one of his colleagues, but unfortunately, as far as he was aware, it was the last year The Bahamas participated in that course.

During that time, it was common for officers to be promoted before going to England, so Henry suggested to the Commissioner that instead of sending them as Sergeants, he should promote them to Acting Inspectors with the understanding that if they failed the course, they would be reverted to sergeants. The Commissioner did not accept his suggestion, and they were sent as sergeants. However, The Commissioner tried to encourage him by saying, "Wemyss you can't come first, but whatever you do, we will be proud of it." Although Henry believed the Commissioner meant well, his words haunted him. "His words resonated in my head from the moment he said them to the moment I arrived in London," Henry recalled. "I became so restless that I could not sleep on that long flight. Even though I was not a Christian, I prayed to God to help me to prove the Commissioner wrong."

On arrival in London, they were met by the then High Commissioner, Honourable Anthony Roberts, now deceased, who later became an Anglican Priest and one of Henry's close acquaintances. "I considered him to be an honourable gentleman indeed," Henry said. "He took us to his residence and entertained us to the fullest, making us feel at home. As we had arrived a few days before the course began, he provided us with hotel accommodations, breakfast the following morning, and transportation to take us to Hendon."

When they arrived at the Metropolitan School, they joined officers from every part of the Commonwealth, including Montserrat, Anguilla, Bangladesh, Hong Kong, Mauritius, Lesotho, Seychelles, St. Vincent, and St. Lucia. It was the most culturally diverse environment Henry had ever experienced. As he settled in, he was still thinking about what the Commissioner of Police had said to him. One of the first things he did was to check the past participants' bulletin board. He was surprised to learn that, except for a few, The Bahamas never made the top ten. "While The Bahamas was still a colony, Officer L. G. Roberts attended the course sometime in the 1960s and placed first," he noted. "Following that, the Assistant Commissioner of Police Addington Darville placed second when he participated sometime in the 1970s." As Henry stood there staring at the board, he prayed once more for God's assistance in achieving his goal of returning to The Bahamas with the baton of honour.

As their first assignment, they had to write a biography. Listening to the other participants, Henry realised that most of them were superintendents or heads of their country's forces. He and the two other Bahamian officers held the lowest rank and were the only ones without a college degree. Despite this, when he introduced himself, he affirmed, "I came to England with one intention in mind, and that is to carry the prestigious baton of honour back to The Bahamas." Most participants had never heard of The Bahamas and asked where it was or whether it was a part of the United States of America. Henry found it amazing that even though Bahamian officers had attended the course since the 1950s, The Bahamas remained unknown. His statement was both ambitious and bold because for about 40 years, the officers from Hong Kong had taken the baton home twice a year.

METROPOLITAN POLICE TRAINING SCHOOL, HENDON
No. 73 Overseas Police Officers' General Course 4th July, 1982 to 19th November, 1982.

Top row from left to right: D.A. James (Montserrat), R.R. Webster (Anguilla),
H. Wemyss (The Bahamas), I. Bissessur (Mauritius), J.M. Ramoholi (Lesotho),
J. Pillay (Seychelles), M.G. Didon (Seychelles), W.M. Francis (The Bahamas),
K.M. Major (The Bahamas)

Bottom row from left to right: D.E. John (St. Vincent), K.C. Dey (Bangladesh), Lo Chuan Man (Hong Kong), C.A. Williams (CPM), R.B. Wells, P.F. Cornish, M J.D. Murray, Li Tak Chung (Hong Kong), Chang Dim Chee (Brunei)

Henry found the program to be an exciting and challenging experience. It was intense and covered every aspect of policing, including law, fingerprinting, crime scene analysis, evidence collection and presentation, prosecution of cases in courts, physical fitness, oral presentations, class discussions, and much more. After each class, he would study extra hard by doing additional research in the library or reviewing his notes in his room. As a student, he had never crammed or studied that hard for any exam, but he was willing to go the extra mile to reach his goal - to take the baton of honour home. Giving up leisure time, he concentrated entirely on the course. "I wanted to prove that winning the baton of honour was not dependent on who you knew," he stated.

The first of three exams came after four weeks of class. Despite studying for many hours, he was still nervous and prayed earnestly before taking the exam. When the results were in, he was anxious to learn his grades, but because they were handed out alphabetically by surnames, he had to wait longer than others. Every time a participant walked out of the office, he asked, "What did you get?" or "How did you do?" They all shared their grades. Finally, it was his turn, and as he walked in, he felt a tight knot in his stomach.

"Henry, how are you doing?"

"I am fine."

"Are you relaxed?"

"Yes, sir."

"Are you enjoying England?"

"Yes, sir."

"Have you been to France?"

"Not yet, sir."

"Are you going out?"

"No, sir."

"You need to go around and see the place. You did not only come for these courses, but also to see the place."

"No, sir. I came here for these courses. If I finish and I have time, I will see the city. If not, I will come back on my own time."

"Well, you are doing something right."

"What is that sir?"

"With your grades."

Henry was pleased with himself when he got his grades, but knew it was just one exam. Feeling that they were the underdogs, he urged his Bahamian colleagues, "Let's study together and share notes. If the three of us work together, I may pick up something, you don't pick up, or you may pick up something, I don't pick up." However, they turned down his offer.

After the first results, the tone was set for his studies, and he spent a lot of time in his room. It was a lonely experience, but Henry stayed focused and committed to taking home the baton. Noticing that he was not doing any sightseeing, the instructors continued to express their concerns, encouraging him to take a break and enjoy the historic country.

"I don't have time, sir," Henry maintained.

"What are you doing?"

"I am studying, Sir."

"You need to go out and see the place because when you get back, no one will ask you about the exams but what you saw while you were here."

"I was sent here on an assignment to do studies. Once I have completed my studies, I will go and see the place. If not, I will come back another time. I am not going to compromise my studies."

As part of the curriculum, Henry also attended a two-week attachment at Wakefield, North England, to participate in a detective course. He would always value this international experience that enhanced his development as an officer. In the end, his commitment and dedication paid off, as evidenced by his accomplishment. He became the first Bahamian under the independent Bahamas to attend that course in England and make top grades. He was ecstatic and called home to share the good news with his wife and parents.

"Against the odds, I brought the baton of honour back home to The Bahamas," Henry reflected. "It was a very proud moment for me and my family, especially my father. I was convinced that if God never answered a sinner's prayer, he did so that time." An officer from Hong Kong placed second and asked him to share the baton with him. Because he had concentrated on studying, Henry never got to do any sightseeing on that trip, but when he and his wife travelled to England twenty years later, he was able to relax and enjoy the sights he had missed.

When Henry returned to The Bahamas, the Commissioner of Police held a press conference at the Police Headquarters and introduced him to the press. He spoke so highly of him that Henry felt certain he would be promoted, especially since he knew of officers who had been promoted after taking the course. Some of whom received double promotions while still in England. However, that was not Henry's fate. "I did not receive a promotion that year," he stated. "But in 1983, I became an inspector. Unfortunately, my father never got to hear my good news. After a long battle with cancer, he died that year - 6th February, 1983 - at the age of 73. He would have been very proud of my accomplishment."

Sergeant Henry Wemyss Received the Baton of Honour from Commandant R. B. Wells Metropolitan Police Training School, Hendon, England, in 1982.
No. 73 Overseas Police Officers' General Course.
In the Background: was Instructor C. A. Williams CPM.

**Sergeant Henry Wemyss Presenting the Baton of Honour
to Commissioner of Police, Gerald Bartlett in 1982.**

CHAPTER 9

The Heart Of A Leader

After 1974, Henry spent most of his time as an instructor at the Police College. From there, his name became legendary, and many of the officers he trained attribute their success to the six months they spent at the college under his leadership. Interestingly, he had taken on that position with little enthusiasm, owing to his disappointment at being suddenly pulled from Eleuthera. He was more passionate about front-line policing, as he believed being out in the field would allow him to rise through the ranks, positioning him to make a more significant contribution. Although he was not concerned about the role of politics in policing, he would eventually come to believe that political connections had some bearing on promotions.

Perhaps, his superiors saw things differently. Henry possessed the "attributes of a good police officer," and was an excellent choice to shape the next generation of officers. Not only did he have the experience and expertise, but, as one of his former recruits emphasized, "He was clean, his leather belt was shiny, his shoes were well slicked, and his uniform fitted well. He was just a sight to behold, grabbing your attention." Unquestionably, he looked the part. Despite his personal feelings, Henry always followed orders and committed himself to duty, but he never anticipated the tremendous influence he would have.

He spent his early days at the college training supernumerary police squads comprising beach wardens and local constables. These were applicants who did not qualify to sit the entrance exam for the Force or took it and failed, but the Force still wanted to employ them. The local constables wore coveralls with their numbers instead of regular police uniforms. They were responsible for guarding the inmates coming down from the prison and maintaining the station cells and grounds. Some of them later upgraded their qualifications and joined the Force. Recognising that academics alone did not make one a good police officer, Henry pointed out, "There was a beach warden—652 Oscar Sands, now deceased—from my first squad, who advanced to the Force and eventually became a superintendent of police. He had street smarts and applied himself."

As he transitioned to training regular recruits, Henry was a bit timid, especially in 1975, when the first female squad joined. He never forgot the conversation about his fears which he had with the then Sergeant 352 Akel Clarke, now deceased, who retired as an assistant superintendent, "I asked him, do you think they'll know that I'm a new instructor? And he said, how will they know? They met you here. If you act like you're new, you'll show them." Quickly adapting, Henry demonstrated the confidence and demeanour of a well-seasoned police instructor. He made such an impression that his first squads would have found it difficult to believe that he was still getting his feet wet. Retired Superintendent Philip Don Wilson, a 1976 recruit, whom Henry nicknamed "Father Boy," recalled, "When he entered the classroom, it was clear that it was his domain. And he was in charge. He spoke in a loud booming voice." Wilson also recalled Henry's warning to the recruits, "I am not going to let you exit these gates to embarrass the Royal Bahamas Police Force!"

Being young and impressionable, most recruits entered the Police College uncertain of what to expect. Some were drawn to the profession because of the uniform and others because it represented a stable income. However, from day one, Henry unpacked the nature of policing as a disciplined, patriotic calling. Many of the recruits came from humble beginnings, and Henry was determined to mould them into individuals society would be proud of. "I took my job seriously and wanted to instil enough fire in the recruits to keep them burning throughout their entire career," Henry said of his time as an instructor. "I considered the Police Force as a golden opportunity for young individuals to become disciplined, productive citizens. And to this day, I believe the fire is still burning in many of them."

Henry walked around with an instructor's cane under his arm or in his hand, wearing tinted eyeglasses that rested on his nostrils. He was an intimidating figure known for shouting and acting crazy. Whenever recruits saw him walking around, they immediately jumped at attention. He did not have to be near them; he would just shout their names and wherever they were, they had to respond. His voice was distinct and, as one recruit recalled, "Sometimes we marched a good distance away, and he did not follow us but stood in one spot, and when he called, "Parade!" you could hear it down the streets."

In 1979, former Commissioner of Police Ellison Greenslade joined the Force. Appearing much younger than his 18 years, he was dubbed "baby of the squad." Recalling his first day of training, he said, "I was petrified upon meeting Henry Wemyss. He sized me up on our initial inspection parade and asked the squad, 'What is this little boy doing here?' He went on to say that the Force hired men and women, not children and exclaimed that the training school administration had made a grave mistake. His remarks were harsh, direct, and they stung. However, my agony was slightly relieved as he continued to assess other squad mates during his inspection of what he called, 'a miserable and sorry-looking bunch of misfits.'"

"He was a commanding figure, clean as a whistle and looked like he had been dipped in a box of Argo starch," said Retired Inspector, Edric Poitier, a 1980 recruit. "Many of us wondered how he was able to walk around and keep his shirt so well tucked. He had this mean look on his face, and the sound of his voice was no less inviting. He immediately struck fear in us by saying, 'I'm going to be your worst nightmare for the next five months. If any of you make it.' My initial impression was, where did they get this crazy man from, and why did we have to get him? We soon learnt that everything about training was a show; instructors regularly put on an act designed to prepare us for things we would have to deal with on the streets once we left the training school. I soon found out that we didn't only have a great squad instructor, we had the best there was then and still is to this day."

113

Clayton King, another 1980 recruit, recalled his initial impression of Henry, "Being a young recruit at 17 ½, my first impression was that he was crazy. As a young recruit entering an organisation, you had no idea that these folks were strict and, as instructors, they poked your mind. As you grew through the weeks, you realised they only wanted the best for you. The information they gave you and the life lessons they taught you carried on to this day."

Irrefutably, Henry Wemyss was an extremely competent and capable classroom instructor, as Greenslade attested, "He understood the law and was able to explain it in ways that were easy to understand. His vast knowledge of front-line policing, coupled with his experience, further illuminated his competence in the classroom. Of note was his uncanny ability to demonstrate critical thinking skills and to pass this skill on to young recruits."

Retired Deputy Commissioner of Police, Ismella Davis-Delancy, a 1983 recruit, nicknamed, "cry-baby" and "mother hen," recalled. "Mr. Wemyss was firm and knowledgeable and like the old Chinese proverb says, 'he prepared us for a lifetime'. Mr. Wemyss' knowledge of the law and his experience in life taught us and prepared us well. The old saying, 'train up a child in the way he should go and when he is old, he will never depart' was our life during training. You were prepared for what awaited you on the outside."

Retired Superintendent of Police, Mary Mitchell, another 1983 recruit, also recalled, "As for his knowledge of general policing, that was unmatched. He could have just drilled off the law, it just rolled off. He just knew those law books. So, during the lecture, you could ask him any questions and there was hardly anything that he did not know." Always willing to give of his personal time, Henry arrived at work early in the mornings and left late in the afternoons. Mitchell added, "If any recruit went to him after class and explained that they did not understand what he had taught in class, he would break it down into layman's terms."

Henry's skill as a drill instructor placed him "right at the top" in respect of his contemporaries, all of whom were fiercely competent at drill and deportment. Retired Superintendent Randy Lightfoot, a 1981 recruit, shared his memories, "What I remember most about him was being on the drill square. He was immaculate on that drill square. He was 'dangerous' on that drill square. They had Mr. Wemyss, Mr. Akel Clarke, Mr. Arlie Forbes, and Mr. Henry Thurston. Those four were the best instructors I ever saw, without a doubt. When they were spinning, if your eyes caught their shoes, it was blinding. You could see glitter coming off."

Mitchell also remembered the precision drills, "We had to get used to drilling what we call left, right, left, right, up, and down, and all those precision movements. There was no room for misguided steps. Your feet had to be up at a certain height and then you had to bring them down in a certain way, and your hands had to be at your sides. And he was a perfectionist at what he did. Then, he had the stature, the demeanour, the cleanliness, and dress code to go with it."

Thinking back, Poitier said, "His escapades on the drill square were the most exciting. He always found a way to make us laugh inside, because we dare not make a sound in his presence. He was not playing mean; he was mean. We always dreaded hearing the words, "Parade! At a jump, attention!" What soon followed was a "double march." It meant that we had to put our riffles over our heads and jog up and down the drill square in full uniform until he told us to stop, which was usually some five or ten minutes later, but seemed like a lifetime." Retired Sergeant, John Pople, a 1977 recruit, stated, "If he was giving drill commands and you didn't get it right, he would chase you out of the line and make you run to the far end of the training ground, break a leaf, and bring it back, and you had a certain amount of time to return."

When it came to conducting muster parade inspections, Henry was not a favourite, because it meant no one would pass the inspection that morning. Compared to other instructors, his standards were extremely high and rightly so. It was difficult being as clean as he was. Recalling the morning inspections, Davis-Delancy said, "They would go around and check your nails and hair for proper grooming, moustaches were not allowed, and the inside seams of the shoes also had to be cleaned. Your skirts and pants had to be properly ironed and your shirt cleaned. The females wore hats, and the males wore helmets, and the helmets had to be white, not beige. It was an art to be clean."

Assistant Superintendent of Police, B. K. Bonamy Jr., a 1983 recruit, also shared his memories, "One time, I don't know who got him mad and he stood like 100 feet from us and said, 'All of them dirty, from what I could see all of them dirty.' And everyone looked at themselves and said, 'This man even ain't close up.' And we were so scared because he shouted it out. And he said, 'I'm not doing any inspection this morning because from where I stand, all of you'll dirty.' So, we had to go back to the drawing board and make sure we were clean, clean, even though we were clean. We just had to make sure that when he came closer, we had no problems." He also shared a more humorous memory, "He teased me one time during training. Before I joined the Police Force, I wore Jheri curls, and the perm turned my hair reddish. I cut my hair and when he was doing the inspection, he asked me if I used to dive quarters off the dock for the tourists. I wanted to laugh so badly but I was on parade, and I said, No Sir!"

When describing their six months of training with Henry, his former recruits commonly referred to him as a disciplinarian. He took a tough stance, demanding only the best from them. There were no excuses because he did not merely say what one should do but modelled the behaviours, skill sets, and attitudes he expected from them. In essence, "he lived what he preached." They knew they were in trouble when he broke out in his zombie walk or took off his cap, crushing it in his hand.

Believing in the "hot stove" approach, Henry dished out swift punishments. Any recruit who dared to nod off during his lectures was ordered to run to the fence and back to the classroom until class ended. He expected them to study and frequently tested them to see if they did. "He once asked us to write down the 200 minor offences, and one of the recruits remembered all but 75 of them. As punishment, that recruit had to run from the classroom to the fence 75 times, but it worked. The next day, he was able to cite all 200 offences," Pople recounted. "On another occasion, a whole squad had to fall in dressed in short blue pants, police boots and socks, and a white t-shirt; carrying a 303 rifle over their shoulders, they had to walk around the flag area, bending down—this was known as 'crab walking.' It was also one of the punishments dished out during his inspections if he could not see his face in anyone's boots."

Whenever one of the recruits was dirty or late, the entire squad was punished. To save themselves, they were then forced to work as a team, assisting each other in remaining clean and punctual. Knowing how much the recruits looked forward to getting passes to leave the premises, Henry restricted that privilege as another form of punishment. He once withheld passes for an entire squad after a recruit faltered during the practice session for a passing-out parade. He belted out the punishment, "You'll pass stop! The next time you'll see Bay Street, you'll think you're downtown Miami."

Other forms of punishment were extra fatigue duties, picking up trash of all kinds, and cleaning classrooms, public spaces, and bathrooms. "When he told you to scrub the 100 ft. x 100 ft. showers, you knew the only tool you used was your toothbrush," said former Superintendent of Police Clarence Russell, a 1976 recruit. Henry's preferred method of punishment was a verbal rebuke, done publicly, as it left recruits feeling diminished and less credible in the eyes of instructors and squad mates. If a recruit complained, his response was, "We didn't send for you. We sent for your pa, but you came."

Holding fast to the slogan, "It never rains on the Police Force," he expected recruits to show up on time and ready to work, rain or shine. Intolerant of tardiness, he once made a recruit return to the dorm to get his mattress, then run to the fence, with it over his head, repeatedly shouting, "I love my bed." That recruit never overslept again. Henry's work ethics were very strong, and he was both firm and fair. He was also quick to publicly recognize good behaviour, outstanding performance, and excellence.

Henry also trained the Royal Bahamas Defence Force recruits, including Retired Chief Petty Officer, Luke Bethel, a 1977 Marine Recruit. As one of his mentors, he remembers Henry as, "An individual who broke and mended individuals mentally and physically, all in the cause of becoming productive police or defence force officers." He also noted that Henry "does not really know how many lives he directly and indirectly touched through his sometimes intimidating presence." Reflecting on Henry's methods, he said, "His leadership style leaned towards being coercive, with a mixture of authoritarian, because of the nature of our jobs, which required continuous focus, concentration, professionalism and representation of the Royal Bahamas Police Force and Defence Force." He also recalled that Henry, "Did not fail or hesitate to advise and share information and experiences with subordinates and peers."

The recruits also admired Henry for "his spiritual life and his strong family values." He took the time to learn about their families and their problems. They initially wondered who he was and why he needed to know all of this, but they soon realised he was more than an instructor and was genuinely concerned about their well-being. "We went to church together some Sundays. As a family man, he always emphasized the value of family. He frequently talked about his family life, bragging about his children," Davis-Delancy recalled. "During the period of our training, I got to know his family and his children and his youngest daughter, Kiki, became my baby. When she came there to the Police College, she would come to the dorms and I would take her over and over. Everywhere I went, she went with me. Then we started to go to his home and Judy took us on and we became his second family."

Mitchell also agreed, "He was also family-oriented and brought his family in. He spent so much time at the Police College that, at first, we thought he had no family. Mr. Wemyss always had the fear of God in him because there was also a spiritual side to him. We would have devotions, and he was engaged in everything we did. It was a thing about being one big happy family. We got to know the kids, and they got to know us, and even his wife came down to counsel us. We had no other instructor who went beyond the call of duty to make sure that our welfare was taken care of."

"He used to take me down to the Police College and sit me on the console in his car. Most of the officers he trained remember me because he used to pick me up from Dandy Lions Preschool and have me there with him." Acribba, who was very young at the time, recalled. Keisha also remembered her father balancing his career and family, "It wasn't hard because Daddy was always a family man. He easily integrated family and career, and there was never an issue. It was either work or family. We would go and watch him do drills with the recruits and attend all the graduation ceremonies, where he commanded the passing-out parades. Mummy always accompanied him to the balls and other events. We also went to the kids' parties at Christmas, Thanksgiving and so on. So, a lot of his recruits knew his family, first-hand—many of them who were close with him."

When they discovered that Judy was the reason why Henry's shirts were so stiff, they wanted her to do the same for them. On Friday afternoons, Henry would bring the shirts home to her, and she accommodated many of the recruits, who wanted to look as stiff as Henry did. With four squads in training, at any given time, she did shirts for about 75% of the recruits for a lot less than what the laundromat was charging and included delivery. Judy had devised a method for getting the job done. After washing the shirts at the laundromat, she dunked them individually in an Argo starch mixture, which she made. She sun-dried the shirts before she steamed and pressed them with Niagara starch. When she was done, the shirts were stiff, and the creases were as sharp as blades. She delivered them to the recruits in a laundry bag, complete with name tags.

Speaking about that experience, Judy said, "The recruits wanted to look like him, so I did all their shirts. Every week I would start on Saturday mornings, go to the laundromat, and work my way through the evenings until 2:00 a.m. I would iron and bag about 400 plus shirts. Every recruit had two uniform shirts." Although it was hard work, it was a labour of love for Judy. On Sundays, at about 5:00 p.m., they would load up their hatch-backed car and deliver the shirts to the recruits, sometimes having to make two trips.

Unlike the other instructors, Henry desired a more holistic approach to training. "Knowing that most recruits considered me to be a hard lecturer, I decided to prove to them that I could also engage them in a more informal setting, without fear of jeopardizing my standards as their superior. Basketball was one of the few sports I enjoyed playing and had become skilful at doing all sorts of spinning tricks with the ball. Thinking that it was a good idea, I invited the recruits to join me in a friendly basketball game." However, Henry was chastised by the then Commandant, who saw it as compromising his role.

Bethel was one of the officers, who played with Henry and recalled, "While playing basketball, he ordered me to always pass him the basketball and I was what we called a 'ball hog', therefore this was a big problem to which he said the solution was to just pass him the ball." Bonamy also humorously recalled Henry's love for basketball, "He loved basketball. He loves sports. If he believed you could play basketball, he would pick you. And when he picked you, you knew who should do all the shootings—it was him. I remember the first time we played basketball with him, and I took a shot and I missed. And he stopped the game and said, 'Listen to me lad, 910, you're not supposed to shoot any ball, I'm the shooter. You're supposed to grab the rebounds and give it back to me.' I was so scared, I gave him all the balls; no matter how many times he missed, I gave him all the balls."

Russell also shared a humorous incident, "I recall a day on the college's basketball court, where all men were suggested 'equal', the senior team headed by Inspector Wemyss was losing the game and a recruit dared refer to Wemyss as the "Goose", the cardinal sin for a recruit. I think after 43 years of graduating, that misled recruit is still doing 'punishment crab walks' with a 303 rifle over his head today. That was the discipline and honour we learnt on his watch." Despite Henry's strict and disciplined demeanour, it was always clear that he wanted them all to succeed. He was regarded as a mentor and father figure. Russell described him as, "Our worst nightmare as our leader, but in the same breath our mentor and father figure on campus. He would mould me and my additional 29 all-male squad mates into a formidable team of soldiers, forming a bond that has lasted a lifetime."

Davis-Delancy recounted, "From the onset, I found Mr. Wemyss to be a strong disciplinarian and a very strong father figure. Mr. Wemyss and the other instructors mentored and moulded us for leadership. They ensured that we learnt the basic application of law and presented ourselves as young ladies. We were not allowed to leave the premises wearing shorts, but had to be properly dressed. Some Sundays, we went to church as a group and every morning we started the day with worship." Mitchell recalled, "Because of some of the things that he would have done for us—for me—he immediately became a father figure. Despite it being a military organisation and him being militant and stern, he became like a father figure to many of us. As young persons, some of us were 17-18, and one or two of them might have been 19. We were young and impressionable teenagers, and for the most part, well a lot of us, needed father figures, like your Daddy was there, but your Daddy wasn't there when it came to guidance and nurturing. He would tell us about life lessons, not just the military part of it. It was like how to take care of yourself. The things that you should do, and the things you shouldn't do as a young person."

Attesting to that, Russell said, "Most male recruits came from basically the same socio-economic background, fatherless homes with single mothers. Mr. Wemyss taught us how to shave, dress, proper hygiene, rap to girls, and how to make the best choices in life. He also taught us the value of money, investment, and insurance. Bought our first piece of property on his advice in training—best investment ever." Also attesting to his sound advice, Poitier said, "What stands out to me the most about Mr.

Wemyss is the time and effort he put into, not just being an instructor, but being a mentor. He gave us financial advice about saving our money and buying property at a young age, while the price was much lower, instead of waiting until we got old and couldn't afford it. He even gave us advice on the good career moves within the Police Force." Reflecting, Wilson said, "He spoke to the entire squad like a father, telling us things that we will encounter and how not to respond speedily when confronted by someone, who is tempting you to act in a manner that you would consequently find is wrong and suffer consequences for it."

Henry had great leadership ability, as summed up by Davis-Delancy, "Mr. Wemyss had the ability to pull so many components and be able to come out at the end of the day with a puzzle. In the training school, there were 21 young persons, who came from varying backgrounds, environments, cultures, biblical installations, and ideologies. For a leader to be able to adapt to those 21 individuals, coupled with the other instructors, and his immediate boss, and to be able to transform the lives of those 21 persons, he is a leader par excellence. He had to be able to see what our strengths and weaknesses were and to take on the responsibility to develop and transform our young minds into full-pledged officers, who are now serving in their respective rights successfully and the credit is due to him. He was a man who was able to translate, transcend and environmentally pull some things to form an individual. He was a leader, who had so many skills. Mr. Wemyss had a purpose. He had a passion, and he loved his job."

Henry Wemyss embodied such positive attributes that he became a role model many recruits wanted to emulate. Greenslade acknowledged, "As my squad instructor, I wanted to emulate him, to be smart and alert, like him, to walk and talk, like him, to exude the confidence that he did, and to garner the respect that he did. I fixated on these things. I read, I practised, and I prepared for each new day in training. I began to visualise myself as his protégé." Reflecting, Pople said, "I emulated him. I wanted to be just like him. To see the kind of respect he garnered, I wanted that. He was my first mentor. Mr. Wemyss got me to see policing as a science—get to know your job, learn the laws you are expected to enforce, know the policies, and be professional." Lightfoot explained, "He was an individual who you could follow—how he conducted himself; how he behaved; how he kept himself clean—these were some of the qualities that he had that, as a recruit, you could model yourself based on what you saw in him."

Throughout their individual careers, the recruits continued their efforts to emulate Henry Wemyss. Poitier shared, "I have been fortunate enough to follow similar paths within the organisation, and as an instructor at the training school, I tried to emulate him as much as possible, to the point where I was told on more than one occasion that I sounded like "Goosie Wemyss." As a takeaway from his training, Bethel said, "I modelled his personal bearing, professionalism, commitment to task, integrity, and focus on getting parade training jobs done at a standard. I modelled his style on having everyone feel a part of accomplishments on parade training, even though mistakes were made, and the road was rough at times. I retained the techniques instilled into me during parade and general training under Wemyss and transferred basically everything into the Royal Bahamas Defence Force where in people's words, I was a "very effective training instructor and parade drill sergeant."

Henry has a rich legacy as a former instructor of the Royal Bahamas Police Force. Recruits were prepared after going through his training. So much so that whenever it was known that an officer trained under him, expectations were high. King said, "Even after recruits left the college and you sit down and talk about how your training was, anybody who said, 'Wemyss was my instructor' would hear, 'yeah, you had a good instructor.'" He added, "Because of Mr. Wemyss and the discipline and the hard work I learnt on the Force, I was able to transition from the public sector into the private sector." Reflecting on Henry's legacy, Bethel remembered him as one, "who encouraged each recruit to apply self-safety, respect, honesty, hard work and continue education upgrade for these will set the tone for a progressive and successful career in both the Royal Bahamas Police and Defence Forces."

Henry succeeded in igniting a passion for excellence in his recruits, and their eventual promotion to senior ranks within the Force is proof. According to Mitchell, "Double entry squad C & D of 1983 made history in the Force for having the most senior officers at this time. Some of my squad mates were the former Commissioner of Police Paul Rolle; the Deputy Commissioner of Police Loretta Mackey; retired Deputy Commissioner of Police Ismella Davis-Delancy; retired Superintendent Joy Bosfield; present Chief Superintendent of Police Kimberly Taylor; present Chief Superintendent of Police, Linda Moxey; retired Woman Chief Superintendent of Police Belinda Missick; and current Superintendent of Police, Robert Simmons. It had to have started somewhere, and it started right at that Police College with Mr. Henry Wemyss and the other instructors, who were there, who would have fed into our lives and embedded us for excellence. He encouraged us to pursue academic excellence. He always encouraged us to educate ourselves; to be the best we can be, be at the top of the class—do not sit on our laurels. He was one of them who made a real transformation in our lives as young teenagers."

Reflecting on his tenure, Henry said, "I really enjoyed my time as an instructor and embraced the opportunity to invest in the young lives that entered my classroom. Today I am proud to see that some of my former recruits hold or have held prestigious ranks within the Force, up to and including Commissioner of Police. It gives me a sense of pride to know that when they came to me as new recruits, I must have instilled in them enough fire to keep them burning." As noted by Davis-Delancy, "I think Mr. Wemyss has done very well in his period, and he was destined by God to do what he was supposed to do. He was someone, who was called for his season, and he operated in his season."

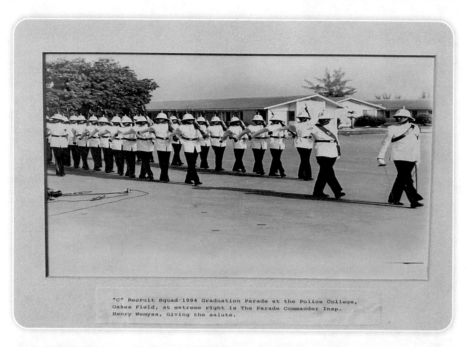

"C" Recruit Squad 1984 Graduation Parade at the Police College, Oakes Field, at extreme right is The Parade Commander Insp. Henry Wemyss, Giving the salute.

Henry Wemyss and Members of the C & D Squad of 1983 Lunch at the Hilton.
Front Row L-R: 900 Ismella Davis-Delancy (First female Deputy Commissioner
of Police, Retired); 902 Denis Colebrooke-Rolle (Retired Sergeant); Henry Wemyss,
President of WemCo Security; 806 Linda Forbes-Moxey (Retired Chief Superintendent);
564 Barrington Miller (Retired Assistant Superintendent); and
761 Noami McPhee (Retired Sergeant);

Second Row L-R: 366 Robert Simmons (Retired Superintendent); 862 Melrose Similien
(Constable); 755 Mary Mitchell (Retired Chief Superintendent); 783 Telinda McKinney-
Missick (Retired Chief Superintendent); 881 Gaynell Hudson-Peterson (Retired
Sergeant); 734 Melvern Deveaux-Roker (Retired Sergeant);

Rear Row L-R: 753 Sophie Austin-Farrington (Retired Corporal); 898 Claudine Atwell-
Hutchinson (Retired Superintendent); Acribba Lightbourne, Assistant CEO,
WemCo Security; and 949 Deborah Allen-Knowles (Retired Corporal).

**Henry Wemyss Attends Church Service at New Destiny
Cathedral with members of the C&D Squad of 1983.**
L-R - ACP Paul Rolle; SUPT. Mary Mitchell-Rolle; SGT. Denise Colebrook-Rolle;
C/SUPT. Linda Forbes-Moxey, Rev. Dr. Delton Fernander; Henry Wemyss,
ACP Ismella Davis-Delancy, CPL. Melvern Deveaux-Roker;
CPL. Debbie Allen-Knowles, ASP Barrington Miller.

CHAPTER 10

Confronting Biases and Setbacks

Henry found great satisfaction in serving as an officer in the Royal Bahamas Police Force, but a dark cloud hung over him. Since he was brought up to believe that performance should match rewards, he expected to be fairly assessed and compensated when he performed well or reprimanded when he fell below standard.

As far as he knew, promotion within the Force was based on three basic criteria: punctuality, compliance with instructions, and proper deportment. Additionally, officers were expected to pass proficiency exams. Taking all of this into account, Henry could not figure out why, year after year, his name was consistently left off the promotions list.

"As far as I knew, I met those criteria. I never had a complaint made against me by the public. There were no disciplinary actions within the Force. I was always clean, and I continued to pass my promotion examinations," he reflected. However, none of this helped him rise through the ranks. After gaining more life experience, Henry's perspective would shift. "At that time, I was unaware of Psalms 75, which speaks about promotion coming from God and not man," Henry explained. "And it took me nearly 31 years to realise this truth."

Henry had been in the Force for four years when he was promoted during a large promotion exercise under the British system in 1970. "I became a corporal, and my brother-in-law, who was a lance corporal and had joined the Force long before me, also got promoted to a corporal that year," Henry stated. "Many officers were promoted to corporals, sergeants, and above. The promotion board thought so highly of some of us that we were placed on the accelerated promotion list, which meant that if there was a vacancy in the upper rank, the next day after promotion, we could get it without having to take any further exams."

Knowing that first promotions within the Force were not easy, Henry became confident that he would quickly advance through the ranks. His family was so proud of his accomplishment, especially his father who said, "You must have done a commendable job." They, like him, saw it as a good indicator that he had a promising career within the Force. Henry felt optimistic about his future and wanted to be like the senior officers who showed so much promise. However, he would soon feel differently about the rate at which he would advance.

Henry's previous experience as corporal and officer in charge at the Grove Police Station in Nassau, Central Andros and North Eleuthera should have been advantageous for him. As an officer in charge, he had already demonstrated to his superiors that he could perform at a higher level. Despite feeling overlooked, he persisted in his efforts, hoping to be recognised for all his hard work one day. He never wavered in his commitment to serving the Force to the best of his ability and was committed to doing so for as long as he was there.

During his tenure at the Police College, Henry worked under four different commandants, each with their distinct style. They were aware of his performance because it was said that he made them all "look good." However, no one seemed to be looking out for him. Being passed over so many times, Henry soon felt like the stone the builders rejected. "I worked hard, and long hours and each year lived in expectation of making the promotion lists," Henry said. "But whenever the lists came out, I was left standing as a Corporal while others moved up the ranks. My chances of promotion appeared bleak, whereas persons who took the exams after me, some juniors, received two and three promotions."

Two years after Henry's first promotion, a fellow constable was promoted to corporal and then received promotions every year thereafter, rising through the ranks, and in eight years, when Henry became a sergeant, that officer was then an assistant superintendent of police. While Henry did not begrudge the officer's success, it was difficult to ignore the disparity between them that had nothing to do with performance.

After years of being overlooked, Henry spoke up, questioning his superiors about his chances of ever being promoted, only to be told, "Promotions are for officers who need money. You don't need a promotion because your pa rich." Although it was said in jest, Henry took it seriously, especially since he appeared to be stuck within his rank. Still, he continued to press his superiors to determine what, if anything, he was doing wrong. Several times, he was told that he had been recommended for a promotion, but they could not explain why it had not been approved.

Performance reviews were even more discouraging for Henry, as his ratings were significantly lower than he expected. It was also disheartening that his additional duties were never mentioned in his evaluation reports. As part of his responsibilities, he did a lot of report writing, and when the Senior Commissioner of Police, Headquarters, noticed how well he wrote, he transferred the responsibility for vetting applications to the Police College—most of which ended up being done by Henry. He did not mind the workload but just wanted to be recognised.

Despite continuously refuting the reviews, Henry got nowhere. Year after year, promotion exercises were carried out, but he was overlooked. "I was never concerned about politics," Henry reflected, "but it became clear to me that to be considered for promotions, you had to be politically connected." It was also no secret that the Force had a buddy system in place, but Henry never played police politics or tried joining any cliques. While some officers may have benefited from associations, including political affiliations, Henry was not looking for handouts. He stated, "Whenever I socialised, I remained within my rank because I wanted to be promoted based on hard work and merit." Even though he never joined in the political discussions or shared his political persuasion with his colleagues, his silence was interpreted as being in opposition to the then-governing party.

Henry once spoke with Deputy Superintendent Alphonso Marshall, who was the Assistant Commandant at the time, to find out why he was always passed over for promotions. Henry highly respected Marshall and considered him an officer and a gentleman. He sought Marshall's advice because he was concerned that he may have been doing something wrong. However, Marshall assured him saying, "You have not done anything wrong. It's just not your time, yet." Henry reminded him that he had already spent eight years in the Force, but Marshall told him that he had received his first promotion after thirteen years of service. He also assured Henry that he still had plenty of time to catch up, even if he started late.

Reflecting on that pep talk, Henry noted, "I trusted what he said and felt a lot better because of it."

Sometime later, Marshall met with the Chief Class Instructor and all instructional staff to discuss a performance report. He then cautioned them against destroying the careers of bright young officers. He urged them to inform officers of their mistakes and give them the opportunity to improve before writing negative reports. The Chief Inspector and Inspector, who was also the Chief Class Instructor, claimed that they were usually "batting" for officers and wanted to see them promoted, but could only write reports based on what they saw. Sitting in the meeting, Henry listened to the Chief Inspector and Chief Class Instructor defend themselves but had no idea why the meeting had been called or whose performance report was being discussed.

Within a week of that conversation, Henry was summoned to the Chief Class Instructor's office and being handed a performance review, he was told, "This is your half-year report." He was confused because he had already received his performance report—a negative review—the week before. Again, he had disagreed with the comments and walked away, feeling that his words had fallen on deaf ears, like always. Surprisingly, the revised report was one of the best reports he had ever received.

"This is the report I should have received last week," Henry said.

"Last week's report was based on your performance up to that point, but you have shown remarkable improvements since then."

"I have improved in less than a week?"

"Sign off on the report and take it up to the Commandant."

Even though he felt that he had finally received a report that reflected his true performance, Henry explained, "I left the office feeling both pleased and uneasy because I realised it could just as easily be changed back." Despite not being recognised for his efforts, Henry was driven by the nature of his work and never had a dull, routine day. "I prided myself on being a police officer and acted as though I was on duty twenty-four hours a day," he stated. "I felt as if I was born to pursue that career, and my father had received that revelation. It became a way of life that was also reflected in my private life."

Eight years after his first promotion, Henry became hopeful again, when in 1978, he was promoted to sergeant. "Even though I felt it was long overdue, I was relieved to finally receive some recognition for all the hard work I was doing," he recalled. As a sergeant, Henry worked behind the scenes for the then Chief Class Instructor. He would set the exams for the squads, detailing which instructor would administer which exams. He would then give the information to the Chief Class Instructor, who would rewrite it and pass it on to each instructor, including Henry, as a folded piece of paper. Once the instructors executed and marked exams, he would give Henry the file to compile the examination results and assign grades for all recruits. This was one of the tasks Henry would never be recognised for doing.

Others, who worked closely with Henry, also felt that he was unfairly dealt with in the Force, especially as it related to his movement up the chain of command. A former colleague noted, "He did his job properly and knowing his ability, I was surprised that he did not make any further progression. When I became an inspector, Henry might have still been a sergeant, and he was my senior." That colleague would also go on to become commissioner of police.

As an instructor, Henry was always open to respectful criticism from recruits who spoke out. He always wanted to know what they were feeling or thinking. Admitting to speaking out himself, Henry said, "Although I was vocal, I never spoke out of turn or tried to make my superiors, or anyone, look bad. It was just my thoughts about where I saw we could improve." However, his colleague pointed out, "In these military organisations, sometimes people, persons, or supervisors take a dislike to you, especially if you speak up, and Henry was one of those who did not hold back. He would tell you what's on his mind, but there is nothing wrong with that, but sometimes people don't understand that speaking out helps to grow the organisation."

Setting aside biases and setbacks, Henry loved his job and never wanted to quit. "After signing the first one-year contract with the Force, I continued signing the contracts at three-year intervals. Even though I was not being promoted, I remained optimistic, believing that it would happen the next time," Henry shared. "The years went by so quickly that I had already been in the Force for eleven years before I realised it. After devoting my youthful years to an organisation, it became difficult to leave with nothing in return, so I began looking forward to receiving a pension. The Force was my life, and I took much pride in myself and the organisation, as a whole".

Henry seemed caught up in police politics, but this became more evident when, one year, the then Commissioner of Police, Salathiel Thompson, sent word through the Commandant at the time, the then Deputy Superintendent Keith Mason, that he wanted to see him. "Henry, you should have been promoted to an inspector a long time ago," the Commissioner told him. "But you have to get the Commandant to recommend you for promotion." Having previously worked with Henry, the Commissioner was fully aware of his capabilities. While he could have recommended Henry, he no longer wanted to stick his neck out because he had previously promoted officers who he claimed had "let him down."

He did not know what else he could possibly do to be promoted because he was already working as hard as he could. When he returned to work, the Commandant wanted to know why the Commissioner had summoned him. Henry was reluctant to divulge what the Commissioner had said, but the Commandant insisted. Finally, Henry told him, "He said that my performance reports are preventing me from being promoted, and I should get you to recommend me for a promotion." To Henry's amazement, the Commandant replied, "The Commissioner of Police has a lot of confidence in me," and that was the end of it.

The then Sr. Assistant Commissioner of Police, Stanley Moir, approached Henry after observing his performance as a parade sub-commander during one of the graduation parades and said, "Henry, I want to tell you something. I don't see you as someone looking for special treatment in the Force, but I think you are someone who only wants what you justly deserve. And if they had given you that, you would have been a senior officer on this Force a long time ago. But don't give up."

That conversation stayed with Henry because he realised that he could not give up. Eventually, he was appointed as chief class instructor, a position previously held by a chief inspector. And in 1983, after 18 years in the Force, he was promoted to the rank of Inspector. It had taken him a long time, but he had not given up and hoped to advance even further before hanging up his career.

Inspector Henry Wemyss Receiving His Good Conduct, Efficiency, and
Long Service Award from H.E. The Rt. Hon. Sir Gerald Cash,
Governor General of The Commonwealth of The Bahamas, at a Ceremony
Held at Government House, 1983.

CHAPTER 11

Finding A Sense of Purpose

In early 1988, Henry Wemyss was on three-month vacation leave, but three weeks in, it got cancelled. The then Commissioner of Police, Bernard K. Bonamy, called him back to work to spearhead the newly revamped Police Cadet Corps. The two-year program had been reintroduced as part of the Force's strategic approach to attract some of the brightest and best young talents as career police officers. The goal was to train, nurture, and inspire high school students to pursue a career in law enforcement after graduation. "I was excited to be a part of what I felt was an excellent program for the Bahamian youths," Henry said about being hand-picked to lead such an important initiative. "I welcomed the opportunity to teach once again and make a difference in the lives of young people."

Henry was responsible for developing the program and syllabus for the Commissioner's approval. Despite not having any prior experience, he took on the task with his usual 'can do' attitude. "I felt as if I had been handed a gold mine. I wasted no time preparing the syllabus with the assistance of Sergeant 703 Andrew Huyler, an instructor who worked with me at the college," Henry stated. "I also designed the uniform, which was inspired by that of police officers: narrow striped pants, a striped shirt, blue patches, red patches of epaulettes, and a beret. As we formatted the program, we expounded on what was already being done at the Police College to ensure that the cadets became well-rounded. There was also a program that recognized academic excellence, good attendance, and long service."

Cadets were required to work eighteen hours per week—three days after school from 4:00 p.m. to 8:00 p.m., and on Saturdays from 8:00 a.m. to 6:00 p.m. As an added benefit, they were paid a weekly stipend of

$64.72. After two years, they had the option of becoming police officers or applying for a bonded scholarship to pursue an associate degree in a related field, at the then College of The Bahamas. Following that, they could go to England, as sub-inspectors, and complete the General Policing Course towards becoming full inspectors. If any of them decided not to pursue policing, they were obligated to refund the Force for all expenses incurred. That was Henry's vision for the future leaders of the Force. "I had envisioned that one day the commissioner of police and all the other ranks would come from the ranks of cadets," Henry stated. "And the future Force would be made up of young, intelligent, educated and well-trained men and women."

Henry said, "I also envisioned the Cadet Corps as a farm club for recruitment, used to bring in the brightest and best so that there would be no need to advertise because trained recruits would have passed through the Cadet Program. And if they took advantage of every opportunity presented to them, they would enter the Force fully prepared." Henry believed that, even if the Cadets did not want to become police officers, the injection of trained and disciplined young people into the society would make a major difference and a better Bahamas.

Along with Henry, a team of senior police officials, including the then-Minister responsible for the Police Force, Honourable Paul Adderley, and the Commissioner of Police at the time, Bernard K. Bonamy, scouted the high schools to promote the program. They were looking for the brightest and best students in New Providence, aged 16 and older. Because some of the schools were already closed, they also used the media to reach potential candidates. The program was well received and quickly gained momentum.

When the team visited St. John's College, Gamal Newry, President, Preventative Measures Ltd. and Reserve Assistant Superintendent of Police, who was a 12th grader at the time, quickly made up his mind to join. Newry recalled, "I remember when they would have finished, I lingered. Mr. Wemyss was the one who sold the program. There were other officers who introduced the Police Force, but he spoke about it. Afterwards, I went to them and told them I was interested, and I was ready to sign up right then because I thought it was a good concept."

Waldon Russel, Chief Operating Officer, was months away from his 17th birthday when he learned about the program. "There was an ad in the newspaper, inviting us to come down to Police Headquarters on East Street," he recalled. "I went along with three of my friends and, eventually, we all ended up joining the Cadet Corps. At the time, I was the Head Boy of R. M. Bailey and was just looking for something positive. I was growing up in Black Village, near Bain Town, and there were a lot of opportunities to get into trouble, and I needed guidance to keep me in line. I was doing okay in school, but there were too many opportunities to really lose my way."

Tagging along with friends, 16-year-old Tyrone Archer (Boat Captain) had no intentions of joining until fate stepped in. "During the summer, I just went along with some friends who were taking their applications to Mr. Wemyss," he recounted. "Being with them, he asked me my name and how many BJC's I had. When I told him I had eight, he asked, 'Mathematics and English?' When I told him, 'Yes,' he gave me an application and told me, 'Fill it out, let your parents sign it and bring it back.' I really had no clue about the program and didn't have any interest in joining it. I never had any interest in the Police Force. I wanted to be a pilot, but that same day, my career in the Force began." After 10 years of service, he made a shift, explaining, "Henry Wemyss gave me a passion, and then I found a passion."

Will Hart, Chief Superintendent of Police and Officer In Charge, Abaco, who was 16 years old and in his final year at St. Augustine's College, was encouraged to sign up by a friend who had already applied. Due to his family's financial situation, at the time, he was financing his own school fees and saw it as an opportunity to further his education once he graduated. He was not interested in a career in policing, as he shared, "I wanted to join the Royal Bahamas Defence Force and pursue a career in navigation so that I could work on boats and go out to sea." He would later reflect, "I also believe that because of joining the Cadet Corps, I received an anonymous financial scholarship to pay off my school fees. Looking back at it now, the Cadet Corps was a stepping stone in the right direction in my life and in my career path that I would have never recognized. It was a fertilizer that helped me to grow."

Another student, Deon Simms (Manager, Trainer, Actor and Writer) was on the verge of turning 17 and was just looking forward to graduating. "There was this whole excitement about being in the 12th grade, getting ready to graduate, getting a job, going to the clubs, and all kinds of stuff like that," he explained. "So, I did not have a direction. I did not have a plan in terms of my life. I was not one of those students who were filling out college applications and looking towards the next step. I heard an advertisement on the radio, and I just mentioned to my mother that I might be interested in it. And then she came home with an application."

As the students flocked into Henry's office, he made quick decisions, rejecting on the spot those who did not fit his ideal profile. However, one student refused to take "no" for an answer. Berkley Neely, Assistant Superintendent of Police and Officer In Charge, Andros District, recalled, "When I first went into Mr. Wemyss' office, he laughed at me and told me that I was too small. I did not meet the measurement of the ideal requirement. I was hurt and dejected. I can remember how Inspector Wemyss told me to do some stretching exercises.

"At first, I wasn't really interested, but I think his rejecting me made me more interested. I came back the next day, and I sat with him again and spoke for about half an hour. I came back the following day and the day after that. I was so persistent that I went to his office five times, and he told me, 'You keep coming here, I done tell you, you're too small.' I visited his office every day until he finally took me to see the Commissioner of Police, but the Commissioner wasn't there, so we saw the Staff Officer, Mr. Rodney Burrows. And he decided, 'Give him a chance.' I had always thought it was the comment, 'You measure me from my head down, but you need to measure me from my neck up' that moved him to allow me to join. It is only now, after all these many years, I learnt that what impressed him most was my persistent, dogged resolve to not be dismissed. He said I told him that persistence is a virtue, and that was the turning point when he decided to give me a chance."

The response was so overwhelming that Henry had collected hundreds of applications by the deadline. Carefully combing through each one, he had the tough task of narrowing down the applications to twenty-five. After what seemed like endless screenings and interviews, the selection process was finally completed. On 28th September 1988, The Royal Bahamas Police Force Cadet Corp was officially launched during a ceremony at the Police College, with its first twenty-five participants making up the 'A' Cadet Squad, known as the Alpha Cadet Squad, along with their families, friends, and well-wishers. They would become the forerunners.

**Opening Ceremony for the Official Launch of the
Cadet Corp Program Held on 28ᵗʰ September, 1988.**

Front Row L-R: Inspector H. Wemyss, ASP E Stubbs, Supt. K. Mason, Hon. Paul
Adderley; Commissioner of Police B. K. Bonamy, S/ACP A. Butler, Supt. R. Burrows,
C/Insp C. Sweeting

Second Row L-R: 13 Kahlil Lockhart, 11 Cornell Ingraham, 17 Berkely Neely, 8 Glen
Hanna, 22 Wellington Saunders, 19 Dave Rolle, 25 Jeremy Tucker, 18 Gamal Newry,
9 Will Hart, 15 Lynden Moss, 16 Jermaine Moultrie, 20 Waldon Russell,
6 Franky Edmond.

Rear Row L-R: 10 Reno Horton, 1 Kissinger Anderson, 12 Gerrad Jennings, 24 Terry
Strapp, 2 Tyrone Archer, 14 Thanacious Milford, 21 Jeremy Saunders,
4 Donald Brennen, 7 Dion Hall, 23 Dion Simms, 5 Thadius Cornish, 3 Phillip Bethel.

Cadets at the Opening Ceremony with Family Members 28th September, 1988.

Mixed Cadet (Male and Female) Squad A, B, C & D (1989)

Recalling his thoughts on being selected, Simms said, "I felt like I was special being in the program. I felt like we were the leading coup. They picked the best of the best. They literally had hundreds of applications in the office. Applications were on the desks and the floor—all over the place. The desks were covered with stacks of applications. When you think about it, they picked 25 out of all that, and I was in the first 25. I had to be special."

On their first day, the cadets were brimming with excitement but had no idea what they had signed up for until Henry walked into the room with a stern demeanour and a commanding voice. During that time, Retired Superintendent of Police Elaine Sands was the Corporal assisting Henry and recalling the first day, she said, "He had everyone assemble into the auditorium, and from the moment he walked in, he started disciplining - putting his finger on everything right there and then. If he saw anyone talking, he called them out right away. Before they even knew what the rules were, he had them go to the front and do push-ups. So, he dished out punishment right away. His mannerisms and the way he spoke were no-nonsense. It was like a zero-tolerance for any kind of misbehaviours or infractions within the Cadet Corps. As soon as they entered the Police College, he drove that home to them immediately. And when he was on-site, you could hear a pin drop. The impression he put on them was long-lasting, and immediately they began to fall in line with discipline."

From day one, the cadets realised that Henry was not going to be easy on them, as Newry shared, "You really got to see a different Wemyss. He was a salesman when he came to the school —a good salesman—but when you got in there, it was like, where did this man come from? He had changed but changed in a good way. He was very much a hard-core disciplinarian from the small details, which he emphasized from when you got in there. You had to have your shoes clean, your fingernails clipped off, and you had to be clean. As a young man, certainly, you're not that kind of detailed, and those sorts of things are not something you would focus on. He emphasized those small details to remind you that those are the building blocks. It wasn't the big picture that you see at the end, but the emphasis that you put on the smaller part that gives you the whole."

About his initial impression of Henry, Neely said, "He was the epitome of fear. He had a way of speaking to you very silently, and then he would go into this thunderous roar to a point where he would say some things that would break you down, but at the end of it, you would learn from the experience. It was frightening but also a building experience. Never really met anybody like him before, because he really was focused on what he was doing."

Sixteen-year-old Jeremy Saunders, an engineer, joined because of an interest in police work and the opportunities that would not be available to him otherwise. Recalling his initial impression, he said, "I didn't know what to think of Mr. Wemyss within the first month. I never met anybody like that. Sometimes, at the beginning, I would even think that he was crazy. But when you sit down and think about what he was saying, over time it made sense."

Sands further shared, "Nobody wanted to be punished, so they were in line when they saw him coming on the compound. Everyone is doing what they are supposed to do—even me. It's just that everyone had respect for him, regardless of what he said or did to us; we took it with a grain of salt, so we never got offended about it because we understood." She described him as, "Having a head of fire and a heart of gold."

As a disciplinarian, Newry felt Henry used a mental approach to address the issues or challenges at hand. "If your boots weren't clean or you were late, he would start with that. That's where it started and that's where it ended. It would be a very strong chastisement, but it would be, 'What are you doing? What is your role in this predicament? You can't blame your mother; you can't blame your instructor. What do you think about yourself?'" He recalled, "He was very introspective in his approach, and if needed, it progressed to some physical stuff, running around, doing push-ups, or that kind of thing, but I think the strongest thing in his arsenal was his ability to communicate your wrong and make you introspect as to what am I doing? How can I beat it because I am more than this? Why am I letting myself fail?"

At times, Henry was so comical that the cadets strained to maintain straight faces. This was usually the case whenever they assembled in the auditorium to give their weekly progress reports and receive feedback from him. Remembering those incidents, Simms said, "When he did that, he was an absolute riot. He used to have us crying because we laughed so much, and the thing about it is that you could laugh, but when you laughed you would get push-ups, so the push-ups would start at 25. The first person to go up would get 25 push-ups and the increments would increase by 25 for the next person. But he would just say some things. We cracked up, and if he caught you laughing, you had to do push-ups, and sometimes it would be about 10 of us on the stage doing push-ups. That was the gist of Inspector Wemyss - to get us to control ourselves. Everything was about self-discipline. That was his way. One of the things I learnt from him, too, was self-discipline - being able to see something funny and not laugh."

Henry was firm and unbending, yet the cadets revered him. They were at a crossroads, and he reeled them in, giving them a sense of direction. Newry noted, "Wemyss was a rough guy, but a good rough, a good disciplinarian, and I think what he did was important for men of our age who needed to have that continued guidance as you were influenced by so many other things at that time. At the age of 15, there were so many things coming in; you're either coming out of high school or you're into exploring the world, for lack of a better term, and he kept us grounded for the time that he spent with us."

Learning drills was also an important aspect of their training, but it was more than just a precision exercise. As Russell recalled, it was "an interesting transformational process. It was not just about turning left and right; it was about focus, discipline, listening, and presenting yourself well. Before you got to stand on that parade ground, you had to make sure that everything you were wearing was perfectly cleaned—and you took hours to do that. Then you had to prepare yourself. You had to make sure that you were properly shaven, and your hair was properly cut." They all sported the same haircut, done by a barber of Henry's choosing.

As part of their training, cadets were given the opportunity to observe live policing through postings at various police stations. This allowed them to gain first-hand knowledge of the ins and outs of policing. However, Henry went deeper. He wanted them to examine "the good, the bad, and the ugly" aspects of policing, encouraging them to think critically about what could have been done differently. Later, they would discuss their ideas with their squad mates in the classroom, and these discussions, along with debates, helped them develop effective communication skills.

As Henry envisioned it, "Recruiting young, educated, brilliant men would bring about a new image for the Police Force, changing its outlook and reception throughout The Bahamas." Seeing the potential of the program, he tried to get all stakeholders to buy into his vision. Whenever he made his station rounds and found cadets sitting idly, he became annoyed and reminded whoever was in charge that they were there to learn. He once met a cadet emptying the trash, and becoming infuriated, immediately addressed it. He was always fighting for the program, doing whatever it took to make sure it succeeded.

Russell found his actions inspiring, "It was so motivating to see someone stand up for you like that—for anything—but to see how he believed in this vision, how he believed in what he was telling you and was prepared to defend you anywhere. It is one thing to say that you believe in someone, but when you make them feel that you believe in them, that lasts forever. He made us feel that there was someone out there who believed in us and was willing to go to bat for us."

Simms, who was also encouraged by the way they were being treated, recalled, "My favourite part about the program was the way he made us feel. He made us feel as though we were destined for something. We did not feel that this was just some assignment that they gave him, and he was just going through the motions. He made us feel that, at the end of the day, we were going to be like the crème de la crop. As a matter of fact, he called us the crème de la crop. He always made us feel that we were the best. The best thing in The Bahamas at the time, and we were destined to go far."

Henry redefined the concept of policing from an enforcement agency to a service agency. He explained that police officers served their country, communities, and families. Through community work, they got practical experience serving the country's most vulnerable citizens - the young and the old. On Saturdays, they volunteered with organizations, such as the Red Cross, Children's Emergency Hostel, Ranfurly Home and Persis Rodgers Home for the Aged. They spent time playing with the children, talking and singing with the seniors, washing windows, and working the grounds, pulling up weeds. Henry emphasized that policing was "not just something to do but a way to have an impact on our country and the way our nation would develop."

He was holistic in his approach, exposing them to many of the areas that contribute to a healthy society. They visited the Magistrate Courts, the Supreme Courts, and the House of Assembly. Not neglecting their spiritual well-being, they attended services at about every denomination of churches - Baptist, Anglican, Catholic, and others. Whenever they went to church, it was mandatory that they wear a suit and tie. While eating with them, he noticed their eating habits and taught them proper table etiquette. Russell recalled, "For many of us, he was the one who placed a knife and fork in our hands for the first time. He taught us how to eat with a fork and knife. It was a chicken on the bone, but it was an experience for young men to get into."

Although he was always stern within the group setting, there was another side to Henry, as Newry shared, "If he pulled you into his office, it was a different man again. He would be a bit more caring and understanding. If there was a need to see him, his doors were always open. Any cadet could have gone in there to have a conversation with him about the future and their plans. It was very surprising because, when you got behind closed doors, if there was a critique or commentary debate, he was open to it. You would have that conversation—it was not a shutdown. And that was important too because you understood that there is a time and place for everything, and to keep that esprit de corps, we have to push you to create that team, we have to motivate you, but also, if we need to address you as individuals, I'm prepared to do that as well. I was surprised by some of the stories, and I experienced it personally. When they went behind, he was a different creature. And that is important; you need individual attention."

Simms also observed Henry's sensitive side, "Mr. Wemyss always portrayed that image of a hard officer in charge, and he would act as if he had no concern for your feelings, which is what we were used to seeing from policemen. But I do remember one time there was a young man - who is now an assistant superintendent on the Police Force - who came into the office and said that he wanted to quit. Inspector Wemyss pulled him in, sat him down, and told him they were going to talk it out. When that guy came back, he was ready to stay. It was amazing to see him show that he was not just there to give you orders, make you comply, and pound you into this, but that he also had sensitivity towards your needs. And that's what he always did with us. When the rubber hit the road, when everything was said and done, he was the type to always show that his concern about you was beyond your being a cadet; his concern was about you being a human being."

From all accounts, Henry proved to be the best man for leading the cadets. He embodied that strong male figure who taught them discipline and how to take ownership of their successes and failures. He was the one who pointed them toward the future and told them they were the crème de la crème. Some cadets came from grass-root areas and others from wealthy families; it was a good mix. Henry was "objective," as Russell noted. "He was looking for the best, as he saw it, and he didn't measure that by our current situation in life. He measured it by the potential that he saw in us. That is unique for an individual to be able to see into the soul of somebody and see what they could be, and then kind of very skilfully chip away the rough edges and create something that could be useful and continue a desire to be useful and to contribute."

Some of the young men had positive male examples in their lives, but Henry was a different kind of positive, as Russell shared, "I had a father, who also inspired me, but during that time in my life, Henry Wemyss was around more than he was, as I came from a single-parent home. When I think about those two men—my dad and Henry Wemyss—they inspired me the most. Because my dad was a person who was like, 'you could accomplish anything', and if I could use an analogy: my dad put a nail there, but Henry Wemyss drove it in. He gave me the tools that I needed to succeed. And it wasn't education; it was character. If someone could spend some time with you and mould your character and teach you values, teach you how to behave in society, teach you how to treat people, what to stand for, and what to accept as a standard for yourself - the impact is far-reaching." Archer, who held similar sentiments added, "I've always had my father and always had my uncles, my aunts, and my mother - they all always encouraged me. I've always had encouraging people in my life, but Inspector Wemyss brought something extra. Most of our squad came with discipline, but he just enhanced it. Basically, he added that military discipline to the little things that we were lacking."

"Ironically, during our time in the Cadet Corps, it was never about being a police officer. It was empowering men. It was never just a feeding system to get into the Police Force, but a way to filter out decent young men and feed them back to society to make a positive impact. The program built you first as an individual," Hart explained. "I was always disciplined, but it enhanced who I was and gave me further structure. When I became a cadet, everyone looked at me differently, including my family. It was discipline and grace - like you are someone - and it gave me sort of a status. As a cadet, even if I wanted to do what everyone else was doing, I couldn't because I had a standard to live by."

Hart further added, "Mr. Wemyss, at the time, was not an easy man but he showed discipline in the form of love. He was a straight shooter to the point, and he had a level that he wanted us to operate at. Even though I was always clean, he showed me how to be clean. When we cleaned our shoes, we cleaned our shoes to be clean. When we cleaned our belts, we cleaned our belts to be clean. It caused you to have pride for the uniform. As a young man, the program nurtured me and steered me in a different direction because I never thought I would have been a policeman."

Russell felt it was easy to learn from Henry because "he was also an example of what he was teaching us. If he was telling you that you needed to keep your uniform clean, you just needed to look at him and see that his was clean every time and his shoes were slick every time." Simms felt the same, "Even though Mr. Wemyss would berate us like he scolded us and tried to sharpen and toughen us up, I had the utmost respect for him. He was not one of those people who spoke a good game and played a good game. If he wanted your shoes to be clean, you looked at him, and his shoes were clean."

Summing up Russell said, "So it was a well-rounded type of training and development. I don't know if there was any aspect that was missing. The education was there, the practice was there, and we studied martial arts. Of course, we studied physical education. Your body had to be strong; your mind had to be strong, and your spirit had to be strong. We went to church together. It was a holistic approach and that's the only way you can develop people properly. So, we had to touch body, mind and spirit and the program did that for me, and I could vouch for my brothers that it did that for them as well."

Neely agreed, "The Cadets Corps changed me. It introduced me to 25 young men who had similar interests from diversely different backgrounds, and ultimately, we were the men of the future. He was an architect of a program that moulded us. He made us buy a suit for church visits. We had to eat with proper etiquette, visit the elderly, visit the orphans, and do community work. We were set apart as arrows on the bowstrings of life. He wanted to propel us further forward, further upward, and further onward than our young minds could conceive. He was a teacher, a father, a man to be emulated, and a boss. He had a plan that he worked at with such vigour, that it was superhuman to watch him in action. He was with us all the time and still found time to fight for the direction of the program." He also noted, "It wasn't so much that he was selling policing, policing was secondary. I think he was more about developing the culture of the country as opposed to just thinking about police officers. He sold the fact that this is your country, and you have to be the one to make it better."

By 1989, the Police Cadet Corps had expanded to 125 cadets—four male squads and one female squad. One of the 1989 cadets was Henry's nephew, Truman Butler, an International Attorney. However, his relationship did not get him any special treatment, and at the time, his peers never realised their connection. Reflecting on being a cadet, Butler humorously recalled, "One time I was marching, and I guess I was too erect and too stiff. He said, 'It's marching, not jumping panny cake man.' At the time, I was like, Lord, have mercy; this is what he's calling me in front of all these people. But I appreciate that name-calling, and I think that's what our young people need today."

"The whole premise of the Police Force, and part of it with the Cadet Corps, was to toughen you so that when you're on the streets if someone says something about your mother, your dog, or your wife, you don't react to that. If they break the law, it's a different thing since you have to enforce it. You don't react to the public saying stuff to you. Those things strengthened me so much. When I went off to London and while walking the streets, I had drunk British men say, 'Look at the monkey, look at the monkey, walking past' that meant nothing. So those things strengthen you and build character. That's the kind of thing I would not have been able to do without the Cadet Program."

Further expanding upon his experience, Butler noted, "In terms of lessons, there is so much to pull out. One of the first things was there was so much fortitude in building us up as young men and getting us through the challenges we would have and the things we would experience, for which we have to have perseverance and fortitude. We used to drill, for example, in the rain. He built men out of boys. He's a father to me, a father to others, just an exceptional leader, loving person, big-hearted, altruistic, and will do things for the benefit of others, and I truly think of him as one of our national treasures."

Glennis Knowles, Senior Administrator, Bahamas Global Academy, who was a shy 10th grader at R. M. Bailey High School and went on to become Miss Bahamas 1998, signed up for the program in 1989. "I never thought about being a police officer," she admitted. "But I got excited because all the other students were. I didn't think I would have qualified as an ideal candidate because I was quite shy and didn't feel I had the skill set that a police officer should have. I had expected to get weeded out."

Much to her surprise, Knowles was selected, and her life was never the same. "It was a turning point for me," she said, in reflection. "It took me from being a shy person, who was afraid to express myself or how I thought, to being authoritative, understanding who I am as a person, and being able to execute that vision. It was very instrumental in my personal development." She recalled the first time she met Henry, "I became excited because of his attitude. I saw excellence and a mindset not to settle for good enough but to go beyond what the average person set out to achieve. He was the epitome of excellence in a military organisation." She also remembers the passion and commitment Henry demonstrated in his capacity as a leader.

"He had genuine care, concern, and love. He took on the father figure for most of the cadets. I grew up around my grandfather, who was also an authoritative figure, and I came from a structured environment, but Mr. Wemyss took it up a couple of notches, instilling how to do that for yourself - self-discipline and character building to hold and harness the skill to achieve excellence," she explained. "It was not just about pressing your clothes, but starching them. It was not just about cleaning your shoes, but doing it so well that you can see your reflection in them."

After the program, Knowles served as an officer within the Royal Bahamas Police Force for 12 years, but having gone through the program influenced her decision to expand her horizons outside of the Force, "Your horizons can open beyond the limitations, and you can still contribute and achieve more. Once you have the vision, it is difficult to remain in the same position." As an educator, she said, "I pass on the values and principles I learnt in the Cadet Corps to establish core values, character, and strength."

David Cox (Chief Superintendent of Police and Attorney) was a 16-year-old 10th grader who also joined the Cadet Corps in 1989. At the time, he was the Head Boy of C. I. Gibson Senior High School. According to Cox, one of the most fascinating aspects of the program was, "that both government and private schools were represented and that organization, under Mr. Wemyss, had the most prefects, head boys, deputy head boys, head girls, and deputy head girls ever in the history of any youth program."

As there were not many opportunities for young men back then, he seized the opportunity to join what he felt was a prestigious program. "I grew up Over The Hill, and most of us didn't have a male figure in our homes, and because of his discipline and very high standards, Mr. Wemyss became a father figure," he stated. "My father died when I was 10, and I had never met a man like Mr. Wemyss before. He was so disciplined. I came from a background that was free-spirited, so that program brought some structure to my life. Mr. Wemyss has a lot of children, and he has contributed to their lives and the way they are today.

"He never expected mediocrity; his standards were always high. Even the shorts and V-neck t-shirts we wore for physical education had to be clean and starched," Cox continued. "One of the highlights was that, Mr. Wemyss made sure that every cadet was a part of the Duke of Edinburgh Award Program, now called the Governor General's Award, where, in addition to doing extra classes, we were compelled to learn a skill such as plumbing, mechanic, and karate."

"The discipline instilled in me all started with the Cadet Corps Program. And I could not have gotten that from anywhere else, because no one was setting an example for me. The Cadet Corps helped to guide me in the direction I needed to go. I would not know what I would have been, but I would not have been this far in my life, in terms of my academics. I would not have been this far in life in terms of what I have acquired, even the way I push my kids."

After the program, Cox immediately signed on as a Police Officer so that he could support himself and his mother. Later, he would have the opportunity to return to college to pursue higher education. He also wanted to become and instructor and stated, "After seven years as a Police Officer, I was sent to the Police College where I spent 14 years. I would always reflect on Mr. Wemyss and how he was such a motivator and pusher, and because his standards were so high, it made me the type of person I am when it comes to standards, as well as what I accept from my children and other young people who I have trained and taught over the years."

Henry loved working with the cadets, but his biggest challenge was not having sufficient support to run the program, "The parents dropped the cadets at the College, but I had to ensure that they got home safely at night. The program ended at 8:00 p.m., and I accompanied the driver to collect the cadets from the various police stations and stood up on the bus during the entire drive. They lived all around the island, and after dropping them home, I had to return to the headquarters to park the bus. There was a Corporal working along with me, Elaine Sands, now retired Superintendent of Police, whom I had trained as a recruit. She was responsible for looking after the females and ensuring that they made it home without any incident." From Monday to Friday, every day, he arrived at the Police Headquarters at 7:00 a.m. and left for home at about midnight. He would slick his shoes before going to bed at about 2:00 a.m.

Henry recalled, "It became so hectic that, eventually, he developed migraine headaches that were so intense he had to consult a physician. I was prescribed medication, but the headaches persisted, so on the advice of Commissioner B. K. Bonamy, I went to the United States to see a specialist for a second opinion. Noticeably, as soon as I got on the plane, my headaches went away and during my entire weekend stay, I did not have any headaches. As soon as I arrived back home, the headaches returned. That was when I realised that the headaches were stress-related." Still, Henry remained committed to seeing the vision of the program fulfilled.

"I felt so proud as I watched them grow and develop into disciplined young men and women," Henry said. The parents also noticed the change in their teenagers and often commended me for turning their children's lives around. Among them was a single mother, Marina Knowles, who recalled, "When I looked at my son, I smiled to myself. He took the training in like a sponge and became disciplined and well-groomed. I was well pleased. Inspector Wemyss was like a father to them. He was an authoritarian, but not so rough until you couldn't talk to him. He was rough in the sense that he gave you the real thing. The kind of training that young people need so they won't go astray. I thanked him very much for helping my son."

Her son, Simms agreed, "He was benevolent in that he was all about leading the whole person, not just the cadet. It wasn't a means to an end to

155

get somebody on the Police Force. It was about no matter where you go in life, these are lessons you will carry with you. So, it was a holistic type of leadership." Simms realised that Henry was all about encouraging them when he received an unexpected award, "They were giving out awards, and I got the most improved cadet award. That was so unexpected because normally you do things and don't think that people are paying attention, so that showed that he was paying attention to me."

"The program was gaining such momentum that the government corporations wrote letters inviting me to put together a technical cadet corps program for them," Henry shared. "I wrote back to them, inviting them to write to the Commissioner of Police, but told them that while I could do the disciplinarian aspect of the program, their lectures had to be tailor-made to suit their respective corporations. It was even mentioned that I should have some input in the national youth service program that was proposed by the then Prime Minister, Sir Lynden O. Pindling."

One of the most important things Henry did for the group was to foster a sense of unity among them. As Russell explained, "He knew we were going to face challenges later on in life and made us value each other and understand how important it was to fellowship and stay together." Some 30 years later, their bond is still strong, and Russell described the Cadet A group as, "A brotherhood - it's a fraternity. They're family, and we try to support each other and follow each other's careers. I think it's something that's going to be with me for the rest of my life, and it has been with me all my life." Also realizing this, Henry stated, "What I like about the men of the A Squad is that they have a brotherhood and support each other, and still celebrate every 28th of September, the day they enlisted in the Cadet Corps."

In explaining how he brought them closer, Hart said, "He made us learn each other's names. We had to line up in the auditorium and go around to everyone in our squad and tell Mr. Wemyss their names and numbers. So, you had to learn their names and their numbers. His message to us was that you don't see these boys every day and just come and go home. You must learn who they are, and they must learn who you are. They must get to know you, and you must get to know them. Because of the program, I made some brothers of those 16-year-old boys, who became my lifelong friends."

In speaking about Henry's legacy Russell said, "His legacy is, of course, the Cadet Corps. His legacy is 100s of young men who idolized him, who were willing to transform to meet a standard that someone was presenting to them. And so, there are many more like me - I'm not the only one -stretched across the whole spectrum of society doing different things and this man has left an indelible mark on all our lives. So, his legacy is having produced Bahamians who contribute to society, who are productive, and who he could be proud of. I think if you could gather all these people together from their respective professions and places, you would see a cadre of dynamic young people who are leading wherever they go; they were taught to lead and think like that, and to act in a particular way. So, he has a strong legacy."

On 5th December, 2022, after 33 years, Henry got a chance to sit with some of the former Squad A Cadets. They paid tribute to him, sharing what the program had meant to them, and the long-lasting impact he had made on their lives. Although Henry had kept in contact with some of them, he had not seen the others since they were teenagers. In attendance were Tyrone Archer, Phillip Bethel, Donald Brennen, Glen Hanna, Gamal Newry, Dave Rolle, Waldron Russell, Jeremy Saunders, and Deon Simms. Meeting them as mature men was an emotional experience for Henry that brought tears to his eyes.

His daughter, Acribba, had designed special T-shirts and caps for the occasion to wear with jeans. One of the cadets refused to believe that they could wear jeans, knowing that Henry never allowed anyone to stand before him wearing jeans. When he showed up, he admitted to using an entire can of starch to crease his slacks. He had been too afraid to show up in jeans and was shocked to see Henry in a pair. As each of them spoke, the respect and admiration they still held for him became evident.

"It was an excellent program and if I had to do it all over again, I would and if I had to go back in time I would perfect being a cadet more, and I would have encouraged more students to join," Hart shared. "I stand on the shoulders of some good men and one of them is Henry Wemyss.

We still have a rapport with him, and we still go to him and ask for advice and he's still very much relevant. So, he's still our instructor."

In reflecting, Henry said, "My long-term goals were for all of them to be successful in life, regardless of whether they continued as police officers or not, but in society. I realise that for them to be able to aspire to these things—their goals—I must be able to let them see that there is a goal and what the goal is, so they can focus and be encouraged to continue. I think I would have accomplished that in the first two years, but that was short-lived. Looking at them now and seeing who they are today, to me, that is a success. Not me; not what happened to me, but what they have become— that is where I am successful. As a leader, you have a hard task because everyone has different character traits, but you must be able to know how to mesh them together and get them to work together towards the same goals, regardless of what their characters are, reminding them that no matter what happens, you must continue to be yourself and nobody else."

While Henry had enjoyed his tenure instructing police recruits, working with the Cadet Corps was the northern star of his career, "I enjoyed policing from day one, but I had no purpose. In other words, I had no reason for why I was there or why I was doing it other than just to serve. Sometimes you need to be able to spread your wings and let them go. When you work under someone and have to report to them, you can't prove who you are because you must follow their instructions. As the leader of the Cadet Corps, I was able to spread my wings because I only reported to the Commissioner of Police. So that allowed me to use my own ingenuity. It took me 22 years to find my purpose in the Force. That Cadet Program was my brainchild, so I gave it my all." Cadets were also distinguished from police recruits by the fact that they were all hand-picked. Henry was also able to "bend the trees while they were young," making the program even more effective.

Henry's commitment to the job was unquestionable. Undoubtedly, he was the moving force behind the program. Sands noted that he went above and beyond, "He used to live, drink and sleep cadets. He used to make sure to tell them that when he's home, he's thinking about how he's going to deal with them." Henry had taken the program to heart. He felt that great confidence was placed in him, and he did not want to disappoint anyone. In Henry's words, "I had to try to make it a success because if the Commissioner of Police, the government of the day and the Minister of National Security had placed the confidence in me. I had to do whatever it took, even sacrificing social and family time to make it work, and I couldn't fail those young men and women, who believed so much in me."

The hard work and sacrifices made by Henry and the team working along with him paid off. The cadets were presented to the public during the 1990 New Year's Junkanoo Parade. The moment they entered Bay Street, the crowd exploded into a resounding applause with standing ovations. The international media was also there, and later they saw themselves marching on international news.

It was an intoxicating feeling, and Henry could not have felt prouder, "As I stood on Bay Street alongside the cadets, I knew that the Force had successfully attracted the crème a la crop. I felt that a bright future loomed ahead for the program, the Force, and the country. I looked forward to taking it to the next level. I was proud of the young Cadets and were honoured to be their leader."

Two months prior, he was at Three Queens Restaurant, which was then located on Wulff Road, when two senior police officers walked in—a Senior Assistant Commissioner of Police, now deceased, and a Chief Superintendent of Police, now retired. On seeing him, they called him over and gave him a heads-up that the Minister of National Security was so impressed with his performance with the cadets that a decision was made to promote him to the rank of assistant superintendent of police during a special promotion exercise in January of the following year. Thinking back to that conversation, Henry felt that, finally, things were turning in his favour; but sadly, the promised promotion would never materialize. Instead, something entirely unexpected happened next that shattered the reputation he had worked so hard to build.

**Henry Wemyss Greets Dion Simms as Tyrone Archer,
Glen Hanna, and Donald Brennen look on. (5th December, 2022)**

Members of Cadet A Squad of 1988 Reunite with Henry Wemyss.

L-R: Donald Brennen, Philip Bethel, Glen Hanna, Jamal Newry,
Henry Wemyss, Tyrone Archer, Dave Rolle, Jeremy Saunders,
Waldon Russell, Dion Simms. (5th December, 2022).

CHAPTER 12

An Unexpected Twist of Fate

Tuesday, 1st January 1990, was the first working day of the year, and as usual, at 7:00 a.m. Henry arrived at Police Headquarters. The year had already begun with a bang, and he was feeling inspired. Many senior officers and members of the public were continually congratulating him for his work with the cadets. He was on such a high that nothing could bring him down. Before that day was over, he thought differently.

Around 8:00 a.m. the Staff Officer from the Commissioner of Police office called Henry. After congratulating him on the successful parade, he explained that he had been instructed to inform him that the Superintendent In Charge of the Drug Unit in Oakes Field wanted to see him. Becoming concerned, Henry wanted to know why but the officer said that he did not know. Before leaving, Henry also questioned the Senior Assistant Commissioner of Police, now deceased, the one who had told him about the planned promotion, but he explained that he was not privy to such information. He did, however, tell him that if he was called in, he would have to go.

As he drove away, Henry had the strange feeling that it would be his last day in uniform, because he realised that getting called to the Drug Unit was never a good sign. Also, sometime prior his banker had called and questioned why the Attorney General's Office was investigating his account. He had brushed it off, knowing he had nothing to worry about since an investigation would only disclose his mortgage, a few personal loans, and a $1,000.00 fixed deposit he had held for several years.

At the Drug Unit, Henry met with the Superintendent, an Assistant Superintendent, and an Inspector:

"I just wanted to see you. There are one or two questions that I want to ask you," the Superintendent said.

"Questions about what, sir?"

"About a drug transaction that went down in Cat Island."

"When did it go down?"

"Sometime in 1985."

Henry had been back from Cat Island for four years, having spent less than a year there. He was confused because he was not aware of any drug transactions that had occurred under his supervision.

"We don't believe it. We don't believe what he said. But we just needed to see you so that we could write it off because the Minister of National Security said, as there is no evidence, it needs to be written off."

"All right, sir."

He then gave Henry the particulars of the case and the persons, who claimed he had been involved in a drug conspiracy, but Henry confirmed that he did not know the names or recalled ever meeting them but asked:

"Did they say that they gave me money?"

"No, they did not say that they gave you any money. They just said that they knew you and your brother."

"Where did they know us from?"

"They said they saw you and your family in a place, laughing and appearing to be quite happy."

"How was I supposed to know them? Are there any peculiar markings that would distinguish them from any other Caucasians? Are there any charges being brought?"

"No. No charges are being brought."

"If there are, I will be vindicated. Because I don't know what you are talking about."

"No Goose. We are writing this thing off."

Without being cautioned, Henry left and returned to his office, but his earlier enthusiasm had faded. It was difficult to concentrate, without knowing what was really going on. He went to see the then Assistant Commissioner in Charge of Police Headquarters to get answers.

"What is going on, sir?"

"What do you mean?"

"They sent me down to the Drug Unit to be interviewed as a suspect."

"I don't know anything about that. They won't tell me anything like that."

"So, who is doing it?"

"I don't know anything about it."

Henry thought it odd that he would not know anything despite being in a higher position than the Staff Officer. Disappointed, he wondered about the motives behind the false accusations. He disliked having his character tarnished in any way and thought back to an incident occurring in 1987, when he was falsely accused of trying to buy voters' cards. He had been working as a Courts Prosecutor, at the time, and there were two sisters from Andros, female constables, whom he had trained as recruits. They were then working as court clerks, with one of them working directly with him. With the elections approaching, everyone was taking time off to get registered.

"While the sisters were filing into the office, I asked if they had registered," Henry recalled. "And they said, 'no.' So, I asked if they were going to vote, and they said, 'no.' I then encouraged them to exercise their constitutional and God-given right to vote and told them to notify me when they were going to register so I could arrange their schedules to have time off." The sisters did not respond, but he did not think anything of it.

"Later, on my way to my car, I passed the Superintendent, who was the then Officer In Charge of Central Police Station, now deceased, standing in Bank Lane. I saluted him as my superior, and he called out to me, referring to me as 'homeboy' because we were both from Andros. He then informed me that the officers had said I was attempting to purchase voters' cards for the opposition. I told him that was foolishness because I don't get into politics and asked how does one purchase a voter's card. But he cautioned me, saying that if the then Prime Minister heard what I was doing, I would be in "big trouble."

Henry saluted him and walked away, unable to believe that the officers had misinterpreted his intentions as anything other than an encouragement to exercise their right to vote. "I felt that it was my duty to arrange time off for them to go and register," he explained. He took that accusation seriously, especially as he never publicly expressed a preference for any political party. But as serious as he felt the accusation of buying voters' cards was, it paled in comparison to being accused of drug conspiracy.

Throughout his career, he had always been careful and worked hard to maintain a good record and reputable character. That accusation jeopardized everything he stood for, and he could not afford for it to ruin his career. At the time, he had his sights set on becoming the Commissioner of Police. Relieved that it did not turn out to be his last day in uniform, he believed the Superintendent's promise that the false accusations would be written off. However, as it turned out, that situation was not so easily resolved. Living in such a small community, it did not take long for rumours to begin circulating about the accusation.

"The next day, one of my former colleagues, then employed at the Road Traffic Department, Fort Charlotte, Inspection Centre, contacted me and asked me to see him, which I did. He told me that he was at a Consul General Meeting, the night before, where it was said that they would be charging the two Wemyss brothers, even though there was no evidence, and it was said that they would let the Courts throw it out." Despite knowing that his colleague would not make something like that up, Henry could not see that happening.

While working with the cadets that Thursday, one of the instructors approached him:

"Man, Chief did you hear anything?"

"No. What?"

"Those guys trying to charge you tomorrow."

"What!"

"Yeah, man they are going to charge you."

"Charge me with what?"

"Conspiracy."

Henry assumed he could have heard it from a sergeant, who at the time worked at the Drug Unit and later became assistant commissioner of police, now deceased. He frequented the Police College to play squabbles in the Sub Officers' Lounge. "That killed my spirits," Henry said. Recalling his reaction to the news, "I took the cadets in training, but I couldn't function. So, I packed them up and bused them home. That was difficult." He had no idea what to do or whom to talk to. He could not understand what was happening or how it could happen to him. "I had done nothing wrong and had never been involved in any drug-related activities," he stated emphatically. "But no one in Headquarters, from the Commissioner of Police on down had said anything to me before or after I was charged."

Just as the Instructor had forewarned him, everything happened the next day. Henry was called back to the Drug Unit and was informed he would be charged. He was also advised to seek legal counsel. Although unaware of the full scope of the charges, he remained certain of his innocence. "As I needed someone to represent me well, I chose Thomas Evans, an attorney, who I considered as outstanding and of a good reputation," Henry explained. "He was also someone I respected highly, so I wasn't concerned about his political persuasion."

On Friday, 5th January, 1990, Henry and his brother, JD, who was charged along with him, were arraigned before the drug courts. They pleaded not guilty and were released on $35,000.00 bail. The case was adjourned, and they were informed of the date to return for the trial. Henry's career, which he had taken painstaking pride in building for 25 years, had come to a crashing halt. He felt betrayed by the institution he had pledged allegiance to since his youth. Judy, having observed his love and devotion to his career over the years, shared his disappointment, "His career was everything to him. He didn't want to have anything holding him down or to do anything, out of the way, that would hold him back. He would do everything to his best, and I thought his career would end at a more senior rank, than an inspector."

Henry was ashamed and did not want anyone to see him. Although not guilty, he felt as if he had let his family down. The pressure intensified when the charges went public and made headlines in all the daily newspapers. With all the negative publicity, Henry tried to maintain his sanity. His primary concern was the well-being of his family, especially his children. He stayed strong for them and never allowed them to see him down. While he waited for the trial, his life changed drastically, and after his salary was automatically reduced to half, he was forced to pinch the remaining half.

"One of the first things I did was write to the mortgage company and another financial institution, where I had a debt, and explain my predicament," Henry recalled. "I also pulled Acribba from the private school and placed her at Government High School where Judy taught. It was a difficult decision because she was doing so well in that environment, but the school administration was not willing to exercise any leniency regarding school fees." Reflecting on that time, Acribba said, "I didn't quite understand how my dad's career ended because I was in school, but it was nerve-wracking, and a lot to deal with. Because it was on the front of papers and people realised that it was my dad, I dealt with a lot of pressure at school." As Keisha was in her final year of high school, she was allowed to remain at the private school where she attended.

"I remember when he took Conrad with him to the office and brought all his stuff home," Ingrid, who was almost 19 at the time, recalled, "I was wondering and trying to figure out what was going on because my parents never talked about such things with us." At the time, she was attending college in the US, but her life was about to change, "I was supposed to be heading back to college. I was on a partial scholarship and my parents had to make up the difference. I felt it was a strain, and as I had already completed two years of college, I said 'Mummy, I finished my associate degree so I could come back, but she was like 'No, stay at school.' So, I started my junior year and had gone off campus because I was trying to save some money - to cut down. And I said, 'Mummy, this is too much, this is really too much.' So, I decided to come home and work off and on at different places."

"Well, I know with the accusation, the kids were ashamed. They felt bad about it," Judy recalled. "They were young and never expected those things to happen to their father because they knew he was an upright guy, and he did everything with honesty. And that's how he wanted his kids to be, to do the same thing. To be honest in everything they did and wherever they went; in whatever job they took on. And I said to them, 'Honey you all don't worry, go to school, and relax. If anyone confronts you, let me know because I'll put an end to it.' I went to school about my business and stood there with my head held high because I knew it wasn't true."

While Henry's half-pay went towards the mortgage, Judy went above and beyond to fill in and assist as best as she could. As she had always supplemented her income by breeding pedigree dogs and selling them, she began doing it more frequently. She even bought a lawnmower and began cutting the grass herself. Whenever any plumbing work was needed around the house, she would first watch the plumber and do it herself the next time.

"My mother was always the cost-saver in the family," Keisha said, recalling her mother's cost-cutting efforts. "Before she allows my Daddy to spend money if the toilet is clogged and the outside pipe or the septic needs to be cleared out, Mummy would go outside and open that up and take the snake and clear the toilet, so we don't have to call the plumber for it. She would go and change the pipes if they needed to be changed. The only thing she never touched was electricity. She's a little Mrs. Fix-It. She will make it happen."

Being raised in a home where his father took on the family's financial responsibilities, Henry had followed in his footsteps. "I felt emasculated," Henry said, recalling when he was no longer able to fulfill his role as head of his household. "The quality of our life changed, and we could only afford the essentials. We juggled what little income we had and tried to cut back on an already tight budget. Things got so bad that I couldn't even maintain the car I drove, and the driver's door couldn't close properly, so whenever I turned corners, I had to hold it to keep it from swinging open. When it wasn't raining, I'd leave the glass down so I could reach out and hold the door."

As Henry waited for his day in court, it was difficult watching his wife carry the burden of the household. He was desperate to find a way to supplement his reduced salary. For years, he had observed people collecting bottles from the garbage or the area around his father's restaurant and bar. At that time, Vitamalt bottles could be redeemed for fifty cents and beer bottles for twenty-five cents. Knowing this, he saw it as a lucrative way to make money and decided to give it a try. Needing a truck, he reached out to a Constable, an officer whom he had trained, nicknamed 'Rambo.'

Rambo, who was also one of the police officers who had worked with Henry in Cat Island, readily agreed to accompany him. "When he first asked me, it freaked me out a little because I knew him to be a 'dicty' kind of person," Rambo said, recalling that day. "Things were rough with him, so he decided to collect bottles, which was the thing back then. But I thought it was a small thing to go and help him, but he never appeared desperate, as if he had to do it. He wasn't working and I think it was just something he wanted to do.

He continued, "We rode around Carmichael Road and got thousands of bottles. He ducked down whenever we saw a car coming because he didn't want people to see what he was doing. I helped him and did not think anything of it. I asked myself why he would do it, but it didn't change my image of him, and I didn't think any less of him. I still admired him."

After driving around the outskirts and garbage dumps for hours collecting bottles, Henry was satisfied to return home with a truckload of bottles, which represented much-needed cash. He and Rambo had just finished unloading the bottles when Judy arrived home with the children. On seeing the bottles, her countenance quickly changed:

"Honey, what are you doing?"

"What do you mean?"

"What are you doing?"

"I'm not doing anything. What do you see me doing?"

"Why did you bring these bottles to my yard?"

At that point, Judy started crying and returning to her car, she got a baseball bat and smashed all the bottles, telling him he did not have to do that. Henry felt humiliated and hurt, especially as all the neighbours were watching. Seeing all his hard work destroyed, he thought of all the hours he had spent in the sun, getting wet in the rain, and driving for miles. He walked away and went to the bathroom to cry. He was at the lowest point of his life, but all he wanted to do was support his family, "I felt that she did not understand how tough it was for me, as a man, not being able to support my family."

Judy vividly remembered that day, "I broke all the bottles he had piled up. I told him, 'Don't you do this kind of nonsense around here.' He said he had to do something to take care of his family. I told him, 'Your family will be taken care of. If we have to eat corn beef and white rice every day, that's what we are going to eat, so forget about this bottle thing.' He had gone out on the road wearing a big, wide hat, trying to disguise himself."

Acribba also shared her memories of what life was like back then, "My Daddy had so much pride he still wanted to support his family, so he wanted to collect bottles, which we did not like because it was another thing we would have to face if someone saw our dad on the side of the street. But we felt it, and my mother mated dogs to make extra money."

It was a lonely time for Henry, especially as he was shunned by colleagues and so-called friends. As Ingrid put it, "It was like Daddy used to have all kinds of friends, but the minute that happened, he didn't have any friends." Word got back to him that when one of his friends, with whom he often hung out, now deceased, learnt of the allegations, he had said, "That's his business. He got his dope money and did not give me anything. So let him suffer on his own." Whether or not those were really his words, Henry never heard from him.

So many rumours were circulating that Henry did not know what to believe. He had heard that the Commissioner of Police had warned his senior officers not to associate with him and lose their jobs. If that was true, two senior officers had defied those warnings. One of them was 'Rhod' Coakley, a brother and close friend from the day Henry joined the Force. At the time, he was a superintendent and had been stationed in Grand Bahama for almost 20 years, but had returned to Nassau shortly before Henry was interdicted. He worked at Police Headquarters and every day after work he took Henry out to make sure that he had something to eat or drink or whatever he wanted. Most nights he would allow Henry to keep his car. It meant so much to Henry to have a friend, like Coakley, when he needed one. And that took some of the burden off him.

The other person who reached out to Henry was someone he never thought would do what he did—Assistant Commissioner Ashton Miller. As his superior, Henry considered him to be a hard, no-nonsense man. Occasionally, he would take Henry to the beach, where they would go swimming and then have breakfast. Sometimes, he would take Henry home with him and every time he got fish, he would share it with him, saying that he was giving him a meal. He did that so many times. "What stood out the most was that he encouraged me and told me that I did not do anything to be ashamed of or to hide from," Henry recalled. "Although I never understood why he was doing it, I appreciated him so much and never forgot his kindness."

Although he was concerned about his own future, Henry also worried about the fate of the Cadet Program. "We saw his car and stopped him in the middle of the road - me and my mother - just so we could let him know that we supported him," Simms said. He recalled running into Henry during that time, "The first thing he said was, 'So what's going on with the program?' and then when I told him what was going on, he said, 'No that's not how it's supposed to go.' Even then, he was concerned about what we were supposed to be doing."

After only spending a year and a half with them, Henry often wondered what would have been different if he had been able to continue the program to its intended duration. Despite this drawback, he felt, "They did exceptionally well, and I'm so proud of all of them. Some from that program decided to take a chance on joining the Force and stayed, achieving senior ranks up to superintendent. But most went into other fields: some became religious leaders, executives, entrepreneurs, engineers, builders, medical doctors, and international lawyers. So, what might have become of these young men and women had they not been interrupted? I believe the Force would have benefited tremendously, as many more of them would have chosen to pursue careers in law enforcement. But when you take the captain off the boat, the crew becomes headless and unsure of what to do. It affected all of us—me personally for a lot of reasons, their careers and what they wanted to become or thought they were going to become; they saw it interrupted or cut short."

Eventually, when news about the allegation against Henry made the rounds, one former cadet recalled, "It was heartbreaking. There was no other leader who came and could rise to the level that he rose to in terms of the value that he brought to the program, in terms of the buy-in and the commitment that I saw from him. I think I even rebelled a little bit because the seriousness of the program had diminished. He was like a father to us. He was like a lot of things to us, and to take that away from a young man was heart-breaking."

The cadets maintained their respect for Henry, "I looked up to him and I never thought anyone with his standards would have been guilty of the things they said so I continued to look at him, not in the light that the legal system put him in. As I always tell people, when someone has shown you so much good, it's hard for you—if you genuinely believe in what they are saying to you—it's hard for anything, anyone, or any organization to turn you away from that person. For me personally, I always had the utmost respect for him and always admired him."

Another former cadet shared his feelings about the situation, "I never even regarded what they were saying because of how he presented himself to me, how he presented himself to us and while, at the time, there was no evidence to say from my perspective, I just chose to continue to hold him in the esteem that I always held him in. There is a dark spot in the story that really served to disenfranchise something that was supposed to be much bigger, and they moved a lynchpin. The Cadet Corps continued to survive, in some form, but I don't think it ever realised the vision of Henry Wemyss, and I think that's a loss to the nation."

The Tribune: Friday, January 5, 1990

Policeman & his brother face drugs charges

By MARK SYMONETTE

A SENIOR police officer and his brother were today charged with drug conspiracy before Magistrate Cleopatra Christie. They were each released on $35,000 bail.

Inspector Henry Wemyss, 42, and his brother, Jo— Wemyss, 47, pleaded not gui— conspiring to import a quantity of cocaine into the Bahamas between March 1 and August 21, 1985. No quantity was given.

Inspector Wemyss, a former court prosecutor and presently the officer in charge of the Cadets Corps, was represented at this morning's arraingment by Mr Thomas Evans.

Mr Joseph Wemyss was represented by lawyer Algernon Allen. Inspector Victor Brown prosecuted. Trial date has been set for Wednesday, April 25. Both men were released on police bail of $35,000 with one surety before they appeared in court today. Both counsel asked the magistrate to allow bail to continue.

Before the court adjourned today Mr Allen said he had a request to make on behalf of Mr Joseph Wemyss. Mr Allen asked that a "full disclosure" of the evidence which the prosecution intended to lead against Mr Wemyss, or at least a resume of that evidence, "so that my client can properly prepare a case so that he can answer his accusers."

Mr Allen said that the charge against his client was very serious and that it was not right for the prosecution to hold the evidence "so close to its chest to disclose when it appears before you (magistrate.)"

For his client to properly prepare a defence Mr Allen said that he must know who made an allegation against him about events which allegedly occurred almost five years ago that he conspired or "criminally agreed" to traffic drugs with others.

Mr Allen submitted that if a confessed drug trafficker was making an allegation against Joseph Wemyss the defence would like to know so that it could properly investigate and prepare. He said that that was required in the interest of justice.

Mr Allen again asked that either a resume or each material witness or a statement that related to the material

Continued Page 12

174

From Page 1

particulars of the charge be made available to counsel.

Mr Evans said he wished to identify with the submissions made by Mr Allen, and that this was a difficult area. In the Supreme Court accused persons would have depositions taken out at the preliminary inquiry and would therefore know what the prosecution's case was. That was not the case in a Magistrate's Court.

Mr Evans said that a magistrate had the power to order that the prosecution give further particulars and dates of the alleged conspiracy.

The particulars of the charge against both Insp Wemyss and his brother "are as bald as they come," and the accused were entitled to more particulars than were presented.

Mr Evans said he had no doubt that the prosecution knew who the "others" alleged in the charges were, and that they must say who the others were.

He asked the magistrate to order that the prosecution give more particulars if only in light of the fact that "we are dealing with allegations that are almost five years old."

The defence would encounter "great difficulty" if further particulars were not provided it. He said that courts still operated on the principle that a man was innocent until proved guilty, and that that was one of the prime reasons why the particulars were needed in this case.

Prosecutor Brown said that it was the "custom of the court not to, if I may say, allow so much of the information pertaining to the charge before the matter is in fact brought before court for trial."

He said that the men were only being arraigned at this stage and "we are not prepared to go on with the evidence," today. He said that if Mrs Christie requested more particulars they would be provided.

He argued that providing further particulars at this stage would be like "putting the horse before the carriage."

"At this time, Your Worship, I would merely rely on the court to, of course, deal with the normal procedure...."

Mrs Christie recalled the Treco drug conspiracy case when the prosecution and the defence were able to meet and listen to certain tapes and

The Nassau Guardian: Saturday, 6th January, 1990

Police inspector faces
cocaine charges

By KATHRYN FORBES

Police Inspector Henry Anslem Whymms, officer in charge of the Police Cadet Corps, and Joseph Whymms, a building contractor, denied charges of conspiracy to import cocaine in the drug court Friday morning.

Magistrate Cleopatra Christie set bail at $35,000 for the two men and ordered them to return to court for trial on April 25, 1990.

There was hardly standing room in Magistrate's Court Five when the charges were filed. Senior and junior police officers in uniform and plainclothes, attorneys, relatives of the accused and curious onlookers packed the courtroom from 10:15 a.m.

Avoiding the lenses of photographers alike, the accused, to the surprise of many gathered in the courtroom, entered through the western entrance of the magistrate's office.

The charge levied against the men alleges that between March 1, 1985, and August 31, 1985, at Cat Island, being concerned together and with others, they conspired to import a quantity of cocaine.

Defence attorney Algernon Allen, who represents the 47-year-old building contractor, requested a "full disclosure" or a "resume" of the evidence which the prosecution intends to lead in the case.

Reflecting on the five-year period since the incident is alleged to have occurred, lawyer Allen said it is "unfair" that these cases, which are as "serious" as capital offences of murder and treason, can have such "serious" penalties and the prosecution "holds the evidence close to the chest."

Mr. Allen said "in the interest of justice," his client "must know who, five years ago, is making allegations that he agreed with others to traffic dangerous drugs." And, he added, if it is a convicted drug smuggler, he would also like to know.

Identifying with the submissions of attorney Allen, defence lawyer Thomas Evans, on behalf of Henry Whymms, 42, told the court that there is an area of difficulty as they are, in effect, dealing with an indictable matter.

Mr. Evans pointed out that in the Supreme Court accused persons have access to depositions during preliminary inquiries, but this is not the procedure in the Magistrate's Court.

He, however, pointed out that the court has the power to order the prosecution to give further particulars which, he added, "are as bald as they come."

Making reference to the dates, lawyer Evans said, "Certainly the accused are entitled to more particulars — who precisely were the conspirators; they know who they are and ought to say." He also submitted that specific dates should be provided to the defence.

"I ask the court to order that the prosecution give more particulars, if only in light of the fact that we are dealing with an allegation (Continued on Page 3A)

Police inspector

(Continued from Page 1A)

of five years," he said. And, he added, "we always have to move on the premise that we represent a man who is innocent until proven guilty."

Sgt. Victor Brown, who was recently appointed prosecutor of court number 5, said it has been the custom and practice of the court not to allow so much of the information pertaining to charges before the matter is brought before the court.

He said the defendants were brought before the court on Friday to be arraigned and the prosecution was not prepared to present the evidence t   ay.

"If   ourt requires additional inform....., we can arrange a date when the Attorney-General's office can peruse the file more and supply the court with information ... We rely on the court to deal with the normal procedures ...it's like putting the carriage in front of the horse," he said.

Responding to submisssions by both counsel for the prosecution and defence, Magistrate Christie said she is familiar with the application, but before making an order she would allow the prosecution time to discuss the matter with the defence attorneys.

Mrs. Christie granted them three weeks, and recommended that they reflect on the application and come to an agreement.

CHAPTER 13

A Travesty of Justice

On 25th April 1990, Henry stood before the Magistrate's Court No. 5, alongside his brother, JD, both charged with 'Conspiracy To Import Dangerous Drugs'. The offence was alleged to have occurred on Cat Island during Henry's tenure as the Officer In Charge of the island, and in which capacity he was alleged to have provided police protection to facilitate the crime. Henry could not explain how he became entangled in a situation he knew nothing about, but he knew that it was impossible for there to be any convicting evidence of his involvement.

"It was difficult to believe that as a former Prosecutor of the Courts, I was standing on the other side," Henry said, describing his emotions that day. "It was also humiliating to be standing before Magistrate Cleopatra Christie, a Magistrate with whom I had worked as a relief Court Prosecutor on a few occasions. As far as I was aware, we had enjoyed a good working relationship." Having been privy to how he ended up before that Magistrate, Henry was a bit curious about why she had been hand-picked for his case. As a former Prosecutor, he knew that "all cases would come down from the Attorney General's Office and a representative or one of the lawyers would bring the files down to the Chief Prosecutor and he, in turn, would assign them to the various Courts Prosecutors, not only drug cases but also assault and whatever other charges." However, information circulated that five drug-related cases for the Courts came down that day and the Chief Prosecutor was specifically told which court the 'Wemyss brothers' file should be sent, but the distribution of the other cases was left to his discretion.

"Prosecutors in the Magistrate Courts were usually police officers but, in my case, Mr. Lee Hing acted on behalf of the Crown," Henry recalled. "As far as I know, I was the first police officer to be prosecuted by a non-

Bahamian." All the other cases going on at that time were being prosecuted by police officers. It was an interesting observation. Nevertheless, with great curiosity, he waited for the case to unfold and the evidence to be presented. He felt certain they would realise that he and his brother were innocent. He could not predict any other outcome.

During the trial proceedings, Henry learnt about the said conspiracy occurring between 1st March, 1985, and 31st August, 1985, and the three alleged plane landings on the airstrip in New Bight, Cat Island in mid-April 1985, mid-June, and early July 1985, offloading cocaine which was later transported by boat to the USA. During the third trip, the boat was intercepted by defence force officers. Subsequently, the captain and two crew members were arrested, and the cargo was seized. Henry would also learn about his alleged involvement that brought him before the Magistrate's Court, as testified by the two key witnesses, both condemned criminals residing in US Federal Prisons.

The first witness was a self-confessed drug smuggler, who admitted to having numerous aliases, and having had 67 charges, including falsifying statements and entering a plea agreement, explaining, "Look I am facing life. I have one life. Would be a fool not to be concerned with life. I believe that my attorney has been given some papers...I have a plea agreement."[1]

According to his testimony, he met the main accomplice, a Cat Island businessman, in March but saw the Inspector in uniform before the first trip, conversing with the main accomplice at a popular beach resort. He claimed, at the time, that the large hand radio with 150-foot-long antennas he was setting up to facilitate his long-distance communication was in plain sight. He later saw the Inspector numerous times at the same resort, drinking in the company of others and once in a jeep driven by the main accomplice.

According to him, the main accomplice, who had promised him police protection so that his plane could land on the airstrip without police

[1] Magistrate's Court of New Providence, Commissioner of Police vs Henry Anselm Whyms/Joseph Whyms Criminal Case No. 5/90 Court No. 5 – Court Transcript page 29

interference, had initially pointed out the Inspector to him. He added that, after the first trip, he spoke briefly with the Inspector, who indicated he was happy with everything that was going on and told him not to do any trips unless he was present on the island.

Later, under cross-examination, he contradicted himself by stating he had met the Inspector sometime between the second and third trip. He claimed that the Inspector and his brother travelled to Nassau on his plane during the middle part of June. He also testified that he had been in communication with the Inspector's brother, and during those several times, they had talked about smuggling and money.

While the witness testified to paying the main accomplice, he confirmed that no payments were made directly to the Inspector, but that the accomplice advised him that in addition to the $250,000.00 agreed upon per trip, a further $80,000 - $85,000 was required to pay the Inspector for police protection.

After the plane had landed on the airstrip, without any police in sight, the witness was satisfied that he had received the promised police protection. Identifying the Inspector, he pointed to Henry and confirmed that he was never asked to identify the defendants from an identification parade but that he was shown photographs by the investigating Inspector from The Bahamas, who visited him at the Florida Correctional Center, where he was residing.

The second witness, the pilot involved, testified that he had travelled to Cat Island and met with the main accomplice and had become acquainted with Bahamian government officials - police and customs officials in their role as associates of the accomplice. He also testified that he was introduced to the Inspector as the resident inspector and had seen him in uniform frequently enough that he had established a casual acquaintance, speaking with him on several occasions.

During that time, the Inspector confirmed that his cooperation in their smuggling nature could be counted on and that he needed to be on the island for the trips to go safely. Stating that the police official he had met was in the Court, he proceeded to point to JD. He added that the police official was present with his brother and that he had gotten a clear view of the brother, whom he had only seen on one occasion. On that occasion, they were all sitting at the bar drinking and having a conversation. He then proceeded to point out Henry as the brother. He also confirmed that he had not been invited to view an identification parade.

Evans objected, telling the Magistrate that the second witness' testimony could not be accepted as he identified the wrong people and should be dismissed, "We can't go any further with this case, your worship because the witness does not know who he is talking about." The Court was also asked to take notice of the description of the two defendants. In comparison to Henry's height of 6'1", JD stood 5'5". At the time, Henry had been bald for the last 30-plus years, while his brother had a full head of hair and had never been bald. There was no way his brother would have been able to fit in his khaki uniform. Contrary to the Evidence Act, the witness' testimony was accepted as corroborating evidence against both defendants.

During one of the Court sessions, Judy noticed a man in the Court, who was telling the witness in the box what to say. Before the witness spoke, he would look to the audience and a small elderly man communicated with him. This was brought to Evan's attention, who informed the Magistrate that someone in the audience was interfering with the witness, and he would like him to stop. He also, had his junior counsel turn aside to see if it was true. When the Magistrate saw that, she cautioned him that the lawyer could not sit like that but had to face the bench.

The Defence attempted to tender a copy of the duty roster, kept in Cat Island, to show the relevant period. They sought to show conclusive evidence that at the material time, Henry was not present on Cat Island. The evidence was, as recorded in the Police Station Dairy, which was kept in Cat Island. According to Henry, it is "a public official record to document everything that happens within your district, be it good or bad, that you have to deal with or come to your knowledge that must be recorded in your diary; leaving the station, leaving the island." When Henry realised that the case against him stemmed from his time on Cat Island, he had secured copies of pages of the diary from the then Assistant Commissioner, District Headquarters., to confirm the dates that he was stationed on Cat Island. When he attempted to present the copies before the Courts, the Prosecution objected stating it was not an official document.

Allan attempted to secure the original copy and wrote to the Commissioner of Police seeking assistance with obtaining the original roster sheets. The Assistant Commissioner of Police responded that he should seek guidance from the Attorney General's Office. However, preferring to make his request from the party who had bought the criminal action, Allan had made his request from the Commissioner of Police but was informed by the Prosecutor that the Attorney General's Office was taking over the proceedings from the Commissioner of Police.

As the original copy of the diary was never produced, and was later alleged to be lost, Evans addressed the Court, citing the Evidence Act as it relates to copies of original documents being entered as secondary evidence. However, the Court ruled that the document did not fall under the cited section. Henry found it disappointing that the Court had thrown out what he considered crucial evidence. He had no doubt that if the copies of the diaries were admissible, it would prove that he was not on Cat Island on the dates in question and that the charges against him were unfounded and they needed to arrest someone else.

Being a former Court Prosecutor, Henry recognised factors of the proceedings that were found lacking. The case would have been investigated, but there were never any police officers appearing in Court to give evidence of their findings against him or to be questioned by the Defence. Nor were any of the police officers who had worked with him on Cat Island called to give evidence for the Crown or to be questioned by the Defence—and there had been at least eight of them. Henry brought this up with his attorney, "Are you not going to call the officers who worked with me to give evidence for the Defence? If they don't call them, aren't you going to call them?" The Attorney replied, "We won't need them, Mr. Wemyss. They don't have any case against us." Later, Henry found out that several officers had been interviewed by the police and gave statements, but they were not called in or turned over to the Defence, as required.

While the trial was going on, Henry had many sleepless nights that continued for years afterwards, forcing him to turn to sleeping pills. Fortunately, during the trial, no photos of him leaving or entering the Court appeared in the daily newspapers. Later, he would learn that a freelance photographer, who worked in the area, was offered payment by one of the major daily newspapers to take photos of him, but he had declined their offers out of respect for Henry. The photographer also mentioned that he could have taken a clear shot of Henry when he exited the car on East Bay Street on the first day of the trial.

On 1st November, 1990, Henry was sworn in to testify. He was not required to give evidence since the Prosecutor's case was never proven beyond a reasonable doubt, but he elected to address the Court to refute the testimonies of the two witnesses. With head held high, he testified that he had never met them "in my entire life until I came here to this Court." As for the place where they had supposedly seen and met him, he said, "Is the only place on the Island where you can get a tyre repair, assistance with petrol or any mechanical help one may need. Everyone on the Island has to go there at some point." He could have possibly seen them, there was nothing peculiar about them that would set them apart from any other tourists who were drinking and eating at the time when they supposedly saw him. He could not say he never saw them, but with reference to the Police Inspector with whom they conspired, he stated, "That Police Inspector was not me." and that everything they had testified about him, "never took place." He testified that he had "never entered an agreement to provide protection for drugs coming into that island." Also, he did not observe any 150-foot antennas at the facility, and if he had, he would have "made inquiries into it." He stated that he had reasons to leave his post in Cat Island but had never flown in their plane and only travelled from Cat Island to Nassau by police plane or the aircraft of a resident who transported locals to Nassau for a fee. Further, he had never been in a vehicle with the main accomplice.

While the two witnesses against him had admitted to a life of crime, he reminded the Court that he had faithfully served the Royal Bahamas Police Force for 25 years. He highlighted the areas in which he worked, including his two years as a Court Prosecutor and placed emphasis on his last assignment where the Commissioner of Police chose him to lead the Police Cadets - those young men and women, who would wish to eventually join the Police Force.

There was never much of a crowd when Henry entered the Court during the trial. On his way to his seat, he would pass Addington Darville, now deceased, a retired Chief Superintendent of Police, who would acknowledge him by bowing. Having sat through the entire trial, he had assured Henry the morning before the sentencing, saying, "Well, Henry, you're a free man today." When Henry asked if he really thought so, he said, "Yes, they haven't brought any evidence yet. What else could they do but let you go?" Henry believed him because he, too, felt that the case against him was seriously flawed. Of Darville, Henry said, "He had been a Court Prosecutor many years ago, and he was a brilliant man. He was also the officer who had placed second in the 1970s for the same General Police Course that I had done in England. And he was also a former Commandant of the Police College—one of the outstanding ones."

At the time Henry never realised it, but one of his former recruits also sat in. "Since I was working on Bay Street, I would often sneak in during my break to observe what was going on with the hearing," the former recruit recalled. "I found the trial so confusing and never believed what the witnesses were saying. Watching that, I felt as if he was being persecuted."

As the trial wrapped up, Henry stood before the Court, waiting to learn his fate, and expecting to resume his life. Before that day ended, he got a startling awakening. Making her judgement, the Magistrate began, "Trial has now proceeded to the stage where all the evidence has been heard and it is now a matter for the Court to make a final determination on the guilt or innocence of the accused men. The Court is mindful of the principles of law that it is not for these men to prove their innocence, but it is for the Crown to prove their guilt. The Burden is on the Crown throughout. Standard is beyond all reasonable doubt. With these principles in mind – the evidence must be examined."[2] After summarizing the details of the evidence, she stated, "But since there are two stories before the Court, it seems that the cases at hand can only be resolved in favour of Prosecution or Defence – either accepting or rejecting one or the other. . ."[3]

"Having considered carefully the circumstances of each witness for the Prosecution the Court accepts the evidence – the Court feels sure that the witnesses were telling the truth of the events and incidents they described. The Court therefore rejects the evidence of Henry Wemyss. . .

The Court feels sure on the evidence that both of these defendants were party to the conspiracy charge. Accordingly, both defendants are found guilty as charged."[4]

Stunned by the Magistrate's words, Henry felt it could only be a bad dream. It was not the outcome he had hoped for or felt he deserved. After a lifetime of holding his head high, his reputation and his good name had been smeared. He was numb with disbelief. "I respected that Magistrate greatly because when working with her, she went by the books and was fair and just in all her dealings, regardless of who you were. But after she convicted us, I was amazed and concerned whether the ruling was hers or a conspiracy.

For her to accept the evidence of two convicted men, who admitted to so many crimes over the years and were facing a life sentence, and to

---

[2] Magistrate's Court of New Providence, Commissioner of Police vs Henry Anselm Whyms/Joseph Whyms Criminal Case No. 5/90 Court No. 5 Court Transcript – pages 65-66

[3] Magistrate's Court of New Providence, Commissioner of Police vs Henry Anselm Whyms/Joseph Whyms Criminal Case No. 5/90 Court No. 5 Court Transcript page 67

[4] Magistrate's Court of New Providence, Commissioner of Police vs Henry Anselm Whyms/Joseph Whyms Criminal Case No. 5/90 Court No. 5 Court Transcript page 68

reject the evidence of an outstanding veteran police officer with 25 what the worth of a good name or character was in The Bahamas."

Evans labelled it "an absolute tragedy that the Court finds itself in a position to impose a sentence for this gentleman." And requested the "Court to consider passing a sentence that does not involve a period of custody,"[5] asking the Court to be as lenient as possible in all circumstances. Earlier he had reminded the court that, "They are bringing a prosecution based on evidence, not only of accomplices who are not corroborated but accomplices who are absolutely of no character."[6] He had also stressed that their evidence was against "the evidence of a 25-year Police Officer in this jurisdiction"[7] and highlighted his outstanding career. He also pointed out that there was evidence before the Court that Inspector Wemyss was not the only Officer In Charge at the time.

On 8th November 1990, judgment was made and before handing down her ruling, the Magistrate said, "It does not please me to pass sentence on a man who obviously played a meaningful role in the Police Force. . . Court finds a custodial punishment must be imposed."[8] For what was deemed a serious offence, the sentence was imprisonment—three years for Henry and two years for JD. What was more unsettling was that even before the Magistrate had handed down her sentencing, Henry had already been informed through a Consul General about the exact amount of time he and his brother would get.

In the final analysis, the case was about which testimony the Court would accept—Henry's word against two convicted criminals. According to the Magistrate, "whose evidence to accept depends wholly on the credit

---

[5] Magistrate's Court of New Providence, Commissioner of Police vs Henry Anselm Whyms/Joseph Whyms Criminal Case No. 5/90 Court No. 5 Court Transcript Page 69

[6] Magistrate's Court of New Providence, Commissioner of Police vs Henry Anselm Whyms/Joseph Whyms Criminal Case No. 5/90 Court No. 5 Court Transcript Page 63

[7] Magistrate's Court of New Providence, Commissioner of Police vs Henry Anselm Whyms/Joseph Whyms Criminal Case No. 5/90 Court No. 5 Court Transcript Page 64

[8] Magistrate's Court of New Providence, Commissioner of Police vs Henry Anselm Whyms/Joseph Whyms Criminal Case No. 5/90 Court No. 5 Court Transcript Page 69

worthiness of the witnesses for Prosecution and Defence."[9] Sadly, the testimonies of two witnesses, convicted men from the US prison were accepted over that of a police officer with 25 years of impeccable record for outstanding character in the Royal Bahamas Police Force. Evans informed the Magistrate that he was going to appeal the decision and she advised him that he had seven days to file his appeal.

Henry could not accept the Magistrate's verdict, and the Supreme Court became his only hope for justice. The appeal was filed, and their bail continued until the case could be heard. After reviewing the transcripts from the Magistrates Court, the Supreme Court Justice Neville Smith, wanted to find out who was Henry and who was JD, maintaining that he could not see how the two could be mixed up. He also noted that he did not find anything in the transcripts that would convince a jury that they were guilty.

Henry sighed with relief when he heard the Judge's words and believed that justice was finally being served. The hearing was adjourned for sentencing and convened about eight months later. That morning, as he was getting dressed to return to the Supreme Court, Acribba had greeted him. She was always interested in what he wore and questioned him when she noticed that he had stopped wearing his police uniform. As she always looked up to him, he could not tell her what had happened, so he told her that he was attending meetings.

"Daddy, what are you putting on today?"

That day he wore a blue suit, a light blue shirt, and her favourite tie— one with fishes on it. As he prepared to leave, she stopped him.

"Daddy, you are forgetting your ring, chain and watch."

"I did not forget them, honey. I am coming back. I'll get them later. I just don't need them today," he had promised her.

She knew he never left the house without his jewellery, but his lawyer had advised him not to wear any to the Court that day. He found his

---

[9] Magistrate's Court of New Providence, Commissioner of Police vs Henry Anselm Whyms/Joseph Whyms Criminal Case No. 5/90 Court No. 5 Court Transcript Page 67

advice strange because he had never told him that before during the trial, which had lasted over a year. Without questioning him, he decided to do as he was told. "I asked him, 'When are you coming back? And he never answered," Acribba recalled. "But he never returned home and that was the last time I spoke to or saw my Daddy. He was just gone."

Surprisingly, on 13th July, 1992, that Supreme Court Judge had a change of heart and decided to support and uphold the conviction of the Magistrate Courts stating that he did not find that the Magistrate "improperly considered anything she ought not to have so as to cause any injustice."[10] And that there were "ample grounds for the Magistrate to reject Henry's evidence."[11] About the witness's failure to identify the Inspector, he said, "This however was a mistake as between the Appellants both of whom were said by the witnesses to have been together in the conspiracy and present together in discussions about smuggling."[12]

However, he did note that, "I would only observe that parts of the Magistrate's judgment were not crouched in the best terms, and I do accept that there were better and less confusing ways to have set out what was intended. Even so, however, there is nothing to show that the Magistrate did not properly deal with matters, particularly relating to the admissibility of evidence from co-conspirators that should have been addressed."[13]

In the end, the Judge set aside the sentences of two years for JD and substituted it for one year but affirmed the sentence of three years imposed on Henry. Henry found the decision mind-boggling, especially after he had agreed earlier that he had not seen any evidence to support their conviction. As he stood there and digested his words, the hope he had

[10] Commonwealth of The Bahamas In The Supreme Court Joseph Whymms & Henry Whymms vs Commissioner of Police – Page 7

[11] Commonwealth of The Bahamas In The Supreme Court Joseph Whymms & Henry Whymms vs Commissioner of Police – Page 8

[12] Commonwealth of The Bahamas In The Supreme Court Joseph Whymms & Henry Whymms vs Commissioner of Police – Page 4

[13] Commonwealth of The Bahamas In The Supreme Court Joseph Whymms & Henry Whymms vs Commissioner of Police – Page 9

been holding onto for months quickly died. Nothing about the situation was lining up the way he had expected. He recalled, "At that moment, I felt so numb that I did not know what to think or what to believe."

Uncuffed, Henry and JD were escorted from the Supreme Court, leaving behind family members who were wailing uncontrollably. "After being convicted, a memory of my time as a constable in the Supreme Court escorting inmates from the Court across to the cell at the Police Station crossed my mind—now I was being escorted," Henry said. When they arrived at the Central Police Station, there was a patrol car waiting to transport them to Her Majesty's Prison. Without sirens, the Inspector, driving the car—who was well-known to Henry—did not appear eager to drop them off. Driving slowly, he even stopped to buy himself a sandwich.

"Can I buy you a sandwich, Chief?" He asked.

"Sandwich? Do you know where you are taking me? I can't eat now! You are taking me to prison," Henry reminded him.

"Chief I know how bad you feel. I feel bad with you and a lot of other people on the Force feel bad about this."

Henry felt worse, knowing that he was the highest-ranking officer to ever be sent to prison. Years later, he would reflect, "Sometimes the only thing that can keep you going is believing that one day everything is going to be okay. Never stop believing because one day it will become a reality." At the time, he felt his life was over. Later, he would reflect, "If I had only known God's purpose and plan for my life, it would have made it easier."

The Nassau Guardian: 26th April, 1990

Cocaine conspiracy trial in drug court

By KAREN SANDS

The conspiracy trial of Police Inspector Henry Anslem Whymms, 42, and his 47-year-old brother, Joseph Whymms, opened in the drug court Wednesday. The matter is being heard before Magistrate Cleopatra Christie.

The two, who are represented by attorneys Thomas Evans and Algernon Allen, respectively, were arraigned on Friday, January 5. They are presently out on $35,000 bail.

Particulars of the offence allege that some time between March 1, 1985, and August 3, 1985, the Whymms brothers, along with others, conspired to import a quantity of cocaine while at Cat Island.

(Continued on Page 4A)

Cocaine conspiracy trial

(Continued from Page 1A)

Setting the foundation for the case against the two, prosecutor Lee-Hing tendered three witnesses. They were Forensic scientist ASP Quinn McCartney, Petty officer Perry Romer and Chief Petty officer Michael Hutson.

Royal Bahamas Defence Force Officer Hutson told the court that on July 8, 1985, he commanded H.M.B.S vessel P35 as it made a routine patrol in waters off New Providence.

About 2.3 miles south of Conch Rock, Hutson allegedly noticed a blue and white fishing vessel — Water Sprout II. And a boarding party consisting of Petty Officer Romer and others was subsequently instructed to carry out a routine search of the vessel.

In his evidence to the court, P.O Romer said that he discovered what appeared to be a makeshift well containing a number of duffle bags that he suspected contained drugs. He later reported this information to Hutson.

Hutson said that on recieving the information from Romer, he boarded the craft and discovered that a captain, Edward Lockhart, and a crew of two — Clement Pintard and a Hosea Cruiz — were on board.

"I observed some large duffle bags in the cooling section of the vessel," said the witness, who said that he did not examine the contents of the bags. But, as a result of his suspicion, he cautioned and arrested the captian and crew. They were later taken to the Defence Force's Coral Harbour Base and handed over to officer 1133 Dames. The vessel was also formally tendered to the police.

Under cross examination, the witness said he did not remove the bags, nor did he examine them. However, he counted them as they were removed from the craft by another officer, but he could not remember the exact number.

Further, he revealed that prior to the Whymmses's trial, he had testified in Court number before Magistrate Joseph Alfred in the matter.

In addition, the prosecution witness said it was about 10:15 a.m. at the time of the interception with Water Sprout II.

Asked if he knew whether the three men arrested in connection with the matter were acquitted by appeal to the Supreme Court, the defendant replied, "I don't know, sir."

He also said that the Whymms brothers were not present when he gave evidence in the matter, nor were they present during the arrest of Pintard, Lockhart and Cruiz.

Also testifying, ASP McCartney said he acted on information received when he travelled to the police drug store house in Oakes Field and spoke to Corporal 1133 Dames, who imparted additional information on July 9, 1985.

As a result, the officer was reportedly shown 22 canvas bags, each containing a number of taped packages, containing a white substance. Samples were taken from each of the 22 bags and later analysed. They tested positive for cocaine, the court was told.

The Tribune: 8th November, 1990

Police inspector jailed in Cat Is. drug case

By MARK SYMONETTE
Tribune Court Reporter

POLICE INSPECTOR Henry A Whymms, accused of providing police protection for drug smuggling operations out of Cat Island, was today sentenced to three years in prison by Magistrate Cleopatra Christie.

And his brother, Joseph Whymms, a contractor, was sent to prison for two years. The magistrate found both men guilty of conspiracy.

"It does not please me to pass sentence on a man like Inspector Whymms," Mrs Christie said, "but the court is always under a duty in these matters."

Lawyers Algernon Allen and Thomas Evans informed the court that their clients would appeal the conviction and sentence.

Mrs Christie, who steps down as Magistrate of Court #5 tomorrow, extended the bail of $35,000 for both men. However, she required that they surrender their travel documents to the court.

Today's conviction and sentences came after Mrs Christie rejected no case submissions put forward on behalf of the Whymms brothers. She called on them to answer the charge. Inspector Whymms took the stand last week and denied that he had ever

taken part in a conspiracy. He said he had never met the two key prosecution witnesses, Tito Dominguez and Jim Brackette. Both men claimed that Inspector Whymms provided police protection and received payments for this protection through Allen Russell, whom they claimed was in charge of the Bahamian side of the operation.

Joseph Whymms elected to remain silent. A number of police officers gathered in Court # 5 today for the sentencing of a colleague. Many of them described Henry Whymms, a police man of 25 years, as an "ideal officer." Whymms, who was in charge of the cadet corps before he was arrested on the charge, has also received various honours for his work as a policeman.

Mrs Christie said that the case against the two men turned on the credibility of witnesses, Brackette and Dominguez. Both men admitted to the court that they were drug traffickers, were sentenced in the United States and came to the Bahamas to tell what they knew.

Dominguez told the court that he set up sophisticated radio equipment on Cat Island as part of the operation. He also claimed that he did so

CONTINUED PAGE 11

Police officer

FROM PAGE 1

with Henry Whymms' approval. Mr Whymms denied this. He also denied that he met with Dominguez on several occasions to discuss plans to import drugs into the Bahamas.

Mrs Christie said she reminded herself of the principles of law that the burden was always on the prosecution to prove the case against the defendants.

She said that the credit worthiness of the witnesses for the prosecution and the defendants was a matter for the court to determine.

Tied into the issue of the credit worthiness of the witnesses was the question of corroboration. She said that the court had reminded itself of the dangers of convicting on uncorroborated evidence.

She said that the position of defence on the evidence of Dominguez and Brackette was that they were convicted drug traffickers whose evidence was not to be believed. The prosecution commended their evidence to the court.

Mrs Christie said that the court accepted the evidence of Dominguez and Brackette and found that they were truthful in their description of the events they told the court. The court felt certain that both Henry and Joseph Whymms were a part of the conspiracy. She convicted them of conspiracy to import cocaine between March and August 1985.

Mr Evans, outlining the achievements of Henry Whymms as a police officer, and other mitigating factors, asked the court to consider not imposing a custodial sentence. If the court intended to impose a custodial sentence Mr Evans asked that it be as lenient as possible.

Supreme Court Justice Joan Sawyer sentenced Nicholas "Nick" Stuart to 16 years in prison today for the rape of a 14-year-old girl in April. The evidence showed that Sturart offered the girl a ride and took her to North Bahamia where he is alleged to have raped her.

CHAPTER 14

Struck Down But Not Forsaken

Henry will never forget the day he was stripped of his freedom and dignity. It had been the most difficult day of his life. The one solace he felt was knowing that his father had not lived to see that day. His siblings had also ensured that his critically ill mother, who died on 27th November 1991, never learnt about his misfortune. The ride to Her Majesty's Prison was especially tough since it was his usual route home, which was nearby.

That afternoon, when Henry and JD entered the prison, it appeared as if they were expected. Inmates were shouting:

"You all were set up!"

"You all are innocent!"

"They're using you all as scapegoats."

"They're two FNM Boys!"

"We were placed in the prison hospital, where about eight other inmates stayed. The room was clean with fresh bedding, bathroom facilities, and a television," Henry recalled. "I tried in vain to relax, wondering how my family was coping and how my children had reacted when my wife told them what had happened. I wanted to speak with them and assure them that, despite being in prison, I had done nothing wrong."

Darnely Sealey, who was the then Sergeant in charge of the Prison's Medical Department, received a call "from someone who had informed me that two brothers—Henry and Joseph—were sentenced to prison for drugs and asked me to assist them during their time in prison," he shared. "I had first heard of Henry Wemyss when I was the Corporal In Charge of First Offenders Prison, which at the time accommodated inmates who were detailed to work at the various police stations. The inmates always had good things to say about Henry, who was the only police officer that I can recall being mentioned. Throughout the years, I heard various people in the community talking about Henry, always having something positive to say but I had never met him in person."

When Henry and JD arrived at the prison Sealey was there, "I remember seeing these two well-dressed men in suits being escorted to the reception area, where inmates were processed before being taken to various cells. They appeared to be very nervous and scared, like they were about to have heart attacks. I spoke to the Officer In Charge to send the brothers to me in the Medical Department as I could accommodate them in the prison hospital. The next day, they saw the doctor and with my recommendation, the doctor gave permission for them to stay in the prison hospital."

Henry cried like a baby that first night and many other nights that followed. He remained awake, tossing, turning, and thinking. "As I tried to make sense of the situation, so many questions ran through my mind—In what year did the offence occur? In what year was I appointed to head the Cadet Corp? Did the Commissioner of Police, at that time, know that I was being investigated? What was the evidence? Should the case be continued if the witness was unable to identify the accused? Why were none of the officers who worked with me at the time ever called to give evidence for the prosecution? Should the Court consider evidence of two convicted criminals serving sentences in the US? Shouldn't a third witness corroborate their statements against the evidence of a 25-year police veteran with impeccable records?"

"Why didn't the investigating officers give evidence and be questioned by the Defence Attorney? Why wasn't I told by anyone other than the drug unit officers that I was going to be charged? How did the situation get from a write-off to a charge? Why did the Courts refuse to accept documents from the diary? Was my case one of a conspiracy and by whom? And why? I believe my lawyer did his best to represent the facts of the case and pointed out the flaws in the prosecution's case, but he could not do more than he did. I chose him because of what I knew of him. He was not a corrupt lawyer who would pull deals. Something else had to be wrong."

Henry also thought back to an earlier case that was brought before the Courts, where a Police Inspector was charged with nine drug charges, along with an Immigration Officer and a Customs Officer. One of the accused persons decided to give state evidence and testified against the others. There was also evidence to show that the Inspector had come to Nassau and purchased brand-new vehicles with US cash. Despite the overwhelming evidence against them, they were found not guilty of eight of the charges and convicted of only one of the charges. They were fined $5,000 or one year imprisonment. They were also given time to pay. It was a *prima facie* case straightforward as all the evidence was there. In comparison, Henry observed, "I had one charge, no evidence, and was found guilty and sentenced to prison for three years with no fine."

Throughout the night, thoughts troubled Henry, and the next thing he knew, the 5:00 a.m. siren was going off, signifying it was time to get out of bed. Staying in the prison hospital, their meals were brought to them. After breakfast, they were escorted to the barbershop. Henry got a shape-up because he did not have any hair, but JD went in with a full head of hair and walked out bald. Having always sported a full head of hair, he was devastated.

It was also one of the most traumatic nights for Henry's family. Acribba recalled that painful memory, "When my mother came home around 6 p.m. that day, I asked, where is my Daddy? She just started crying, and I asked her what was going on. And she called the three of us together and said, 'Your dad is going to be gone for a while.' Gone where? Well, she had to break the ice, which was rough on her and rather stressful on my oldest sister, who had to go out and find work to help support the family." Ingrid recalled, "Nobody slept that night. Everybody sobbed. I sat up and thought, I can't believe this is true. I can't believe this is true."

"I know the day that it happened when he had to go in without jewellery and I had to go to school," Keisha said. "I couldn't concentrate in class that day, and I failed both of my exams. I was eager to get home and when we got home, Mummy tried her best to tell us that 'they convicted your

Daddy.' I skipped school for the rest of that week. When I returned to school the following week, I didn't know how to look at anyone because I was afraid that everyone looking at me knew or had heard something, but none of my friends approached me or said anything about it. I'm not even sure if I went to graduation, but I probably did—Mummy and me. That was probably one of the worst years of my life."

At school, Acribba's experience was not so pleasant, "I ended up at a government school where I couldn't have friends because people's parents told them not to hang out with me because my dad went to prison or some would ask if that was my dad on the front page and they would say that I would get them involved in the wrong things, even though I told them my father never took drugs. My mother cautioned me not to answer them, but I had no choice because they were talking about my Daddy."

Henry's imprisonment also sent shockwaves throughout the Force. Despite the conviction, many officers, particularly those he had trained or worked closely with, did not change their perception of him. They refused to believe he was anything other than the honourable officer he had always proven to be.

During his second week there, several police officers of all ranks—seniors and juniors—visited him, expressing their concerns for his well-being and their desire to provide him with whatever he might need. Several even claimed that they were attempting to get him out of there. Although Henry appreciated their desire to assist him, he believed there was nothing they could do.

He was surprised by visits from some of the cadets' families. "They were upset over the ordeal and wanted to know what they could do to get me out," he recalled. "Even though they could not help me, I was relieved that so many people cared about me and believed in my innocence."

One of the officers, who had worked with him on Cat Island shared his reaction to the news, "I was hurt. I never believed what they said. Up to this day, I still haven't. When he was incarcerated, I used to go to the prison to see him. He cried and said, 'I didn't do the things, they said I did.'"

And I told him, "I believe you." Up to this day, I still have faith in him. No one could change my mind about the Henry Wemyss I met 38 years ago."

Many of the officers he had trained reached out to his family as well, as one officer recounted, "I was broken. When I say broken, not knowing the truth of what he was accused of. I knew it was unlikely that he would have done what he was being accused of—knowing the person that I knew. I think all of our squads really rallied around Mrs. Wemyss and the children to give them support and encouragement. We couldn't communicate with him, but we stayed close to Mrs. Wemyss to find out how he was doing. That really affected me a great deal. I knew what the allegations were. I won't say he wasn't capable of it, but I did not see it in him."

The Prison Superintendent, a former Assistant Commissioner of Police, Lawrence Major, now deceased, also sought Henry out, telling him, "Wemyss you should not be in here. I know you should not be in here" and abruptly walked off. Hearing those words almost drove Henry crazy, because he realised that some kind of conspiracy must have happened, but no one was speaking out.

Henry could not cope with being on the wrong side of the law. He had spent too many years as a committed police officer, careful not to tarnish his reputation or that of the Force, "The Force was my life. I lived to be a police officer, I lived to be an instructor and I lived to know that I could share knowledge. I never sat down in my tunic to mash it up. I wouldn't let anyone come close to me to mess up my shoes. I had to represent the Force, and I just couldn't go without looking right. When driving my car, I was cautious of how I drove or where I went because if I was in uniform, I didn't want to bring disgrace to the uniform."

Everyone knew that Henry was a proud person, and some believed he would not survive prison, fearing he might commit suicide. Some senior officers raised these concerns to the warden, who instructed the Officer In Charge to keep a close eye on Henry. Admittedly, Henry felt he should have died instead of having to endure prison, but he had no way of escaping.

He was always depressed because, as far as he was concerned, his life was over. He tried to pray but could not—the words would not come.

The television was always on in the room, but it stayed tuned to talk shows or sitcoms. There was nothing inspirational, uplifting, or religious to watch, and there was never anything positive going on around him to keep his mind occupied. He was hurt and could not think straight. His brother, Sam had warned him, "The worst thing to do is to try to talk, make decisions or plans when you are in prison because you will only do that to satisfy yourself because they would never become a reality."

"Almost every day, there were lots of tears and hurt over being in prison," Sealey recalled. "I felt that if they were locked in cells or separated from each other, they would have had a heart attack or go into mental depression. Henry was very hurt and often talked about their wrongful conviction. I told him that he should appeal his conviction and if freed, he can start his own business."

Henry recalled his conversations with Sealey and how he had sat in his office for several hours. "He told me that he had heard some good things about me and tried to encourage me with some prison survival tips."

"You have to block out the outside world and think like you are in prison and you can't think like you would out there. That's the only way you can make it," Sealey had suggested.

"How am I supposed to think like that? I can't do that."

"Behind bars is a new culture and you have to conform to that culture. If you don't do that, you are not going to make it."

"What do you mean conform?"

"Just try to live like you are in prison and not like you are living on the outside."

"I could never change who I am."

"You should not be here, but now you are here."

"Well, I am going to die now. I want to get out of this place."

Sealey also recalled that, "Henry and JD assisted with cleaning the hospital and with other inmates who were admitted by the doctor for medical treatments." Despite his own discomfort, Henry remained true to his character and still found time to mentor others. "Henry assisted an inmate with his appeal, due to his experience in law enforcement, and today that former inmate is a doctor," Sealey stated. "Henry was always helping the medical officers with advice."

Even though they could not vote in the upcoming General Election, which was scheduled for 19th August, 1992, the inmates actively discussed politics. While Henry remained silent, JD constantly talked about politics, freely expressing his political preferences. He even stated that he would be released from prison once the opposition gained power. His remarks frequently offended an inmate, who was the prefect in charge. They had lived in the same neighbourhood but never got along.

Following the election, he teased JD, "Well, your party won, and you're still here." Their back-and-forth squabbles continued for weeks until the prefect complained that he could not live with JD and requested that he be removed from the facilities. Although Henry was not required to leave, he did not want to be separated from his brother, so both were transferred to medium-security after spending a few months in the hospital.

"As soon as I walked in, all I saw was iron and concrete walls everywhere, including the roof," Henry recalled. "The hospital facilities were luxurious in comparison to medium security." They were assigned to a dorm with about 25 other inmates, each of whom had their own beds. Because there was no new mattress, Henry slept on a piece of plywood over the spring. "I cried all night, especially when I thought about my warm bed at home," he recalled of that first night. "As usual, I stayed up all night trying to figure out where I went wrong or what I did to deserve what was happening but came up blank."

The next day, he was confronted at least four times in the yard by inmates who claimed he had sent them to prison while he worked as a Court Prosecutor. As they were all bald, none of them appeared familiar to him.

"Chief, do you remember me?"

"No."

"You don't remember me? You sent me to jail."

"I'm sorry, man," Henry said, fearing retaliation.

"No man. I don't hold that against you because you did not lie on me. You were just doing your job. But if anyone tries to bother you, just let me know. I'll take care of you."

"It was a humiliating experience, to end up in the same place as others whom I had prosecuted for crimes," Henry stated. "But none of them treated me disrespectfully."

Despite his best efforts, Henry could not adapt to the prison environment, especially as he was accustomed to good hygiene. He could not eat, and his stomach was always queasy. "The food was basic, usually fried sausages, oats, or some other porridge for breakfast; hard bread and water or sometimes 'switcha' for lunch and rice, some kind of 'no name' meat, chicken, fish, or so-called pork for dinner." Flies infested the yard, landing undisturbed on the bread and food. There seemed to be a fly epidemic every day, except Sundays when visitors came. In preparation for visitors, they sprayed repellent, and the flies vanished. One day, Henry saw a truckload of fish being dumped on the grounds between the dormitory and the kitchen, where the inmates played basketball and visitors came. He could not believe they expected them to eat it, but the inmates cleaned and cooked it for dinner.

While Henry never considered himself self-righteous, he always had a sense of pride and never imagined being banished from society. He remembered when the inmates came by his office at the Barracks. They had strong odours because they never wore arm deodorants, and he always complained that, "These guys smell so green." When he had to live with them, he could no longer freely comment on their scent. When they returned from work, drenched in sweat, and raised their arms, he had no choice but to move away. "I was not foolish enough to say anything because I feared becoming involved in a fight," he admitted.

A prison officer came every day and took Henry to the garden for some fresh air. He gave him water and allowed him to pick vegetables for snacking. Instead of working like the other inmates, Henry was allowed to sit under a shady tree, but the officer warned him that if he saw any other officers approaching, he should get a bucket and pretend to be busy. Although Henry was curious about the officer's motivation for what he did, or whether he had been instructed to do so, he never questioned him. He was grateful for the kindness shown to him during such difficult circumstances and looked forward to returning the favour at a future date.

However, another prison officer from one of the Caribbean countries tried to degrade him. Later, Henry would learn that they were connected through his in-laws. One day, he called Henry to the guard house by the entrance to the medium security:

"I hear you are corrupting my officers."

"How am I doing that?"

"You brought cell phones into the prison."

"Is that what they told you, sir?"

"Yes. That's what I was told."

"Well let me tell you what they told me about you. They said you came to work on a Saturday and pretended to be sick. You went to the restroom and left the gate open for the Colombians to escape because they had bribed you with a lot of money."

Henry retaliated because the officer's accusations hurt, especially when he was already being punished with a prison sentence for something he did not do.

"That's not true!"

"I'm not saying it's true, but that's just what they told me."

That officer became so upset that he carried out a search, pulling up all of Henry's personal items, bedding and rumbling through his clothes, but found nothing. "I suspected that he was just trying to belittle me and show his empowerment at the time," Henry explained.

Despite that isolated situation, Henry realised that life in prison was not as difficult as it could have been. Even as a prisoner, he gained respect, and whenever he went to the bathroom, nobody else went in until he came out. Judy kept him supplied with groceries that he shared with the other inmates. When everybody knew he had sweet milk and peanut butter, they brought their bread to him. Judy also brought in cigarettes—the prison currency— which Henry used to gain the inmates' favour. He paid them two cigarettes whenever he needed anything done, including laundry.

"It was really a taking away of my freedom," Henry said of his time in prison. "Being locked up affected my spirit in a way that is difficult to explain. Unlike in a free society, I could not live my life—it was dictated to me. Everything about the system was designed to continually remind me that I was no longer an individual, but a prisoner. When you know where you came from, it's difficult to drop that drastically, having to sleep in a dormitory with 30-40 other men, with no door to close and only one open space, sharing a shower with so many other people. That was new to me.

I had to walk from the dormitory to the kitchen to get my food, tow a line, and then return to the dormitory to eat. The food didn't taste like anything I'd had before. It was just too rough for me because I remembered who I used to be, how much pride I had in myself, and how I had been thrown to the bottom of the basement. Where do I go from there? How would I make it when I re-enter society? How do I face people who think so much about me?" He often reminded himself that, "I could only go up from here, but getting up would be difficult."

To cope with their circumstances, the inmates used their ingenuity. Henry observed them concocting rum from fermented sugar and grapes. He even met one of the officers he had trained there, who began smoking because the pressure was too much for him. "When I saw him smoking marijuana, he became embarrassed and came to me. He apologized saying, 'Chief, I am sorry, but I am not as strong as you—this is what I have to do. Please forgive me.' I told him that it was fine because he should do whatever he needed to do to survive. Because I didn't smoke, I never judged him nor

206

felt morally superior to him. I realised we were in a situation where it was impossible to judge a man's character. It was all about survival one day at a time, and I was trying so hard to keep my own sanity from being so close to home and unable to go."

Henry and JD were among the dorm's older residents. Henry, who still had a heart for young people, even then, tried to make a difference, "The prison was full of young people, so I did a lot of talking, counselling with them, telling them about what life is about, even before I gave my life to Christ, telling them what they had to do. Some of them were wearing dreadlocks, but I told them they couldn't go back out there like Rastas because of the stigma attached. That was before it became fashionable. When officers see you with plaits on your head, they have two thoughts: you're a Rasta and all Rastas smoke dope. You must change because you will be arrested. Seek a better way of life."

Night-time was always the most difficult for Henry, but the darkness allowed him to release some of his sadness. When the lights went out at 10:00 p.m., he cried into the morning. He lost weight quickly because he barely ate enough to stay alive, and his clothes hung on his body. Despite the favour and respect he received from the other inmates, he found it difficult to let go of the odds of being incarcerated. He would eventually come to realise that "things don't happen by happenstance. There's a reason for everything that happens in life." However, he had to survive some of his darkest days before he could appreciate this truth.

Every day, Henry would look at the street in which his house was located and pray to catch a glimpse of Judy and the children as they drove by, even though he did not want them to see him. He constantly worried about what his children were going through, but he never wanted them to visit him there. When Judy came to see him, she brought letters from them, and he also sent letters back to them. He looked forward to reading their letters and found comfort, knowing that they were coping.

As soon as Henry got convicted, he was taken off the payroll, so Judy supported the family with her salary and the extra money she earned from breeding dogs. She tried to make everything at home appear as normal as possible. "Religiously, she would wake up to make our breakfast, make his breakfast and take it to the gate, drop us and pick us up from school, get dinner for him and take it to the gate," Keisha recalled. "She did that every day that he was in there and she never broke down. If she ever cried, she never showed it. She tried her hardest to stay strong."

Reminiscing about the tough times, they faced, Acribba said, "We felt the poverty because the fridge would be empty. Sunday dinner was sardines and grits, and we went from having a big dinner with family coming over to that with Kool-Aid. But it never bothered us because it was something to eat, and our stomachs were full. And I remember the lights got turned off when things got rough, and it stayed the same when he got out until he found something to do."

Explaining how she remained strong, Judy said, "I didn't let anything bother me. It would have bothered me if what they said about him was true, but it wasn't, so it didn't bother me. I just did what I was supposed to do: take care of the kids, the house and whatever business needed to be done, and every day I went to see him and brought him fresh food and other things he needed." During their visits, she said, "He wanted to know how the kids were managing and how I was managing. I said don't worry about that. The kids are coping, I am coping, and we are making sure that you are well." Henry was concerned about his image and appearance, even in prison. "When I went up there, he looked stiff and clean, just as always," Judy stated. Henry kept his prison uniform pressed by placing it under the bed mattress when he went to bed at night.

Acribba was bothered that her father had kept secrets from her and only learnt the reason behind their financial struggles the day her father was incarcerated. She raised this issue in one of her earliest letters to him, "One day I wrote him and asked him why he never told me." He said, "because he did not want me to be hurt, but he just wanted me to know that Daddy did not do anything and that's all you need to know, and Daddy is okay."

"We never really lost it because we tried to make everything appear as normal as possible, but you know what it is to live right here and your Daddy right here and you can't see him, can't touch him, can't say hello," Keisha stated. "You didn't even know if someone was beating him up because he was in a place where he sent people—in jail. Or if they have a problem with him. We couldn't wait until Mummy saw him to come back and say he's okay."

Although she had heard the prison bell many times before, Acribba began to pay more attention to it, "The prison was so close to our home, and every day I heard the bell ring so I knew that Daddy would be getting up and when it rang later, I knew that it was time for him to go to bed. I would tell my mother that Daddy was up, or Daddy was going to bed now." Since Henry had never been an absentee father, it was difficult to cope with his absence.

Rosie reflected on that traumatic time for the family, "When he was forced to leave the Police Force, we felt very bad. Our father had already died, and Mummy was sick, and we couldn't tell her, and she went to her grave never knowing that. I couldn't sleep for nights. My husband told me that if Henry sent for me, I should tell him that I couldn't come because I could not sleep for about five nights after visiting him. I would just stay up thinking about him. That was so difficult, but God saw him through. We never believed what they were accusing him of."

Two months into his imprisonment, his family still held hope that his sentence could be reversed. Judy and Rosie borrowed $7,000.00 from a bank and hired a Jamaican Queen's counsel to review the Court's records and meet with Henry. When they met, Henry noticed that the pages of the transcript—he had brought with him—were all marked in red. "He asked, 'How did you get here? There were no grounds to convict you.' He offered to get me bail and I became so excited, but my spirits crashed when I found out that it would cost me $25,000.00, plus his expenses for travel, room, board, food, and transportation. He assured me, 'If I take your case now, you will be a free man.' Without the means to pay him, my dreams were shattered, and I realised I was in there for the long haul." Having met for what Henry described as, "the shortest ten minutes." The attorney left. Watching him go, Henry felt dejected because he was convinced that his freedom had been within his grasp.

After spending the $7,000.00, Judy faced a major financial crisis. The mortgage company was threatening to foreclose on their home. They had used the mortgage payments to assist with Henry's legal fees for the trial. At the time, they were convinced Henry would be acquitted of the charges and entitled to back pay from the Force. They had to make the difficult decision of selling the duplex they had previously lived in for half of its purchase price—$60,000.00.

When Judy brought him a portable radio, Henry's days seemed brighter "She encouraged me to listen to 1240 am, a local religious station. Despite not being a Christian, I enjoyed listening to Vaughn Miller, a disc jockey, whom I became convinced that God was using to minister to me," Henry recalled. "Every time he played 'God Can' and 'God is My All,' it meant so much to me that I promised myself to find him and thank him as soon as I got out. His program not only inspired me but also kept me sane." Even though he had grown up a devout Catholic and served in the church as an altar boy, this was a new experience for him.

"One morning, I was sitting up in bed listening to the song, 'God will take care of you' and it meant so much to hear that. The words, 'Be not dismayed whatever betide, God will take care of you. Beneath his wings of love abide God will take care of you.' This touched me. Tears began flowing, and I wondered if God really would take care of me, what message He was trying to send to me, and whether this was the only way he could show me. It was difficult to believe that His only way was by dropping me from the top to the bottom." But as Henry continued to meditate, he realised that God had been so good to him for many years, perhaps trying to get his attention. That song began to change his life and his direction. He wrote the words of the song down, placing it above his bed. The more he listened, the more he felt compelled to accept Jesus Christ as his personal Lord and Saviour.

Looking back, Henry said, "There was a time when I attended three church services every Sunday, hoping to find something meaningful. At one of the services, I was moved to tears each time I heard the song, 'Spirit of the Living God Fall Fresh On Me,' but I could not explain why the song stirred my emotions like that. I had always believed I had what it took to become a committed Christian, but had never found the opportunity to do so." But he made the best decision in his confinement, away from worldly distractions. "Right there in the cell, I surrendered to God, and it was a moment that changed my life forever." He was born again and able to release his fears about what the future might hold for him. "I started studying the Bible daily after that, and my faith grew stronger."

It was not a private matter for Henry because he made his decision to follow Jesus Christ publicly known. "The second Sunday we spent in minimum security, Bursil Brown, a prison officer, now deceased, who was also the minister responsible for keeping chapel services, came to our dormitory and invited us to church," Henry shared. "I also learnt that he was a family relative, who had heard that we were in there. When we got there, about sixty other inmates made up the congregation. He told them, 'These two men you see here, I know them, but I don't know how they got here but I will tell you, you will not see them here again.'"

"During the altar call, I went up and made my acceptance of Jesus public. When I did that, I felt a peace I had never known before. After the service, I returned to the dormitory, and the peaceful feeling remained. Even though I still did not want to be there, I felt quite content in my current state. Having committed my life to Christ, my mind changed, and I experienced peace amid a storm. I realised that I was only there for a season and just passing through. I continued my Bible studies and received the spiritual strength to stand firm." Henry continued attending chapel faithfully and assured Brown that upon his release, he would visit Calvary Deliverance Church, where Brown served as a Deacon at the time.

Henry's actions did not go unnoticed, as he explained, "One of the inmates placed a sheet around my bed so I had privacy to pray. My prayer life became a part of me, and I never felt whole unless I prayed. When I thought about my circumstances, I was convinced that God had pulled me out of my usual environment to get me. I understood that God will do and allow whatever is necessary to get our attention and prison is where he got mine."

Henry also took advantage of an opportunity to register for a distance learning Bible study course. All the materials were sent to him by mail and after completing the assignments, he sent them back for grading and waited for the results. After successfully completing the course, he was hungry to study God's Word, "I was determined to know the Bible as well as I knew the penal code when I was an officer and decided to pursue a bachelor's degree in theology when I got out." Later, he would attend the local branch of Christian Life College of Theology. With his newfound direction, Henry felt resolved and at peace.

Henry was pleasantly surprised to learn that Fred Mitchell, an attorney and well-known human rights activist at the time, was there to see him. "He and I met through a mutual friend, and they were both officers on the Police Force and they use to come by my office, which was right next door to the police station, from time to time in the late eighties," Mitchell stated, explaining his connection to Henry. "Then I learnt quite sadly that the government had charged him with an offence, and he ended up losing the appeal from the Magistrate's Court to the Supreme Court. Unfortunately, he had to serve a period of imprisonment that I always thought was unfair. I did not think the charge should have been brought against him, and I thought that the Judge had made a mistake. I certainly could not believe for one minute that he would be involved in any such thing. When I think about Henry Wemyss, I think about a man who is very correct, very organized and strict, who takes his business and himself quite seriously. He is quite protective of his family and very patriotic about The Bahamas."

Not one to stand by and watch injustice unfold, Mitchell decided to step in and visit Henry. "He spoke with me and said it was unfair what had happened to me," Henry recalled of his visit. "He thought the Judge had made a terrible mistake and called my trial a travesty of justice. He shared the contents of a letter he wrote to the government of the day, stating, 'There is no way possible that you can take the evidence of two convicted men against one of your most outstanding officers with an impeccable record, who has never been charged for being late. How could the Courts do that? His name and character must account for something.'"

"When I visited him in prison, he remained dignified as usual and had the respect of the people who were there," Mitchell observed. During his visits, he never mentioned whether he received a response but promised Henry that he would not let the situation die until justice was served and his prison sentence was reversed. "I don't know whether he realised at that time what my political persuasions were, but it didn't seem to matter because he was concerned about justice." Henry added, "If he was going away, he would always stop by to let me know and express his hope that I would be freed before he returned. He left several times, and each time he came back, he expressed disappointment that I had not been released." Even after the party he supported lost the government, he continued to fight tirelessly for Henry's cause. He then used his political alliance with the new government to meet with the then Minister of National Security and the Chairman of the Committee of the Prerogative of Mercy. He then applied for Henry's release based on time served. Henry said he was most impressed by Mitchell because, "He saw me without ever asking for money and he came to see me on his own and proved to be a true friend."

Thanksgiving came, and Henry was still in prison. Judy was allowed to bring pots of peas and rice, salad, turkey, and ham that had already been sliced up, cakes and canned sodas. Henry set up a small table in the dormitory, where he was staying, but inmates from other dormitories joined in on the feast as well. While Henry appreciated what she did, he would have preferred to eat at home. Then came Christmas, which was the first Christmas away from his family. He missed going to church services and being able to buy gifts for everyone. That year, there were no big celebrations at home, but Judy made ends meet.

"We were struggling financially because we didn't have his income. We tried side jobs. Mummy was a dog breeder back then so we would breed the dogs," Keisha recalled. "We always had dogs and she would breed them from time to time, but after his incident, she bred them more regularly to get pups and make a sale. Besides that, Ingrid took on a job at Coral World so she could assist at home during the Christmas break, Kiki and I worked at the Perigord Christmas tree farm on Prince Charles, selling Christmas trees. It wasn't fun, and Christmas was not the same without him. There was no big celebration, but Mummy made ends meet. Of course, the mortgage fell behind, but Mummy held it together until he was able to come out."

Later, Judy determined that Ingrid should enlist in the Bahamas Defence Force, following in her father's military footsteps. While Henry was not pleased with her decision, Judy was counting on Ingrid to generate a more dependable income. "None of my entry knew that my father was in jail until one of the instructors said, in front of everyone, 'You all think only 'niggas' does come here trying to get on the boat so they could deal drugs too, eh? You ain't see you'll have one of the chief drug dealers' daughters right here in training,'" Ingrid said recalling one of her most embarrassing moments as a defence force recruit. "I could only look up at the sky and stare right there, but he asked, 'Wemyss, you ain't talking, eh?' Then one of the instructors, whom Daddy had trained, told him he shouldn't have said that." However, he later apologized for his indiscretion. Ingrid would go on to have a successful career, rising to the rank of Petty Officer and, like her father, she became an instructor and one of the cleanest officers in uniform.

They continued to hope and pray that Henry would soon come home. As 1993 began, the months slipped away, until Henry had been gone for almost a year. By that time JD had already been released months earlier.

Finally, halfway through the year, there was good news. The application to the Committee of the Prerogative of Mercy had been successful and Henry was being prepared for release.

Henry sat before the psychologist for the first time since his imprisonment and was asked, "Mr. Wemyss, have you been rehabilitated?" It was a difficult question for Henry, who explained, "My problem was that I had not done anything in the first place that required rehabilitation. I also wondered how I could have received rehabilitation if I had not been exposed to any such programs. But I considered the situation and realised that if I said no, I would not be allowed to leave. I would have remained locked up if I had given them any reason to believe I was angry, defiant, or resentful. I considered my wife, children, other family members and freedom." When the question was asked again, Henry responded as expected, "Yes sir. I have been rehabilitated."

When Sam found out that Henry was being released, he visited him. He was worried that Henry would no longer be able to live so close to the prison. He promised Henry that he would find him a new place to live within a few days. However, he returned disappointed because the rents for all the places he found were higher than he could afford. He kept looking for another location in time for Henry's release. His greatest fear was that Henry would have to hear the prison siren every day, which would hinder his recovery. Initially, Henry shared his concern but had a change of heart, "I was lying down one day, thinking about that, and reading my Bible. I came across the passage, 'God has not given you a spirit of fear, but of power, love and a sound mind.' That scripture sparked something in me and gave me a sense of confident peace."

Decades later, Henry reflected, "If it had not been for the Lord who is on my side, who pulled me out of the pit, my spirit, my soul and my body, even though I had been released from prison physically, would have remained in the pit and I would have been acting like someone still living in the pit—consumed by anger, envy, hatred, malice and unforgiveness. Thanks to God, who gave me a new mind."

CHAPTER 15

Rebuilding A Shattered Life

On 7th July, 1993, Henry exited the gates of Her Majesty's Prison. He was 60 pounds lighter, exhausted from sleepless nights, but happy. He was released before Sam could find a new home, but that no longer bothered him. "I believe it was never God's will for him to find me another place," he reflected. "I returned to the same street I saw every day from behind bars. Sam drove me, but I stopped at a barber shop before going home. My wife was the only person who knew I was returning home that day. I wanted to surprise my kids, but as soon as the car pulled into my driveway, Acribba ran out, as if she had been waiting for me."

Acribba, who was 13 then, recalled the day her father came home, "We did not know when he would be coming out, but I probably had a feeling because I did not go to school that day. I saw this car pulling up and saw this bald guy. My dad was tall, slim, and light-skinned as if he had not seen sunlight for years. And I ran outside." It was a time of celebration with family members and close friends. Overjoyed about Henry's return, there was a lot of crying, hugging, kissing, and praying.

Miraculously, Henry never heard the prison siren again after returning home. However, being incarcerated had left its mark on him, as he stated, "Prison made me appreciate life and freedom more. No one goes in and comes out the same. It changes everyone for better or worse. I don't care who it is. Some come out angry with the system, and having a criminal record can make it hard to readjust to life on the outside. It's easier for them to go back inside than to stay in the world outside, so prison becomes a revolving door for them." After leaving, he thought about the inmates that he left behind and wanted to pave the way for them.

216

One of his first actions was to write a prison reform paper and send it to the government of the day. It was a master plan for successfully rehabilitating inmates. As part of his plan, he intended to establish an employment agency to assist inmates upon their release. Another aspect of the plan was to avoid returning them to the negative environments in which they previously resided and instead relocate them to new, more favourable neighbourhoods. They would also be required to become actively involved in a church as part of the program.

Henry lobbied for a cooperative relationship between the prison, churches, the government, and corporate Bahamas. He empathized with former inmates and expressed his willingness to spearhead the initiative. Unfortunately, he did not get the response he had hoped for, "I received a response that my recommendations were passed on to an employment agency but that died a natural death." He realised that because he had been to prison there was an automatic stigma attached to his name, but having been there he felt he would have done better at the job than someone who had never experienced imprisonment.

"It was difficult for me to go there. It was difficult for me to stay in there and it was difficult for me to get out of there," Henry explained. "I never believed I would have gone in there, and I never believed I would come back out. After getting in there, what would I do now to come back and face the world after being in there? That was not easy."

One of Henry's first challenges was needing a new wardrobe because the clothes he had left behind were too big for him. Acribba recalled, "When my father came out, my mother bought him a new wardrobe and ensured that he had money in his pocket." Ingrid also recalled taking her father shopping, "I took him to the store to buy some jeans. But he said he didn't like going inside the stores. I asked him what size he believed he was and went into the store and got some jeans for him. They didn't fit, but I figured out his size and bought him about ten pairs of jeans and matching polo shirts. He told me that I was not supposed to do that for him, but rather he was supposed to do it for me."

Henry returned home a changed man. "He knew the Bible from the beginning to the end, and he knew how to quote scriptures; and I mean with his Bible closed," Judy explained. "He loved God and had become a Christian while in prison." Keisha also agreed, "We noticed a significant change in him. Daddy was fully into the Bible and could read it backwards. I think that episode got him closer to God. That's when he gave his life to Christ and went strictly into the Bible, and there was a grave difference." Ingrid also noticed something else, "He wasn't so uptight. When he came back out, after being around a lot of young people, he could relate to us, even more."

Keeping his word, Henry spent his first Sunday out worshipping with his family at Calvary Deliverance Church, "I went there, and they seated us almost to the front pew. Bursil was so happy to see me that he was smiling. He must have told the deacon, who was next in line to become pastor, who I was because Deacon VG Clarke came and shook my hand and prayed for me and my family. Despite us being the same age, he took me under his wings, like a father, and became my spiritual mentor. I was surprised to learn that he had noticed me on Bay Street some years earlier and commented on how clean and neat I was. Eventually, I became an usher, and when he became pastor, I served as his armour bearer. He looked after my family and assisted us in every way he could."

"After Henry was released from prison, he became a parishioner of our church and attended regularly with his wife and family," Bishop Clarke stated. "He adjusted very well and was appointed to our Board for about eight months and served with distinction. During the weekly Bible study session that he led, Henry enthusiastically shared his prison experience. During his time with us, he served in a variety of capacities. He was the president of our men's fellowship and on Wednesday evenings, he led our small group session. He was also an ordained minister and he worked as my personal assistant for nearly eight years, accompanying me on numerous trips to Ohio, Maryland, Atlanta, Rome, Israel, Egypt, and many of the Family Islands."

Bishop Dr. James Newry, the current Senior Pastor of Calvary Deliverance Church, was a minister of the church. He shared, "We welcomed him with open arms and allowed him to feel a part of us, and he was accepted along with his family. I saw the humility that he displayed after being released from what was a false accusation. For us it didn't matter; he was a human being, and the God we serve is a God of a second chance.

"He had the opportunity to go to Israel, and it was very impactful to see his reaction," Bishop Newry continued. "After having such a challenge and a setback, being in the place of the Bible was very transformative for him. He talked about where he was and where God had brought him. God had given him another opportunity and allowed him to travel to the Holy Land, the land of the Bible, which was life-changing for him—to see the Bible come alive."

Reflecting on the role church played in the Wemyss household, Acribba shared, "We were always a Christian family and always went to church and Sunday school religiously—never missed church. We were Catholics and confirmed in the Catholic Church. The good thing was that my dad took us to church right away. So, he knew his faith needed to be grounded in the Lord. We were always church-going people, but it was a different level of churching for us. It was new to all of us because he introduced us to the Pentecostal faith. And I watched my dad rebuild his life through fasting and praying."

After three years of unemployment, Henry was eager to resume his position as head of the household and relieve Judy from shouldering the burden. He was ready to return to the workforce, but that was not a simple task, "I was released from prison in 1993, and every job I applied for after that never materialized. I fasted and prayed until 1995, but all the doors were closed. Even the government had promised me jobs that never came through." Because of what he had to endure, Henry resolved that one day, he would establish his own company to employ people needing work.

In his search for employment, his first stop was an old acquaintance, Sir Albert Miller, the former Deputy Commissioner of Police he had served as a batsman. At the time, Miller was the Chairman of the Board at the then Bahamas Electricity Corporation. Henry knew the importance of making a good impression, so despite not having any money in his pocket, he wore a business suit, spritzed his wife's perfume, and carried a briefcase full of newspapers.

As he drove to the corporation, his anxiety increased upon noticing that the fuel gauge was touching 'E'. However, he was optimistic that the day would end well, "I felt that if anybody would help me, it would be him, especially since he was aware of my qualities as a worker." When he entered the office, Miller's warm reception filled Henry with anticipation.

"How are things going?"

"I am looking for a job, sir."

"You don't want a job here."

"I don't want a job, I need a job, sir."

"I'm sorry I can't give you a job here."

"But you have to help me, sir."

"But I can't help you."

Henry was dumbfounded, "I could not believe that the person I had looked up to as a mentor and friend was saying those things to me. Disappointed, I got up to leave." His expectations were dashed.

"Take it easy, don't give up, keep on looking," Henry recalled him saying. "He reached into his pocket, pulled out $200.00, and offered it to me. Despite my pride, I could not turn the money down, even if I wanted to. I was so grateful for it because I realised I could not have gone any further in the car." Although he did not land a job that day, Henry still walked out on a high, quickly driving to the nearest gas station, "I kept the car windows up and sweated all the way, giving God the praise."

Henry continued his efforts to find employment without success. Pastor Clarke also attempted to assist and got him an interview at an insurance company. Henry did the interview and completed the screening test, but his criminal record prevented him from moving forward in the hiring process. People were aware of Henry's good character, but due to his criminal record, they were unable or unwilling to assist him. "I could not live with that image and decided to do whatever it took to have my records cleaned," Henry stated. "I had no money at the time but made up my mind that with the first job I got, I would use the money to take my case back before the Court."

Despite not offering Henry a position at the electricity corporation, Miller used his connections and referred him to one of the top executives on Paradise Island. Again, Henry showed up dressed smartly and carrying his briefcase. After an outstanding interview, he felt confident that his worries were over. Unfortunately, his criminal history was a stumbling block that caused him to be turned down, once more, "I was so hurt, nowhere to turn, nowhere to go. I did not believe the Chairman would have sent me there if he never thought there was a possibility. The only thing that kept me moving was believing that God was testing my patience, and I had to persevere."

As Henry tried to find work, the bills at home were piling out of control. At that point, he would not have turned down any job offer because nothing was too low for him, "I just needed something to do to support my family, and I did not care what it was, as long as it was legal." One day, as Henry was driving past a gas station close to his house, he pulled over to ask if there were any job openings. He was hoping he could get a job supervising the pump attendants. He met a former police officer he had trained, who was there managing the day shift. When he saw him there, he felt encouraged because he knew the man had also served time in prison. He gave Henry a job application and arranged an interview for him the following day. Henry became optimistic once more, seeing it as a stepping stone until something better came along.

He showed up for the interview on time and smartly dressed. When the interviewer saw his qualifications, he became curious, "Mr. Wemyss, why are you at a gas station looking for a job?" Before Henry could answer, he said, "I see you did not bring your police record. Why is that?" Henry told him that he had been to prison and the all too familiar words followed, "I'm sorry, but we can't hire you."

Henry returned home crushed and cried like a baby. He turned on the television to the Trinity Broadcasting Network (TBN), the only station he watched at the time. It was around 2:00 p.m., and The Benny Hinn Ministry was on. When Pastor Hinn began praying for sick people, Henry forgot about his worries and rested his hand on the television as a point of contact, praying for Sam, who was very ill at the time and could not walk. He would never fully recover and died on 28th March, 2007.

As Henry continued to desperately seek means to support his family, a cousin offered to assist him. She had a taxi plate and told him that if he bought a car, she would rent the plate to him for $500.00 a week. He did not have a car at the time because, while in prison, he promised the prison officer, who was nice to him, that he would give him his 626 Mazda when he got out. He fulfilled that promise and shared a car with Judy, who would drop him off at the church.

Thinking his cousin's idea was feasible, Henry applied for a loan of $10,000.00. He felt the amount would cover the cost of the car and travel expenses to the United States but could only qualify for $9,000.00. He accepted the offer, only to be told by the manager that as $1,000.00 was for his services, he would only receive $8,000.00. Henry could not refuse it, no matter how unfair it seemed, because he was desperate to get a car to make a living. He was already $25,000.00 in arrears at the time.

When Henry shared his plans with Sam, he discouraged him because he did not believe Henry had the fortitude to become a taxi driver and advised him to find something more suitable. Ignoring Sam's advice, Henry stuck to his plans, "I went to the United States with $7,000.00 to buy the car and to clear it. I found a 1985, gold-coloured Mercedes that I liked and bargained with the salesman until he agreed to sell it to me for $5,000.00, which included re-painting it blue. When I returned home, I realised my brother was right—taxi driving was not for me."

Even though the vehicle ran on the more efficient diesel, he still struggled because he could not afford to keep it fuelled. He also had to put up with Sam's criticism for purchasing a vehicle he could not afford to maintain. He drove to the church every day, using the limited diesel in the vehicle and parked there. At one point, he and Judy shared the vehicle, but to save fuel, he waited until the traffic died down before picking her up.

"Watching him rebuild his life was crazy," Keisha recalled of that time in her father's life. "Daddy was so discouraged. He applied for numerous jobs, but was repeatedly turned down. It felt like his life was over, and there was no point of return. I remembered he had a navy blue Mercedes vehicle. So, he got the Mercedes to become a taxi driver, but that didn't materialize. It was a nice Mercedes with chestnut leather seats—top-of-the-line. He took us driving in it occasionally, otherwise, it was parked up at Calvary Deliverance Church where he spent most of his time."

"I remember my dad became like the woman in the house. He would prepare meals and do household chores," Acribba reminisced. "I remember the first meal my dad made for us. He had learnt to cook fried fish and peas and grits. Before that, he never cooked. You would have never found my Daddy at a stove or cleaning a house. I remember him doing these things because I supposed he thought: my wife's going out to work so the least I can do is this."

"Henry never wore his problems on his face. He was and still is a worshipper," Bishop Newry shared "You would have had to sit down and get behind the veil, so to speak, and take away all the hardness to really get to know what he was going through at the time. When he came to church he was like the Psalmist, declaring 'I will bless the Lord at all times: His praise shall continuously be in my mouth', and 'This is the day that the Lord has made, I will rejoice and be glad in it.'"

Realizing that the situation could get no worse, Henry concluded, "God must have been doing something in my life that I was not fully aware of." He kept reminding himself, "If God be for you, no man shall stand against you." He continued plugging in at the church and particularly enjoyed ushering, "I always ask myself about the most successful period in my life and the answer always comes back the same—being an usher, serving the people in the house of the Lord. Greeting people and opening doors for them brought me so much joy." Bishop Newry had also noticed his passion for ushering and recalled, "He flourished at that and loved it. Dancing at the door and greeting people, and the way he welcomed them, everybody was just drawn to him because of his love for people. He was open, transparent, and enjoyed the fellowship."

"I think it was the Lord's will for us to go to Calvary Deliverance Church," Henry stated. "It was difficult for me, just coming out of prison and feeling like a nobody. The men I met there took me in as one of them, and I found my purpose there. Bishop Newry, one of the ministers at that time, worked at Epic Battery, and whenever I was stranded, I would call him, and he would come and lend me assistance, including buying me a battery. Some of the other men, who made me feel at home were Ethan Stubbs, Billy Austin, Oris Campbell, now deceased, and Greg Stubbs. These men became great friends and assisted me greatly with re-entering society. At first, I didn't want to mix with them because I felt out of place and didn't want to tarnish their names, but they made me feel at home and supported me in whatever I did—when I did Bible Studies and when I became the President of the Men's fellowship. I will always be grateful to them."

Although he tried to remain focused, Henry felt that his faith was being tested, "Because of what I was going through at that time, that whole period, not having a job and being unable to pay my mortgage, I really believed that God had withdrawn Himself from me. But as I thought about it, I began to understand that sometimes, when God withdraws Himself from us, He is only testing us and wants us to put our complete trust in Him. So that kept me moving despite what was going on around me. I spent hours in the church basement every day, fasting and praying until it was time to go home," Henry recalled. "I found so much strength and peace from hanging down there that I looked forward to it daily. One of my brothers thought that I had lost my mind because I spent too much time around the church. Because I was there all the time, I was given the keys to open and close the building."

JD took Henry to meet with the then Prime Minister, The Rt. Hon. Hubert Ingram. When Henry got there, he was made to feel special. At the time, his pride was still bruised from being incarcerated, "I counted it such a privilege and honour that every time I went to his office, there would be well-dressed men of all colours, waiting to see him. His office staff would seat me in a large conference room to wait for him. When he came in, he would greet me warmly with a pleasant smile. Being a former prison inmate, I did not take it lightly to be able to sit in the room with the most powerful man in the country at that time. He appeared genuinely concerned about me, and whenever I wondered about it, I could only think that it must have been the favour of God," he reflected.

Learning of Henry's dilemma, Prime Minister Ingraham promised to assist him as best as he could. Initially, he attempted to secure a position for Henry as a director of security at ZNS, but that never materialized. Next, he tried to place him as head of security at the National Insurance Board, but as the job required going to the Courts to prosecute cases, Henry's criminal record immediately disqualified him. After Henry had met with him three times, the Prime Minister became apologetic, "Bro. Wemyss, I feel like I let you down, but give me some more time."

Every attempt to assist Henry was met with setbacks, but although doors remained closed, Henry was not discouraged because he believed the Prime Minister was a man of his word. Henry did not feel that he needed political influence because he lacked qualifications, but because he was being ostracized. The fourth time they met, the Prime Minister assured him that he would soon be hearing from him. Eventually, he would fulfil his promise and provide Henry with a stepping stone that not only got his life back on track but propelled him further than either of them could have imagined.

It had been nearly five years since Henry had worked, and all that time Judy had carried the financial burden of the family. With her teacher's salary, breeding dogs, and other odd jobs she was managing as best as she could. Yet the bills continued to pile up. When the mortgage company threatened to foreclose on their home again, Henry decided to get another loan. He initially sought help from one of the church's ministers, who was also a banker and a friend, but he told him a loan would cost him an additional $10,000.00. He then approached the loan manager from another bank, who had given him his first loan back in the 1960s, but he was also asking for $10,000.00. When Henry discussed the situation with his pastor, he assured him that, "God will never let them take your place and even if they try, they will never find a buyer. Just continue to trust God. Don't pay anything."

Determined to save his home, Henry went to a third bank. After his previous experience with loan officers, he expected the loan to cost him extra. So, he was upfront with the officer, "I am not bribing you, but I just want you to know that I am not prepared to go and ask a fourth bank, so please add $5,000 or $6,000 there for yourself." However, that loan officer completed the application without expecting anything in return. He assured Henry that he was doing his job and that whether Henry received the loan would be based solely on his own merit. Henry was surprised, noting that he was a Jehovah's Witness and the other bank officers, who wanted to be paid, were Pentecostal and Lutheran.

At the end of January 1995, Henry's application was successfully approved, "I received the loan but still had no job to be able to pay it back. When the money was placed in my bank account, I immediately withdrew $2,000 to sow into church as a seed of faith." It was also a testament of faith because at the time he did not have any groceries at home.

When Henry offered the money, his pastor, refused it and in reflecting, Bishop Clarke explained why, "I did not want him to get the wrong impression that if something happened it was because he gave. And that, even if he cannot give, because it was difficult for him at that time, God was going to continue to sustain him." Despite this, Henry insisted on sowing the seed, pleading with the pastor that it was something he had to do. Eventually, the pastor said, "If you really want to do this, and feel led to do it, I will accept it." Henry then asked him to pray over the seed, and he did.

During that time, Judy was also involved in the church, and according to Bishop Newry, "she was very instrumental in running mid-day services on Mondays, which was a huge success." He also explained that "Bishop Clarke was a man of prayer and a lot of fasting. He believed in the power of God to heal and to transform lives. Calvary Deliverance Church is a Pentecostal Church that believes in the old-fashioned tarrying in prayer, fasting, and consecration, and Henry was a part of that."

While ushering people in for a mid-day service in early February 1995, the pastor summoned Henry to the altar while praying for people. Telling Henry to raise his hands, he said prophetically, "God says He is going to bless you and find you a job for your faithfulness." Henry recalled, "The anointing was so strong in the service that day that everybody must have fallen out under the spirit. I knew that I had received a word from God, and that he had a job waiting for me."

The following Monday, Henry returned home after another mid-day service, and the phone rang as soon as he walked through the door. He tried to ignore it, thinking it was just another sympathy caller, but felt compelled to answer. It was a call from the Bahamas Telecommunication Corporation (Batelco), inviting him to an interview. "I was elated because I felt that the tide had changed, and God was working things out."

As usual, Henry arrived for the interview immaculately dressed. As he sat there, it became apparent that the job was his for the taking. Despite not having worked for a long time, he expressed his dissatisfaction with the salary, which was higher than what he had earned as a Police Inspector, after 25 years in the Force. Although it was an answered prayer, he remained hesitant to accept the offer but was assured, "Mr. Wemyss, this job is yours, there is nothing I can do about that. You can think about it for a few days, but when you come back, the job is still yours, starting from today."

That day, Henry walked away holding a job offer. After all that he had gone through, he reflected on the scripture, "If God is for you, who can be against you." Going straight to his pastor, he showed him the letter, saying he would not accept the job because he was dissatisfied with the salary. "Get your backside out of this office and get to work. Man did not give you that job, God gave you that job. Once you get your foot in the door, there is nothing God won't do," Pastor Clarke said, bringing him to his senses.

Henry immediately caught himself, "I felt that I was acting like a crazy, ungrateful man." Pastor Clarke also opened his wallet and took out a paper with Henry's name on it, telling him that he had been carrying that for four years as he prayed for him. On 21st February, 1995, Henry accepted the job. "After five long years, my wilderness experience ended," he reflected. "When the time came for the first payment for the mortgage, I was able to pay it, take care of my family, and other financial responsibilities."

"Bishop Clarke had cautioned me, saying, 'Henry, God has been good to you. Whenever He releases you, testify, but you must be led to testify' I said, 'Fine, thank you,' but knowing our country, I refused to do it. Also, a good friend of mine, who was one of the ministers at the church, warned me. She said, 'Don't ever testify that you've been to prison from that pulpit because if you to do that, all the good things you do, nobody watching or listening anymore to what you've said. They'll say, 'he went to jail.' That got me because I knew it was the truth. Once you've been behind bars in The Bahamas, that's it for you—whether guilty or innocent. You better try make it by your own bootstrap."

Henry did not testify in the church, but as the Men's Fellowship President, he went along with several other ministers and the pastor to TD Jakes' Manpower in Atlanta, "There must have been over 20,000 men or more in that church that night in the auditorium. TD Jakes preached about how people are hiding and how so many people who have been to prison are going around with the burden of having been incarcerated that they are afraid to release it. When he said, 'All those in here who's been to prison before come stand in front of the pulpit.' I think the entire church must have gone up, and I was one of the first to go. I did not feel any way about doing that, but I would not do that here." Although he had landed a job, his past continued to haunt him.

Front Row L-R: David Williams, Oris Campbell, Bishop V.G. Clarke, Minister James Newry Henry Wemyss, President of Men's Fellowship.

Also Shown are Other Members of the
Men's Fellowship of Calvary Deliverance Church.

**Bishop V.G. and Elder Beverly Clarke present Henry Wemyss
with the Award for Unselfish Service and Support to
Calvary Deliverance Church.
– 11th September, 2005.**

CHAPTER 16

The Rough Road Back To Dignity

Batelco hired Henry to be a supervisor in the Security Department. He was to be the man on the ground responsible for implementing new policies and establishing procedures to improve what was already in place. Lawson Ferguson was the Senior Manager, and he had two senior supervisors working along with him, "When I met the Senior Manager, he reminded me that he was one of the police reservists whom I had trained. He also asked me whether I would mind wearing a uniform, even though none of the other supervisors did. I told him I didn't have a problem with that, but it never happened," Henry recalled. "I was so relieved to finally be working again that I was willing to do whatever it took to keep that job so that I could support my family."

Ferguson was about to retire, which led to some early conflicts surrounding Henry's employment. The two senior security supervisors, whom he had met there, were concerned that his background as a former Police Inspector would hinder their progress toward upward mobility. The situation became so intense that it reached the parliamentarian level, and Henry was immediately transferred from the Security Department. As he was leaving, a security foreman, Rev. Clifford McKinney, now deceased, assured him, "You are leaving, but it won't be for long. You would be back. God's speed and God's grace go with you. I will be praying for you." Henry never forgot those words.

Due to his experience as a Court Prosecutor, Henry was next considered for a position in the Fraud Department, handling fraud cases. At the last minute, the position was withdrawn. With his criminal record, he could not represent the government in the courts. He was then transferred back to the Security Department to assist with training, but that position was blocked. After all the shifting around, he was finally placed in Fleet Management working out of the Perpall Tract location, "I didn't mind where they placed me because I just wanted to work, and I believed that whatever was happening to me was orchestrated by God," Henry explained. "Swallowing my pride, I showed up for work at 7:00 a.m. every day, even though I wasn't required to be there until 9:00 a.m. I spent my time meditating, praying, and reading the Bible.

Henry met two men he characterized as "honourable gentlemen" on his first day in fleet management: Arlington Rahming, Senior Manager, and Ivan Knowles, Manager. Knowles, who once worked with his brother, Sam, assured him, "You'll be working with me, and I'll take care of you. I'll do for you what your brother did for me." Henry immediately felt better, "From then on, he looked after me and treated me like a son, even taking me home to meet his family."

Rahming, who knew the Wemyss family said, "We both grew up in the Coconut Grove area. I was friendly with his brother Michael, and I had met Henry through him. Being a young policeman, Henry was always on the move, so the relationship was very limited at that time. The next time I saw him was at Batelco, where I was responsible for Fleet Management. He came to me as part of the Fleet Management staff. With politics being played, he was pushed around a little bit. The moment I saw him, there was a connection back to Michael. I knew that he had gone through a lot of things as a police officer with being incarcerated, and knowing the Batelco system, I knew that he was not welcomed. I was quite familiar with that because I was also not welcomed when I first went there. I said to him that the worst thing they could have done was to put us together because only success could come out of this."

Everyone else in Fleet Management had an office, except for Henry. He was allocated a desk in the corridor, where employees would pass him on their way to and from the mechanic and electrical shops. "I felt like a public spectacle and could hear everyone passing and whispering, 'That's Mr. Wemyss now,'" Henry recounted. "The men who sat in the office in the workshop area, next to where I sat, knew whenever I was there. But they openly gossiped about how I went to prison, came in as a senior supervisor, and would soon become their boss. This bothered me so much that I would occasionally go and knock on the door and ask for water. I didn't want the water, but just wanted to let them know that I was there and hoped that they would ease up on me."

"From where I sat, I could also hear my co-workers in the other sections openly discussing me. They said I was only hired because of my political connections," Henry recalled. "Some employees would pass me on purpose to say 'hello' just to see what I looked like. I could hear laughter and conversations going on, but as soon as I walked in, everything stopped.

It was easy to assume they were laughing and talking about me. When co-workers smiled at me, I could not tell if they were genuine or not. I decided to take them at face value because I knew if I tried to think about what was going on in their heads, I'd become resentful. I often left my desk to go upstairs to the restroom, close the door to pray, and have a quiet talk with Jesus. I tried to stay focused on the things of God rather than the thoughts of men, while I concentrated on doing the job I was paid to do."

As much as he tried to remain optimistic, there were moments when he wanted to pack up his belongings and go back home, but he needed to work to provide for his family. He felt he was being treated unfairly, but he understood that perseverance is a virtue and that he had to endure certain things. "Whenever I got discouraged, I went into the restroom and locked the door. I prayed, asking God what He was doing and whether what I was going through was the reason He had brought me there."

Admittedly, Henry knew very little about fleet management, but stated, "God always has a way of filling in the gaps. I didn't know where to start, but I knew who to call, and I contacted the then Superintendent Ellison Greenslade, who was able to assist me with some ideas, which I tweaked and combined with information about how rental companies operated in the US. From that, I was able to customize a structure for the corporation and presented it to the senior manager, which he approved."

He was also responsible for training drivers in defence management. He was sent off to complete a fleet management, train-the-trainer defensive driving course in Atlanta, Georgia. When he returned, he began the training process, but it was less effective than it could have been because when it was time to train the senior managers, the General Manager suggested that he first teach the managers and line staff. However, Henry's strategy was to teach from the top down so that they could buy into the vision and enforce it once it was implemented.

Even though Henry had finally landed a job, he was not out of the red financially. "If you did not know that he was down on his luck, you would never know. He came to work every day looking better than me wearing a suit and tie. He was as clean as could be with his briefcase and shined shoes," Rahming shared. "You would never know if he had lunch that day because that was the kind of person he was. We had some tearful moments when things were down. I remember one Christmas, and everybody was preparing to do what they had to do, and in talking with him, it became evident that there was not going to be a celebration because it was not there. So, I called him over to come by my house, and I gave him a ham and a turkey, and that was a tender moment that brought tears to his eyes. He said, 'Sir you would never know what you did.' It was a private time because you see a big man dressed up, and looking like he has it all together, but there are times when we cry on the inside."

After a while, the men in the office next to him eased up a bit. Henry occasionally accompanied Reverend Michael Hinsey, Senior Manager, for morning devotions with them. Sometimes, Henry spoke and prayed as if he had no idea how they truly felt about him or what they were saying about him. He stayed in the corporation and endured the persecution, "I always believed that God does not do evil, but he allows evil to happen. I felt that despite my challenges, something good would eventually come out of it."

"He was a person, I found to be considerate and compassionate. He mentored a lot of people, who were under him, and always fathered them,"

234

Rahming stated. "There are two people who come to mind—John Taylor and Perry Brooks. These gentlemen reported to him and worked closely with him. It was a normal thing to mentor them and there was always some class or school going on. Whenever you talk to him, there is a lesson going on."

Henry did not stay in fleet management very long. But while there, he focused on bringing about much-needed changes. "With the corporation's approval, I implemented control measures to restrict vehicles from being used for personal purposes. Before this, employees would sign out vehicles and keep them indefinitely, using them on holidays and weekends, costing the corporation millions of dollars. With the new measures in place, whenever vehicles were issued to any individuals, the cost was deducted from their departments' budget. As a result, people were cautious not to use the vehicles for personal use. Any employee requiring vehicles for work purposes, after hours, needed permission from their department heads."

As the corporation had its own gas station, employees had been requesting gas whenever they wanted to, even on weekends. Henry changed that, and vehicles were not allowed to be fuelled up on Fridays, which discouraged employees from taking the vehicles home on weekends for personal use. The system worked for a while, but the employees pushed back, accusing him of bringing his military-style into the corporation. Despite the criticism, Henry and his team transformed Fleet Management, saving the corporation over a million dollars in the first two months.

"He was always a standout with the way he carried himself. He was a stickler for detail and insisted on things being done with excellence. He always had an opinion, and there was always a solution to the problem or another way of doing it. That distinguished him. The fact that he always had a view, whether it was a good one or bad, is immaterial. There was a drive, and he always discussed his goals. It may have been because of the whole prison scenario and losing status, losing physical things, and not having what you want—not even lunch some days. Those things became a driving forces because we were always discussing goals, the philosophy of life, and how to better oneself. From that point of view, he was different."

Securing a job held great significance for Henry, and the persecution he faced just strengthened his resolve to clear his name. He could no longer live with a stained reputation, "As soon as I had saved enough money, true to my promise to myself, I turned my full attention to placing my case before the Court," he stated. "I went to see The Right Honourable Dame Janet Bostwick, the then Attorney General. I asked her to assist me with getting my case back before the court. But she said, 'Brother Wemyss, there is nothing I can do, and there is nothing that anybody can do. My own father was falsely accused and convicted, and he died fighting his case without having his conviction overturned but be encouraged.'"

Others could not understand why he wanted to fight his conviction and reminded him that his record would be expunged after seven years. Henry felt differently, "I did not want my record to be cleaned automatically after seven years. I wanted my record to be cleaned by the system that convicted me. I understood what everyone was telling me. They were looking at the natural and logical events of things, and the history of the court system. But I wasn't taking no for an answer - God is bigger than that. I asked Him to make a way and allow it to happen for me. I was convinced, and I believed with all my might that it was not impossible for God to clear my name with the truth."

After receiving a job from the government, he knew he was taking a risk, "I decided on my own, with God on my side that I was going back to Court to fight for my name, no matter what the consequences were." He went to his attorney and laid out his intentions. His attorney also questioned his rationale after serving his sentence and getting a job. Henry remained undeterred, so he agreed to assist him for $5,000.00.

On 13th April, 1996, Henry was advised by the attorney that his hearing before the Court of Appeal would be the following day, which also happened to be his birthday. He was also informed that if he did not pay the outstanding legal fees, he would not have representation in Court and would not be guaranteed another date for the hearing. Henry could not pay the fees because he was waiting on a bank loan that was still in process, but he realized he could not jeopardize the opportunity he had been waiting for. As usual, he sought advice from Sam, who advanced him a cheque until the loan was finalized.

The next day, Henry appeared before the Court of Appeal, facing two foreign judges and a Bahamian judge–Dame Justice Joan Sawyer. He knew of her reputation for being intolerant when drug-related charges were brought before her. In her ruling, Justice Sawyer referred to his case as a "travesty of justice," and questioned, "How could they send an innocent man to prison? How could he get his life together again? You could not give him bail?" Addressing Henry, she said, "You are a free man." When Henry heard those words, he recalled, "I cried like a baby and felt as if a heavy load had been lifted off my shoulders."

After leaving the Court, Henry returned to work. As excited as he was, he did not tell his wife or anyone else his good news until he got home. They cried and shouted for joy, and when Sunday came, the family went to church to thank God and receive prayers. That was the beginning of a new chapter in Henry's life, "I was happy but sad because of all I had to go through. And I realised that so many other people never got justice because they could not afford it. After the trial, I thought about what the attorney general had said about her father's case, how he was never able to get justice, and how many people had advised me not to appeal my conviction but to wait until the seven years were up. I was also warned that if the judges were told what to do and were unwilling to do justice and ruled against me, then I would lose my job."

91

COMMONWEALTH OF THE BAHAMAS   19 92

IN THE COURT OF APPEAL   No. 38

CRIMINAL SIDE

HENRY ANSELEM WHYMMS   Appellant

Vs.

THE COMMISSIONER OF POLICE   Respondent

NOTICE TO THE AUTHORITIES OF
RESULT OF APPEAL

This is to give you notice that the abovenamed having appealed against his conviction(s) of the offence(s) of

.........CONSPIRACY TO IMPORT DANGEROUS DRUGS...........

and his sentence(s) of

.............THREE YEARS IMPRISONMENT ....

passed upon him by the Supreme Court for the said offence(s), The Bahamas Court of Appeal has finally determined the said appeal and has this day given judgment therein to the effect following:

"Appeal allowed. Conviction and Sentence set aside."

DATED the 25th day of April   19 96.

Registrar,
Bahamas Court of Appeal.

TO:

Superintendent of Prisons,
Attorney General,
Registrar, Supreme Court,
Commissioner of Police.   (Conviction and sentence)

238

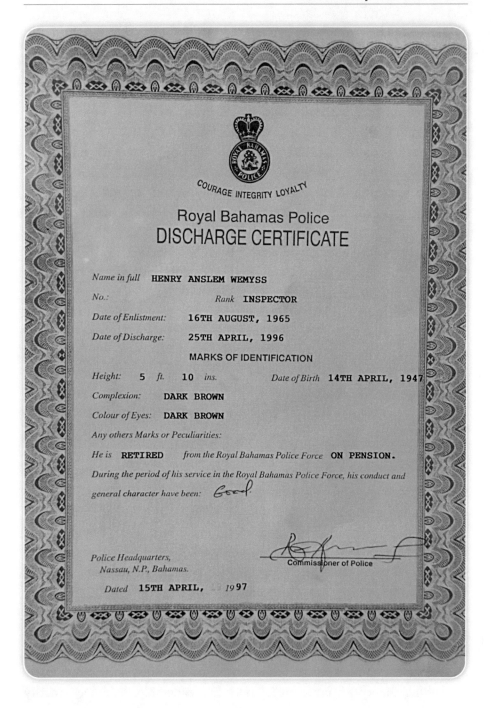

COURAGE INTEGRITY LOYALTY

Royal Bahamas Police
DISCHARGE CERTIFICATE

Name in full **HENRY ANSLEM WEMYSS**

No.: *Rank* **INSPECTOR**

Date of Enlistment: **16TH AUGUST, 1965**

Date of Discharge: **25TH APRIL, 1996**

MARKS OF IDENTIFICATION

Height: **5** *ft.* **10** *ins.* *Date of Birth* **14TH APRIL, 1947**

Complexion: **DARK BROWN**

Colour of Eyes: **DARK BROWN**

Any others Marks or Peculiarities:

He is **RETIRED** *from the Royal Bahamas Police Force* **ON PENSION.**

During the period of his service in the Royal Bahamas Police Force, his conduct and general character have been: Good.

Police Headquarters,
Nassau, N.P., Bahamas.

Commissioner of Police

Dated **15TH APRIL,** *19*97

239

Following his exoneration, Henry received full compensation from the Force, including all back pay, vacation entitlement, and a good discharge certificate for 31 years of service. "I didn't have to think twice about saying "No" when asked whether I wanted to return to the Police Force," he said. "I felt that my time with the police had come to an end, so I took my full pension and gratuity and closed that chapter of my life." After waiting a long time, that money worked wonders for him. "That was the first time I had ever had so much money, and when I got the check, I deposited it to my bank account and laminated the deposit receipt," he reflected. "After a long struggle, my life was falling into place, and God's plan was being executed."

Sadly, his brother, JD, would not share the same destiny. It had been too late by the time he had accumulated sufficient funds to take his matter back to Court. He had hired a lawyer who took his case to the Court of Appeal, only to learn that the correct order was to return the case to the Supreme Court and the Judge who had decided the case. That Judge would then have to grant approval for the matter to be heard by the Court of Appeal. As the Judge was no longer in office, the only remaining option was petitioning the Privy Council, which was not financially feasible. JD died in 2013, without receiving justice. He had lost everything because of his conviction, including his home.

Henry continued to work at the corporation and was eventually sent back to manage the Security Division, but faced some setbacks. Despite the Board's instructions, Human Resources reassigned him to training and directed him to report to the Senior Manager. Later, he was appointed to manage the Security Division, a position he held with distinction for three years and for which he received numerous commendations. He was second in charge to the then Assistant Vice President at the time, Theresa Burrows, who oversaw Human Resources and Security.

As Rahming observed, "Shortly before the downsizing, he was reassigned to security at J.F.K and spent some significant time there attached to Human Resources. It was then that security began to take shape and improved significantly to become more of a security and not someone just sitting there in a uniform." Under his leadership, qualified security officers were also installed as district constables to serve the community in a greater capacity. They were empowered to make arrests, just like ordinary police officers, anywhere in New Providence. Henry was nominated for the Manager of the Year Award and won. The General Manager approached him and apologized, admitting he had no idea what he was capable of, and congratulated him on winning the award.

Ingrid recalled observing her father's return to work, "You could see that he was happy, organizing things, and doing the kind of activities he enjoyed. It was like being a police officer, and he was in his element. When I was in the Defence Force and became an instructor, I frequently used him as an example for not giving up on people or putting them down, rather than giving them a second chance to redeem themselves. I think that's the problem—people don't like giving second chances. Whoever was responsible for giving him a job at Batelco did not have to do that. They could have believed what others believed about him, but they gave him that second chance and I felt that was a good thing for him."

SECURITY OFFICERS INSTALLED AS CONSTABLES
(Photo by Jermaine Burnside)

In an effort to equip personnel with a greater ability to serve their country, 21 Bahamas Telecommunications Corporation security officers were initiated as district constables this week. To qualify, the officers had to be physically fit, between the ages of 21 and 60, and have both a clean character and antecedent record. As district constables, the security officers will be able to make arrests just like ordinary police officers anywhere in New Providence.

The security officers, however, will be required to transfer all evidence of the crime to the local authorities for further investigations. Shown above are the 21 newly initiated district constables along with (from left to right) Anthony R. Thompson, Security Supervisor, Batelco; Henry Wemyss, Chief of Security, Batelco; Magistrate Roger Gomez and Sergeant Daniels of the Royal Bahamas Police Force.

CHAPTER 17

When Promotion Comes From God

In 1999, The Bahamas Government implemented plans to privatize The Bahamas Telecommunications Corporation. The purpose was to focus primarily on telecommunications and outsource the other functions. This afforded employees opportunities to bid for a three-year contract to provide non-telecommunication services such as security, air-conditioning, construction, and auto-mechanics. "At one stage before they decided to pay out, I met with all of the other groups from the corporation intending to form a conglomerate of masons, carpenters, and electricians to create a one-stop shop," Henry recalled. However, nobody bought into his idea because they preferred to do their own thing.

Mr. Shane Gibson, the President of the Union, at the time, met with all employees and advised them to form companies so that they could provide services to the corporation. When he met with the security personnel, he suggested that they come together and form a security company to apply for the security contract. He further suggested that with his track record, Henry would be the ideal person to head the company, but it will belong to all of them. However, Henry was perceived as too strict and disciplined, so the other security personnel were not willing to join forces with him. Instead, they said they would go ahead and form a company without him.

Kenneth Whyms, Henry's nephew, who also worked for the Corporation, became the driving force that pushed him to consider starting his own business. For months, he showed up at Henry's office, every day, trying to get him to see the logic behind starting his own company. "He suggested that I provide private security because he believed it would be more profitable than working directly for the Corporation," Henry recalled. "I was afraid because of the public perception, not because I felt incapable, but because I wondered if it would be supported and if my negative past would hinder its success."

"God put me at the right place at the right time," Kenneth reflected. "I knew my uncle had the expertise. So, it was a no-brainer for me. He doubted himself because he had always been a career civil servant and lacked the entrepreneurial spirit. So, at first, he just wanted a job and was relieved to have one. I kept telling him it was a once-in-a-lifetime opportunity, but he couldn't see it. We used to have tea or coffee together every morning, and he even started ducking me in the mornings because I kept telling him to go for it. I have to give him credit because after all my nagging and bugging, he finally gave in. That opportunity changed his life altogether forever."

Looking back, Henry recounted an earlier memory, "While I was still working as a police officer, the Chaplain, Father Anthony Roberts, an Anglican priest, and former High Commissioner to the United Kingdom told me: 'Henry you are such a brilliant young man. When you retire from the Force, you should start your own security company.' When I asked him why, he said, 'You are so good at what you do. You've been teaching and training, and I watch how you manage and know it's your calling.' I didn't see that happening at the time. So, I didn't take him seriously because it wasn't my thing. Later, if I had later gotten a job as a director of security for some organisation that would have sufficed to complement my pension."

As Henry considered the next step forward, he stated, "I was advised by someone I greatly admired not to take the package but to remain with the corporation to oversee security and provide consultancy services between the corporation and whichever company was selected as the security provider. That sounded great, and I knew that the person advising me had the power to make it happen. But I realised that position would be contingent on the government of the day remaining in power, and if it did not, I felt I would be one of the first people fired by those who had previously opposed my appointment to the corporation. So, when I was asked whether I was going to stay and take the position, I stated my decision to form my own security company. Rahming also encouraged me to start my own company, but I was still afraid."

As I struggled with that decision and my best course of action, I heard a sermon by Elder B. M. Clarke, at church, and she seemed to be speaking directly to me," Henry reflected. "The acronym FEAR was defined as 'false evidence appearing real.' I realised that my fear had triumphed over my faith, and whatever I feared, might never come true. After I heard that sermon, my faith was strengthened, and I ultimately decided to take Kenneth's advice and that of others who had placed their confidence in me."

On 16th April, 1999, Henry founded Wemyss Company, abbreviated WemCo, establishing WemCo Security & Collections Ltd. The staff complement consisted of three office staff, including Acribba. "Before I joined my dad, I worked at an offshore bank. I was 18 going on 19, and my dad told me to leave my job and come and work for him," Acribba recalled. "We did not have a contract yet. Daddy was about to put his bid into Batelco, but we weren't sure we would get it. But we were working as if we knew we would get something."

WemCo began in a small office on Harold Road in an upstairs building. "We had a fax machine and one of the old telephones that you pull off the hook," Acribba said. "At the time, I was the only family member, and there was Mr. Patrick Levarity, a former police corporal, Rev. Clifford McKinney, a former security foreman at BTC, and a girl named Neka. Paul Thompson was there, and although he was employed elsewhere, he worked with Daddy to get the company started." Initially, none of the employees were being paid, but Henry promised to compensate them for their time once the company received its first contract. "Daddy wasn't sure he would be awarded a contract, but he had faith. I designed the uniform and the employment application, using a template. We advertised in the newspapers, and people came in to fill out applications. We were also conducting interviews so that once we got the contract, we would know who to call," Acribba explained.

Henry created a 10-point plan, outlining the benefits of hiring a private security firm compared to an in-house security and presented it to the corporation. The idea was that the corporation would significantly reduce its operational costs by outsourcing the services. He did not know what to charge when determining the cost of his services. He could not ask former police officers or his superiors who were in the business, but God led him to the right source who assisted him with crunching the figures that he presented to the Board.

However, he received feedback that his cost was too high. Rahming was also sent to advise him to reduce his cost. "I told him that I would get back to them and immediately went on a three-day fast. I prayed and asked God for guidance on what to do. I believe the answer was to be still, and I kept praying, and the only answer was to be still," Henry recalled. Interestingly, on the third day of his fast, he was reliably informed that the Board had approved the contract without any changes.

"On the fourth day, The Board met, and the financial advisor to the Board of Directors at Batelco, James Smith, a former Central Bank governor, reviewed my proposal and said that the price I had submitted was in keeping with the cost for good security. WemCo was awarded the contract with no cost adjustments. After that, my life was never the same. I finally realised that God had closed all the other doors for me because he knew that Batelco was the path I needed to take to reach my destiny," Henry reflected. "That day was a new day, having to start all over again from the ground up after 31 years in the Police Force and going through this ordeal. God intervened, and with one contract, I was able to accomplish more in three years than I had done in 31 years. The enemy had kept me from my destiny for a while, but God is bigger than any enemy."

"My dad did not get the first contract until 2000, and WemCo was incorporated on 16th April, 1999," Acribba reflected. "And Daddy got the contract on his birthday, 14th April, 2000. It was so divine. Everything was divinely orchestrated like God has always seen Daddy's heart. He knew that if He blessed this guy, he was going to do what He needed him to do, and he has always had a big outreach heart. Daddy's entire mission was to pour into somebody or to help where they couldn't help themselves—that was always him.

"When I started working for Daddy, he made it clear from early on that he was my employer and not my father when I showed up to work. When we were just building the company, he told me, "I expect you to be better than the people in here; I expect you to come to work on time; I expect you to be an example. You don't have to have a title, but be an example." He established that with me right away. I believe that working with him and being able to part ways with Daddy-daughter and boss-employee made the process go very smoothly. Now, if we were alone having lunch, we would talk as Daddy-daughter, but as soon as lunch was finished, we returned to being boss-employee."

"I was involved from inception, but I played dual roles at that time. When WemCo started in 1999, I was fully enlisted in The Bahamas Defence Force. I never got released until 2001, but during that time, I still ran the accounts department—payroll, receivables, purchases, and the likes," Keisha reminisced. "During the first few years of WemCo, I would go to BDF and being in training, I worked 36-hour shifts. So, if I went to work at 7:00, I wouldn't get off until noon the next day. If it was a weekday, once I got off, I would go to WemCo's office, which was on Harold Road at the time. I would go into the office to see what cheques they needed. I was constantly going.

"At the initial stage, I never did the training because when we first started, we only had the Batelco account, and Daddy trained the officers, along with Paul Thompson. I believe we didn't get another client until 2001. By that time, we had relocated to an office on Dowdeswell Street. When we moved to our current Collins Avenue location, I began participating in the training. I did payroll training to ensure they understood how they were being paid and what they were entitled to." Also reflecting on WemCo's early years, Ingrid said, "Daddy used to be hands-on with patrolling and supervising. That meant he was back on the road again and on the beat, occasionally taking on a few of the shifts. When they started doing credit and collections, I helped in that area."

Casey Wemyss joined the company in 2000 and described his time working for WemCo as a "learning experience." His responsibility was managing the company's alarm business, including installation and service. "He is a giant of a man, a visionary leader, and a man with a lot of knowledge," he says of his father. "I enjoyed working with WemCo" Nonetheless, he desired to work independently of the father-son relationship and stated that he "showed up to work as an employee and not a family member because he wanted to be respected for his abilities and not his relationship." After 14 years with the company, he branched out on his own and attributes his success, both personally and professionally, to his time with WemCo. On a more personal level, he stated that his father "loves his children unconditionally."

WemCo's contract with Batelco provided a solid foundation. The first complement of officers was trained individuals who had previously worked in security at Batelco. Henry channelled the expertise he had gained, as a police officer, into his own security company. From its inception, he set high industry standards for WemCo. Former Assistant Commissioner Paul Thompson, who was there to provide guidance, stated, "Everything he learnt from the Police Force, he put into WemCo. He had baton drills. His officers had pocketbooks, like the police. He introduced diary keeping, handheld radios, a control centre, and security codes. Plus, the officers had to be neat and clean when on duty. WemCo even went as far as to check your personal hygiene. You had to be smelling right to report for duty."

Later, Thompson took on a more active role with the company, "When I left the Force, I was always in touch with WemCo and was invited when they had meetings, and I did some lectures for staff. Eventually, I went back to the Police Force as the Training Officer and spent three or four years there. By then, WemCo was going strong, and Henry invited me to join them regularly.

Eventually, I was made General Manager, and during that time WemCo progressed to become one of the best security firms in the country. The reason is that Mr. Wemyss is a fanatic when it comes to training. He does not want to hire people or put them out there unless they have been trained, and that came from his policing and time as an instructor at the Police College. I think WemCo is the only security company that does not hire people unless they are trained. You must come in and get your training before being hired, and upon completion of the training, you are hired on probation."

Glennis Knowles, a former cadet, served as WemCo's second General Manager. She reflected, "It was the first company that gave me the opportunity to be the General Manager. All of the principles he had taught me, as a cadet, I put into practice. One of my goals, as General Manager, was to establish another office in another location, and we opened the office in Grand Bahama." Her relationship with Henry was quite different than before, as she explained, "As a boss, he was different than when he was a cadet leader. At that age, there was more consulting. So, I saw a different person, but he had the same values outside the military environment. Not authoritative, but authority was understood. He worked with me, and I learnt a lot, but also had the ability to make changes and have a voice in where he wanted to take the company."

Jewel Fulford, current General Manager, was with the company from its inception, having started as a Guard I. She had previously worked in the security department at Batelco. "When WemCo Security & Collections Limited started its operations in 2000, security companies were still operating with 'night watchmen' and 'bouncer' mentality," she reflected. "They just wanted a body on post. It was WemCo Security, who came in and changed the landscape of security in the country. Our employees understand that they are not only hired by WemCo, but are an extension of the clients as ambassadors and, therefore, must be able to complement their standards. Through training, coaching, and counselling, people who started just looking for a job have made a career in security. WemCo has also been a stepping stone for young men, who started with us and, because of developing an interest, transitioned into law enforcement."

In 2003, Security Manager, Administration, Irene Smith joined the company as a Guard I, "I moved from Andros in search of work, and I was on a bus when I was on a bus when I saw a security officer at Batelco,

Poinciana Drive in uniform, and I said to myself that I would look good in that uniform. I searched for the company's name in the phone book, and I was hired on the spot with the assistance of Mr. Howard Smith, Director of Security, at the time," she reflected. "I was trained among some of the best and brightest managers and supervisors—Vincent Forbes, now deceased, Howard Thompson, Cleopatra Woodside, Hilary Taylor, Almarie Taylor, Vivian Ward—they were a force to be reckoned with. They ensured that after working for one week, you would be ready to run WemCo's control room and field. I felt proud wearing my uniform. I was taught to remain respectful, diligent, and focused on one goal—to protect and keep the peace." In response to what sets WemCo apart from other companies, Smith stated, "Our guards are well trained and our uniform."

From the beginning, Henry's vision was to establish a family business, not just in the sense of employing family members but also in the sense of fostering an environment in which all employees had a feeling of belonging. Fulford recalls, "There was work, but there were also occasions to fellowship, not just in the annual church service, but times spent in non-working settings with employees, which allowed for the building of relationships and employees morale." Over the years, WemCo has shown its appreciation for its employees in many ways, including award ceremonies, back-to-school giveaways, and the distribution of hurricane relief supplies. There have been both private and public monetary donations. Smith also attested to WemCo's generosity, "We had giveaways for the kids in the community, donations to the various churches and paid medical bills for some persons."

Smith shared her experience, "I can personally speak about my husband being sick. I was in a managers' meeting when Mr. Wemyss said, 'Mr. Smith is sick and you're to work?' He not only sent me home, but he also paid the medical bills for my husband to go to a private doctor." In describing Mr. Wemyss, she noted, "He's like a shepherd—someone who looks over his sheep. He is always trying to help others without thinking twice about himself." Smith added, "Mr. Wemyss is like a Mufasa in The Lion King.

When he speaks, we listen. He is rough and tough, but a soft and kind-hearted person."

One of the most memorable events was when the company raffled off several of its vehicles, free of charge, to its employees. "Mr. Wemyss would give his staff his heart if he could," Gerelean Medows, Security Manager, Administration, stated. "He is an awesome person who shows love to everyone, and always treats me like one of his own." She joined the company in 2006 as a Security Guard and when she thinks about what made WemCo a family environment she stated, "staff being much more together and staff coming together for fun days and happy hours." As for what sets the company apart from other security companies, she said, "WemCo is a very well-organized company, officers are always well dressed, and the company has high standards."

Terrance Bain, a financial consultant, met Henry at a WemCo employee's appreciation event and was invited to provide accounting services to the company. At the time, he was impressed by how the company was giving back to its employees and noted, "What I found out when I got involved was that he had a list of orphans and widows whom he assisted financially regularly.

He is a generous person who would do just about anything for you. Many times, business owners tend to be so concerned about the business side of things that they forget the people's side. But I think he has always held the importance of people, and that's not just the employees, that's also the clients, that's also the people he meets along the way, that's also those he could assist as a result of having the business. To that extent, it was a means to an end. It allowed him to be able to do a lot more for others than if it had not been for the business. Many people can say that if it were not for the generosity and opportunity that he gave them, they would not be where they are today.

"He believes in order and things being done properly, professionalism and discipline—those are the things he instilled in his officers," Bain said of Henry's business practices. "We have a reputation to maintain; we're going to put a product out there that we are proud of, and people will want: a professional, world-class operation. It wasn't just about being a watchman but being a security officer, which is why training is so important.

He made sure they were trained properly and completely to become an asset to the clients that they were serving, not just about being robotic but being pre-emptive in the way they chose to carry out their duties and I think that, as well, contributed to the success of the company to be one of the largest physical security firms in the country.

"At the end of the day while he would have certainly wanted to run a successful business, in terms of being profit-driven, he cared about the people in his employ. He continued that, even after he was not active day to day, he tried to consider them in the decisions. He wants to see that the employees are taken cared of because, as he put it, they are the ones who built the company."

"What I understand is that success has nothing to do with accomplishment or wealth, but it is all about what you do for others," Henry said when reflecting on his accomplishments. He has always believed that he was blessed to be a blessing. While keeping his promise to create jobs for the unemployed, he also believes in giving back and assisting anyone in need. "He has a heart for people. His outreach is amazing. He's never lost the cause, the mission or the assignment and always understood what his assignment was, and his assignment is Ministry of Help—People," Acribba explained. "If he loses a contract today, Daddy is always worried about what will happen to the employees. How are their families going to eat? People don't always get to see that deeper part of him. He's very concerned about his employees."

Attesting to Henry's Ministry of Help, Bishop Newry stated, "While everyone can get involved in the Ministry of Help, he takes it to another level by giving of his resources, and he does it quietly and if you don't know, you don't know. He is very secretive in the way he goes about it, but over the years, he has taken care of the poor and the widows. I know that for a fact because the widows of this church receive a stipend from him every month."

Mr. Henry & Judy Wemyss, Acribba Lightbourne (daughter), family, friends and the Management and Employees of WemCo Security & Collections Co. Ltd. at Calvary Deliverance Church to celebrate the Company's 5TH Anniversary.

Henry Wemyss, Judy Wemyss and daughter, Acribba Lightbourne, Meet with Widows to Launch the Widows' Fund – 2006.

Henry Wemyss remembers his alma mater and donates to Aquinas College. Shown L-R: Acribba Lightbourne, Henry Wemyss, then-Principal Elizabeth Miller, and Keisha Wemyss.

WemCo Security & Collections gives back to the community by hosting a back-to-school giveaway.

WemCo Security & Collections Ltd. Rewards Students in the Community
for Achieving Excellent Grades.

Henry Wemyss and the Management Team of WemCo Security & Collection
Pay a Courtesy Call on Commissioner of Police, Paul Farquharson
at Police Headquarters in 2001

Former Commissioner of Police Paul Farquharson, now deceased, stated, "Henry built that security firm from the ground up, and by that time I became Commissioner of Police, and Henry continued to build his security firm and contacted me on several occasions to come and share in handing out certificates when he had graduating classes. He was also instrumental to me when I started to bring all the security forces together to help the police so that we can could have one common goal as security officers and police officers.

"And his business was a conduit for several officers who retired from the Force and who contacted Henry, so he provided an opportunity for them in his business. He also provided opportunities for hundreds of Bahamians, and if they produced good work, he retained them. He is a no-nonsense guy in terms of his business and if you didn't measure up, he showed you the road. Henry has a heart of gold for his friends, his church, and people he is close to, and that's why I believe he was blessed in business because of his generosity to his father and friends whom he met."

Brenda Ferguson, a business consultant, also explained, "He does not always care for the limelight. He will do stuff in this community, personally or through the company, and sometimes he will issue press releases. But much of what he does never makes the media, except when he wants to highlight his employees and put them out there." Reflecting on how her initial impression of him changed, she shared, "When I first met him in the capacity of going to Calvary Deliverance Church, where he was a minister, I used to hate when he would get up to collect the offering. He always had a story to tell and shared his testimony, but I just wanted him to get out of the way. After a while, I realised that there are all kinds of people in the church, and perhaps after hearing his story, they too will understand."

About what drives him, she said, "When he talks about growing up, he refers to his father. He describes his father as the person who shaped him to be the man that he is now and to understand that mediocrity is not an option. You must strive to be the best and achieve the best, not that it means in the material sense, but being the best person, you can be. When he puts himself out there, he wants to do it the best. He really wants his company to be the best security company on the island, and that is the standard to which he strives."

"Integrity stands out," Acribba said of her father's business ethics. "My dad never believes in breaking the rules or taking shortcuts; he will do it right even if it takes him a year. He built WemCo on the principles he learnt as a child from his father and the Police Force, as well as its discipline and morals. Through training, he instills all his attributes in his employees. Uniforms and appearance are everything to my dad. He is still radical about that, and everything about Henry Wemyss is in line with WemCo— discipline, appearance, approach. That is why WemCo survived."

Rahming stated, "Henry was fortunate enough to be able to operate in the world he was designed to operate - the security and the whole law enforcement kind of aspect. I think he may have had some aspirations otherwise as far as law enforcement is concerned, but nevertheless this was a window that was opened for him, and he went in and made a difference. He has created what will go down in history as the largest, most effective security operation in the country and that is no small matter.

"I would describe Henry as the embodiment of determination and excellence. He knows God and has a heart for God and a passion for what he does in the security field. He has a big heart of compassion and that is connected from where he came from as well as by his own personal design. I can refer to him in one phrase—as a change agent—for he influences change wherever he goes. He is a success story, and his life is a testimony to anybody who is down that with perseverance, hard work, and whatever else you want to throw into the mix, you can make it even though people will reject you. He is an icon that will affect change in the lives of many people who read his story."

As a child, it was difficult to understand why her father had to experience such a horrible defeat, but as she matured Acribba came to realise that it served purpose, "Now, years later, I see the Biblical aspect of it, that everything was predetermined. You're not going to go about life living perfectly without fires, without being thrown in dens like Daniel or in a pit like Joseph. You don't go through life like that. My dad was supposed to go on the Force, and he was supposed to be falsely accused so God could bless him and bring him out like fire. Even though the public might have thought it was unjust, you can now see the beauty of why he had to go through it. That was supposed to happen. So, I call it unfair on a physical level yet divinely orchestrated by God. As an adult that is how I perceive it today."

"Never lose hope. Because you can be enthusiastic about your profession and your accomplishments, and then you can have some stumbling along the way. But you should never give up but continue moving towards the mark," Anthony Gibson, a family friend, says of valuable lessons drawn from Henry's life. "When I heard about his COVID experience, I said, here again, he has gone through fire and has come out. Character-wise, he is a much better person. I think the worst thing that ever happened to him was the best thing that ever happened to him. He suffered because his career in the Police Force was interrupted, but what happened after that just proves the worth of a man, the character in him. He took whatever opportunities were available to him and turned them into who he is today. He has become a very accomplished person, a very respectful businessman. I'm proud of him. I can point to him when others are facing obstacles in their lives and tell them, 'Well, look at Goose.'"

In thoughts of what drives Henry, Gibson stated, "I think, first love of God and then for his fellow man. And his character is that he knows that he is not a loser. He is a fighter, and I think he knows that once he puts his mind to something, he can accomplish it and he goes after it."

Dr. Fox summed up, "Well, you can come from humble beginnings and still make it, and determination is the key. He is very determined and persistent to be successful and stay on top, so that is one of the lessons to learn: if you have the determination to achieve, then you will achieve and you will succeed." Of his generosity he said, "Yes, he is very kind and gives a lot. A behind-the-scenes man; doesn't like to be at the forefront of his generosity, and often prefers his kids to do it so that the spotlight is not on him. A very generous man."

When she thinks about all her brother has gone through, Millie quotes, "But those who wait on the Lord shall renew their strength; they shall mount up with wings like eagles; they shall run and not be weary, they shall walk and not faint," Isaiah 40:31 (NKJV).

"The fact of the matter is that it happened, and you can't scrub it out," Freddie Lightbourne, Henry's son-in-law explained. "But that's just a point to show people that you could be at the lowest of the low, and God can raise you to the highest of the high. I'm sure when he was in prison, he thought that was it for his life, his career, and his family, but that was just a place for him to be for things to line up, and now Mr. Wemyss is one of the most respected persons in The Bahamas."

"If only I knew the end at the beginning," Henry reflected. "It took me about 20 years after becoming a Christian to realise that promotion comes from above, not from men. If I had known that I would have been quite content that my plans are not always God's plans, and that he would promote me in His own time."

"My daily prayer from the 14th April, 2000 - the day WemCo began - has been for God to keep me humble that I may be a servant rather than be served. I recite Deuteronomy 6:4-10, 'Be careful that you do not forget the Lord,' after realizing what the Lord has done for me and where He has brought me from. If you could imagine how deep God had to reach down to pull me up, and every day he tells me to, 'forget those things that are behind, but press towards the mark of the prize of the high calling, which is in Christ Jesus.' I never accepted credit for the company's success from anyone. Firstly, I remembered Deuteronomy 8:18, 'and you shall remember the Lord your God, for it is He who gives you power to get wealth,' and secondly, I thank God for the dedicated employees he has given to this company he has entrusted to me."

Celebrating the goodness of God, on 26th April, 2023, the Wemyss family, along with the management and staff of WemCo marked the company's 23rd anniversary by worshipping at Calvary Deliverance Church. A week prior, they had celebrated Henry's 76th birthday in worship, as well. Having left the church in 2007, the family returned in mid-January 2023, making it their church home once again. Even though Henry was not an active church member, he had never stopped financially supporting the ministry.

On 19th May, 2023, Bishop Dr. James Newry and Calvary Deliverance Church recognised Henry for his years of contribution and service during the church's 40th Anniversary celebrations. He received the Clementina Stubbs Award and the Eagle Award. "Mother Clementina Stubbs was our first pastor and a woman, and that's the highest award you can get in the church," Bishop Newry explained. "I chose him because of his commitment and dedication. I also chose him because he is a man of honour in Calvary, and he has earned it for his commitment to the work of the church and to the people of God." About why he was also awarded the Eagle Award, he stated, "Our Eagle Award is for persons who have done above and beyond and do not allow the adversities that they go through to keep them down."

One 9th October, 2023—celebrated in the Bahamas as National Hero's Day—Henry was recognized once more, this time at a national level. During an Investiture Ceremony at Government House, he was conferred by The Government of The Bahamas with the honour of Member of the Order of Merit, with all the rights and privileges, in recognition of his exemplary service to The Commonwealth of The Bahamas, as a Public Servant and Philanthropist.

During his remarks, the Chairman of the National Honours Advisory Committee, The Honourable Fred Mitchell, MP, & Minister of Foreign Affairs, referred to Henry and stated, "I remember the injustice that was wrought upon him during his career that brought his career to an end and now today being honoured by the state for his service." Hearing that public vindication was an emotional moment for Henry, "After all I had to go through—after 33 years, while being recognized by the state I never expected to hear anything like that. I could hear the loud applause in the audience, and all I was able to do was cry."

"As I continue to walk this road, this long winding road, I still have more roads to travel and more places to go. I have not yet finished the race that I was called to run. There is still much walking for me to do. I am still not able to see around the bend, but I realise it is not as long as it has been. I hope never to look back because looking back can be death, and I hate to be reminded of what I have overcome. As I stay on this road, it becomes easier and easier every day. I am reminded of what the Psalmist says in Psalm 90, 'Teach us to number our days that we may apply our hearts unto wisdom.' It speaks about how life can change in an instant. I have experienced that personally more than twice, and it says regardless of how long we live, we seldom know what peace is. We try to buy peace; we will give up anything in the world to find peace, but instead of looking for it, peace must be found within us—the peace of God which passes all understanding."

It may have seemed that Henry ended up on the wrong side of life, but it still turned out to be a right turn for him. "He's been through a lot, overcoming two major downfalls, and he's emerged stronger and better from both of them, so he's definitely here for a reason," Keisha said. Sharing similar sentiments, his sister Terry added, "His purpose is not done that's why God raised him up." After reflecting on his life, Henry came to the following conclusion, "If God had not blessed me, prison would have been my end, but God used it as my beginning. IF GOD BE FOR YOU, no one could be against you."

**Mr. & Mrs. Henry Wemyss Pose with Bishop
Dr. James & Elder Queenie Newry – Sunday, 26th April, 2023.**

Henry Wemyss and Family Pose with Bishop Dr. James Newry
In front: Skylar Lightbourne, grand-daughter;
Second row L-R: Keisha Wemyss, daughter; Henry Wemyss; Bishop Newry;
Acribba Lightbourne, daughter; Quanajia Solomon, grand-daughter;
Judy Wemyss, wife; and in back, Freddie Lightbourne, son-in-law.
Sunday, 26th April, 2023.

Henry Wemyss Receiving the Clementina Stubbs Award and the Eagle Award from Bishop Dr. James Newry and Elder Queenie Newry of Calvary Deliverance Church during the Church's 40th Anniversary Banquet on 9th October, 2023.

L-R: Hon. Wayne Munroe, M.P. & Minister of National Security, Mr. Henry Wemyss, Mrs. Judy Wemyss, and Hon. Fred Mitchell, M.P. & Minister of Foreign Affairs in Attendance at the Investiture Ceremony at Government House, 9th October, 2023.

CHAPTER 18

"From The Heart of Henry Wemyss"

Looking back on some of my darkest days, I can see how God, not only had his hands on me but also placed all the right people in my life at the right time; just when I needed them most. Only God could have orchestrated such a plan.

There was no way possible for nine individuals to play such an influential role in my life without coming together or knowing each other. And for that, I give God all the praise and all the glory because it is due to Him and Him alone.

In the same way that pillars support a building during the worst storms, regardless of the damage, the size, the strength or the magnitude of the storms, these pillars had to be structured properly and built with the right material to sustain weight during the worst storms. These people - whom I refer to as the "Nine Pillars" of my life - supported me and held me steady during the most challenging times of my life. These people demonstrated their belief in me and never wavered when things might have appeared difficult.

These are people who never conform to an unforgiving society. I do not think I would have survived my life's turbulent storms had they not each played their respective supportive roles. I want to take this opportunity to publicly pay tribute to them for their profound support, encouragement, and assistance when I faced the most difficult task of rebuilding my life from the ground up. God used them so my story could have ended on a positive note. Using an analogy, these individuals, at their designated times, all played their role as committed parents who cared deeply about the future and well-being of a son—a prodigal son.

Judy Anna Wemyss nee Lockart, my wife, has been an unwavering **Pillar of Strength, Encouragement & Persistence** in my life and that of my family. When we met in 1966, I found her beautiful, attractive, kind, pleasant, energetic, athletic, well-dressed, and full of life. Never had I encountered a woman who was as radiant as she was. Shortly after meeting her, she volunteered to assist me with cleaning my uniform. No other white tunic—long or short—could compete with the ones she did for me. Because of her, I was always well-dressed and earned the reputation of being one of the cleanest officers in the Police Force. We got married eight years later and have been together for 58 years. She has stuck by me for better or worse, for richer or poorer, and in sickness and in health.

Over the years, she has done much more than her share and is still doing heavy lifting. She has been the wind beneath my wings, and I am not ashamed to say that all my success is due to her persistence. Whenever I felt like giving up, she was there encouraging me, telling me, "You can do it," "You cannot give up," and "You're almost there." I can attest that behind every successful man, there is a hard-working woman. I am too afraid to even try to imagine what my life would have looked like without her. God does not make any mistakes, and he blessed me with the kind of wife I needed - one who would faithfully accompany me through the highs and lows of life.

In 1967, I had the pleasure of meeting the late **Deputy Commissioner of Police, Sir Albert Miller,** one of the cleanest Police Officers that I had ever seen or known in a Khaki uniform. I could not think of anyone to compare him with. He had the looks of integrity, intelligence, deportment, size, and build. He was stern and no-nonsense. He left an indelible mark on my life as someone I aspire to be like. I considered him a born leader and wanted to emulate him as much as possible. He knew every police officer by rank, number, and name, and encouraged me to sharpen my skills and get to know as many of those officers as possible. He would frequently put me to the test by asking me to tell him an officer's name. He was reliable, trustworthy, and for him to do something for you, you had to be deserving of it. He did not do favours. He believed in strict discipline. He taught me that when you earn something, you will appreciate it more than someone giving you something you did not deserve.

He was always willing to hear me out and find time for me. Even after my imprisonment, he did not turn his back on me and encouraged me whenever we spoke. He told me, "Don't give up. Keep your head high." When I got the job at Batelco, it was because of two people, and he was one of them. He did anything that he could to assist me. He reminded me of the verse in the Bible that says don't do your charitable deeds before men to be seen of them. Whatever he did, he preferred to do it secretly. He was a **Pillar of Integrity, Loyalty & Fatherly Love,** especially when I needed it most. May his soul continue to rest in peace and rise in glory.

The late **Deacon Bursil Brown**, who became a **Pillar of Encouragement & Fellowship** appeared in my life at one of my lowest points. When I heard his voice shouting out my name from outside the prison dormitory that Sunday, inviting me to attend chapel service, it reinforced my recent decision to follow Jesus Christ. It was there that I realised I had been running from God for far too long, even though He had gifted and blessed me over the years.

Hearing him tell the congregation of fellow inmates that they will never see me and my brother again in prison filled me with peace, and tears began to flow. He was the door that led me to Calvary Deliverance Church, where I found a place of solace, comfort, and fellowship. He was truly a man of compassion and a heart for all people, regardless of their status in life. If someone was in need, he would give away the clothes off his back and continue smiling. Worldly things were never a concern to him all he wanted to do was to work for that day when he would be with Jesus.

Our relationship did not last as long as I would have liked because he soon became ill and was admitted to hospital. We had great conversations, during my visits to him, always about God, and then we would pray. During one of those visits, he told me I would preach from the same pulpit where he once stood, and at that time, I was still an usher. He predicted that God would use me more and that I would have more to offer than he did. What really got to me was when he said he was unsure he would be there to see it. Well, that day really came and like he said, he was not there to witness it. May his soul continue to rest in peace and rise in glory.

After the outcome of my trial, I had lost faith in the judicial system, but my faith was restored when the now **Honourable Frederick A. Mitchell** showed up to visit me in prison on his own initiative. At a time when I felt the system had failed me, he became my **Pillar of Justice, Influence & Friendship.** With no other evidence, the testimonies of two convicted criminals determined my fate and destroyed my career. My outstanding performance record as a Police Officer, serving the Commonwealth of The Bahamas and wearing my uniform with pride and dignity were diminished to nothing by the Courts. However, he upheld it as proof of my personal integrity, and used his influence to fight for my freedom, which meant the world to me. He never cared or asked about my political persuasion. His only concern was that there had been a travesty of justice, and he could not rest until justice had been served. He never asked for payment, and I could never repay him for standing up for me when others refused or were too afraid to. Thirty-three years later, he is still fighting to redeem my name and character to an unforgiving world.

When I first met him in 1980, I would have never guessed the significant role he would one day play in my life. Back then, I considered him quiet, professional, not too friendly, but always willing to help when possible. Prior to meeting him, I had noticed him as a person of high intellect, who never joked around and seldom smiled. Admittedly, I was shocked and happy when he visited me in prison and continued to do so each week. Even the inmates who saw him expressed surprise at seeing him there. After my release, we got to know each other better, and today I consider him not only as a personal friend of my entire family, but also one of my sons. A prominent lawyer, now deceased, once told me that anytime you want any legal action, with good results, let Fred write it, and I am grateful because it worked for me every time. He will be a dear friend until death.

When I re-entered society in 1993, it was not easy, especially since all hope seemed lost as I tried to find work. Thanks to Bursil Brown, who introduced me to **Bishop Vernal G. Clarke,** I found refuge at Calvary Deliverance Church.

Bishop Clarke became my **Pillar of Spiritual Wisdom, Refuge & Counsel.** When I first walked into Calvary, I met this slim, well-dressed minister in the pulpit. He appeared to be friendly, always smiling, and accommodating, but when I heard his fire and brimstone messages, I could not believe it was the same man who smiled and spoke so softly. Sometimes, he would take the microphone and run up and down the church, all over the pews, and all I could say was, "Lord have mercy!" Coming from a Roman Catholic Church background, where there was law and order and quiet, once you entered the doors, it was a new experience for me, and one that forever changed my life.

Bishop Clarke always knew the right words to say at the precise moment I needed to hear them. Sometimes, he offered words of love, other times words of encouragement, and sometimes even words of rebuke. I often wonder what would have become of me if I had never gone to Calvary, but I know it was all divinely orchestrated by God, and he had ordered my steps there to be shepherded by someone he had chosen for that time and season in my life. While I was looking for work to reclaim my position as head of my household, he took me under his wings like a son and provided for me and my family. When my future seemed over, he said to me, "God will reward you for your faithfulness." Bishop VG Clarke left an indelible mark on the development of my spiritual life and more. I thank God for his role as my Spiritual Mentor. He is truly a Prophet. "Believe in the Lord your God, so shall you be established, believe in His prophets, so shall you prosper," 2 Chronicles 20:20-21. To God be all the glory. Great things He has done.

The Right Honourable Hubert A. Ingraham, former Prime Minister of the Commonwealth of The Bahamas, opened a closed steel door for me and gave me a second chance opportunity from which I was able to build upon and expand with God's grace. He became the **Pillar of Generosity, & Care** in my life by leveraging his influence to assist me. I first noticed him in the mid-1960s while he was working at Batelco on East Street and taking driving lessons. We never officially met at the time, but I watched him from a distance. I could see leadership qualities in him, even as a young man. He was always a people's person, and though you may disagree with his political views, you would still like him because of his attitude.

I met him officially in 1991, a year before he became Prime Minister, and a year before I was imprisoned. He was the official opposition leader then, and one of my colleagues and good friend, Inspector Richard Gardiner, made the introductions. He was so pleasant and down to earth that I did not feel inferior in his company. When my reputation became ruined, and so many others despised me, he gave me the impression that

I was still somebody, even though, deep inside, I had given up hope. He promised to assist me, and, in time, he did. Before then, I did not see a way out to support my family or to pay my mortgage. I have proven that he lives up to his mantra that, "I say what I mean, and I mean what I say." God used him to help me, and I would not have been who I am today if it was not for this. He gave me a reason to believe again and to see my life the way God sees it. I do not know if he even realised how much he helped me back then. Perhaps, he may have even placed his own character on the line.

I went to him expecting that he would want to discuss my case, but he did not. The closest he ever came to mentioning it was when he told me, "You did nothing wrong." That meant so much to me. He was quite helpful and always made himself available to sit and listen, and he seemed to understand my position. Through interacting with him, I learnt that the way to accomplish much for Christ is to serve Him in everything that we do. He was different from others in that he did not talk much yet accomplished a great deal. He has a listening ear and is one of the politicians who I have never heard quote Bible scriptures, but his actions spoke louder than words. I learnt from him that words do not have to be many to be meaningful, and kind words from the heart can bring much comfort. He is a gentleman par excellence.

There is nothing I can do for someone who seems to have everything. But the best I can do to show my gratitude on behalf of myself and my family is to pray for him and his family daily that God will continue to give him good strength, good health, happiness, and long life as he continues to do the things that made him happy in his life. And I thank him for believing in me during my time of despair.

When I first started working at Batelco, I was transferred three times in one day. First to Security, then Fraud and finally to Fleet Management. I worked under **Bishop Arlington Rahming**, a God-fearing, dependable gentleman, and later, I became convinced God had placed him in my life as a **Pillar of Spiritual Meekness, Administrative Wisdom & Help.** He played a significant role in my growth and development at the corporation.

He was an excellent team leader, who knew how to get whatever he needed out of you. Bishop Rahming listened attentively, and he could see that I was displeased by the way I was being treated. When I was thrown into a corridor to work, where I could hear all the negative things the employees were saying about me, he eventually made it possible for me to sit in an office space on the 2nd floor. I think of him as a leader, mentor, and someone who truly cares.

Even though I was much older, he encouraged me, supported me, and played the part of a big brother. He sent me away to Atlanta on a Defensive Driving Course—Train the Trainer. Through talking to me, he found out that I liked basketball and made reservations for me to see the Atlanta Hawks live. That was the highlight of my trip, and it was my first time visiting a basketball stadium and watching a live game.

Bishop Rahming has an appetite to help people, and I was one of them. I realised that my trial was God's road to triumph, and he reminded me of James 1:3—the way to great patience is through great trials. Because of his generosity to me, his coaching, and his interest, WemCo became a successful company.

In 1999, I didn't have the insight to see an opportunity to become self-employed when it presented itself. Even if I could, I was too afraid to go after it. But God impressed it on my nephew—**Kenneth Whyms** and he never let it rest. At the time, I needed a **Pillar of Encouragement, Perseverance & Motivation** and he filled that role. He came to me every morning, without fail, to convince me to form my own security company when Batelco was outsourcing its security services. He had faith in me when I did not have faith in myself. He saw the golden opportunity that

273

would allow me to empower myself by running my own business. He was so persistent that I had to avoid him at times. Despite knowing that I had the competence to run a successful company, I was trapped by the fear of my past and having people hold it against me. But Kenneth could only see my talent, skills, experience, and how well I would do. He started it all, and if it was not for him, I doubted that I would have ever established WemCo Security & Collections Limited.

I can remember the day Kenneth was born—he was the first child of my brother, JD. He grew up to be an intelligent young man, who was always serious about his schoolwork. As I watched him grow into a teenager, I told his father, in his presence, that he would become a successful man and that he would be proud of him. At that time, my brother did not take me seriously as Kenneth was different from his other siblings, always drawing. From an early age, he believed in his independence, and after securing employment, he moved out from his parents to live on his own. As time passed, I saw all the good things that I said about him come to pass. He is committed, dedicated and truly a success story. And because of his unwavering determination to help me gain a bright future, WemCo is a reality today.

The late, Retired Assistant Commissioner of Police, Paul R. Thompson, my Pillar of Armour Bearer, Advisor & Knowledge, was a constant support. Since the inception of WemCo, I have benefited from his knowledge, wisdom, and expertise. In life, very few things come full circle, but our relationship is one of them. When I was an 18-year-old police constable, I met Paul Thompson, who was working on attachment at (CID), Central Police Station, at the time. He was always willing to teach young officers, and I remember him taking me along to crime scenes during his investigations and taking the time to explain what had just taken place. His rank never made a difference to him.

When I joined Batelco in 1995, I met Paul there as an independent security consultant. We worked closely and travelled to some family islands for security investigations and assessments for the corporation. When I decided to form WemCo, he supported me, doing everything without complaining, never refusing to help, and never asking for one penny. I believe he simply wanted to see young people succeed. I am willing to admit that without Paul, WemCo Security would not have become the company that it is today. He was my first general manager and advised and assisted all security managers and supervisors on their duties and responsibilities. Until he became general manager, all of Paul's work for me was pro bono, and after he began working elsewhere, all his work was pro bono. I was frequently asked why I would hire him when he also owned a security company, and I would respond that I trusted him and did not see a conflict of interest, as it never interfered with the performance of his duties. He is the bedrock of WemCo, a father figure, personal friend, confidant and what I call the 'all-purpose man.' He has always shown faith in me and WemCo, even going so far as to defend us when others try to use my past to gain business leverage.

These are the people, the nine pillars in my life, who have had a lasting positive impact on my life. I am grateful to have had these contributors in my life. Some fulfilled their roles and moved on, while others remain to this day. It was not planned but simply happened, and everything fell into place. It was one of God's miracles to me because they were all willing and did what they had to do of their own free will, with no strings attached. I know what happened to me through all these people resulted from God's favour. There was nothing particularly noteworthy or special that I did, they just volunteered to help.

Induction Henry Wemyss Order of Merit

The Governor General of The Bahamas, Her Excellency The Most Honourable Dame Cynthia Pratt ON GCMG CB CD JP, Inducts Henry Wemyss into the Order of Merit on Heroes Day, 9th October, 2023

About the Book

The headline splashed across the front page: *Police Inspector Faces Cocaine Charges…*

That Inspector in question was Henry Wemyss, a distinguished officer of the Royal Bahamas Police Force, who had worn his uniform with such pride that he was called "one of the cleanest police officers in uniform."

A legendary instructor at the Police College, Henry was highly regarded as a "father figure" and as a "role model."

Henry was an officer entrusted to lead the Royal Bahamas Police Cadet Corps and groom the future leadership of the Force.

In 1990, that false accusation derailed his career and plunged him into one of the darkest periods of his life. He lost his freedom, his reputation, and the profession he felt was God-ordained.

But this life-shattering experience did not define him. God used it as a turning point and propelled him further than anyone could have ever imagined.

In 2020, Henry faced another dark moment when he contracted COVID-19 and was brought to the brink of death. Yet again, God stepped in, and He became "the miracle patient."

In 2023, Henry was conferred by the Government of The Bahamas with the honour of member in the Order of Merit of The Commonwealth of The Bahamas.

This book chronicles Henry's journey from humbling beginnings in Behring Point, Central Andros. It pulls back the curtains, delving into his policing career, court trial, life behind bars, re-entry into society, pioneering work in the security industry and his remarkable recovery from COVID-19.

It is told, not just through his own words, but also through the perspectives of the people he touched along the way. It is powerful testament to the resilience of the human spirit. It is a story of faith, hope, and perseverance.

Henry continues to have a positive impact on the world around him. He stands tall as a proud Bahamian nation builder, an entrepreneur, a visionary leader, a philanthropist, and a man who is unashamed to declare that Jesus Christ is his Lord and Saviour.

Henry's story is a life changer for anyone facing difficult times.

His message is simple, "Never give up! If God can do it for me, He can do it for you."

About the Author

Henry Anselm Wemyss was born in Behring Point, Andros, on 14th April, 1947. He began his education at St. Mary Catholic School in Andros, and after moving to Nassau in 1959, he attended St. Thomas Moore and thereafter completed his high school education at Aquinas College. He has been a committed Bahamian patriot for 58 years, contributing to law enforcement, youth development, and ongoing financial aid to community and social welfare. He is the President and Founder of WemCo Security & Collections Ltd.

In 1965 at the age of 18, he joined the Royal Bahamas Police Force. During his tenure on the Force, he earned the reputation as one of the cleanest police officers in uniform. This innate sense of pride afforded him the opportunity to travel throughout the Americas and Canada as an Ambassador, along with the Ministry of Tourism.

In 1982, he made history as the first and only Bahamian police officer in an independent Bahamas to complete the General Police Duties Course at the Metropolitan Police College in Hendon, London, and bring home the coveted baton of honor, having achieved first place.

He is a revered and highly respected past instructor of the Police College, where he taught for 12 years, eventually becoming chief class instructor. In this capacity, he was instrumental in grooming the future leadership of the Force, including male and female assistant commissioners of police, the first two female deputy commissioners of police in the history of the Force, the past three commissioners of police, and the current commissioner of police. In his last assignment, he revitalized and led a new Royal Bahamas Police Force Cadet Corp Program from 1988 to 1990, where some of the country's most successful young men and women were trained and they have risen through the ranks to become superintendents of police, assistant commandant of the Police College, assistant superintendents, inspectors, and other ranks of the Police Force. Others became international lawyers, medical doctors, entrepreneurs, and business executives. Before retiring after 31 years of service, he was recognized and received the medals for Long Service and Good Conduct, along with Meritorious Service.

In 1995, he began working at the Bahamas Telecommunication Corporation as a supervisor and shortly after, he was promoted to security manager. In that same year 1995, he was nominated and received the award for Manager of the Year. After the privatization of the corporation, he ventured out as an entrepreneur, and in 2000, WemCo Security & Collections Limited began operations. WemCo became a trailblazer in the security industry and continues to stand out as an industry leader, setting the standard for trained, disciplined, and career-minded security professionals. Over the years, the company has received numerous commendations from the Commissioner(s) of Police, clients, and the general public for outstanding services in going above and beyond.

He is an ordained minister of the gospel and a philanthropist. He has established his personal Ministry of Help. Many, including charitable organizations, churches, widows, orphans, employees, and members of the general community, continue to benefit from his generosity. He has received numerous awards, including being honoured by the Broadcasting Corporation of The Bahamas as a Salute to Legends for his commitment and dedication to The Bahamas. In May 2023, he received the Clementina Stubbs and The Eagle Award from Calvary Deliverance Church for his dedication and support to the church's outreach ministries.

He has been married to Judy Anna M. Wemyss, née Lockhart, for 49 years and has eight children. His life motto is "For with God nothing shall be impossible" Luke 1:37. This has been the hallmark of his life's accomplishments and exemplary service to the Bahamian community.

Made in the USA
Columbia, SC
14 September 2024

b352a752-d9b4-4d5d-92a6-4e8c46f6aeb1R01